ON THE GRAND TRUNK ROAD

O N   T H E

Grand Trunk Road

—

A Journey into South Asia

S T E V E   C O L L

T I M E S   BOOKS

R A N D O M   H O U S E

Library of Congress Cataloging-in-Publication Data

Coll, Steve.
On the grand trunk road : a journey into South Asia / Steve Coll.
— 1st ed.
p.   cm.
Includes index.
ISBN 0-8129-2026-0
1. South Asia—Politics and government. 2. Communalism—South
Asia. 3. South Asia—Ethnic relations. I. Title.
DS340.C65 1994
915.404'52—dc20   93-1944

What Caesar, battling for democracy,
Unasked, relinquished his regime?
What cotton king decried slavocracy?
What cat forwent its dish of cream?

Vikram Seth,
The Golden Gate

Our researchers into Public Opinion are content
That he held the proper opinions for the time of year;
When there was peace, he was for peace; when there
    was war, he went.
He was married and added five children to the
    population,
Which our Eugenist says was the right number for a
    parent of his generation,
And our teachers report that he never interfered with
    their education.
Was he free? Was he happy? The question is absurd:
Had anything been wrong, we should certainly have
    heard.

W. H. Auden,
"The Unknown Citizen"

Contents

Introduction

I f there is a better place for a journalist to work than South Asia, I would like to know about it. I say this not because of the Victorian romance of a New Delhi posting, which is surely part of the bargain, but because of contemporary factors: with the cold war's demise, the Indian subcontinent finds itself today in the midst of a transition from socialism to something beyond, a transition in which nearly all the earlier political and social arrangements are being fiercely contested. This has placed many of the most compelling and universal ideas of our time—revolution, counterrevolution, political religion, separatism, nationalism, and capitalism, to name a few—into a kind of bubbling cauldron of subcontinental conflict and experimentation. Something like that could be said these days of other regions of a rapidly transformed world, such as the former Soviet Union. But in South Asia all this collective groping for the future seemed to me uniquely accessible and enlivening.

Partly that is because South Asian societies are wide open, highly self-conscious, and for the most part deeply hospitable to Western outsiders. Time and again on my reportorial travels for *The Washington Post*, which sent me to New Delhi in 1989, I would wander unannounced to the forbidding iron gates of a princely palace or a seat of governmental power, pass my calling card to the guard on duty, and find moments later

that I was sitting, astonished, in some grand but tattered drawing room, sharing milky tea and intense conversation with somebody I had longed to meet. With repetition, I learned not to be surprised by this sort of hospitality, but to be bolder about the access I sought.

History, revolution, and politics lie around in South Asia like heirlooms and furniture in a cluttered guest room that your host has not had time to clean and sort. You are free—and privileged—to wander about, pick the heirlooms up carefully, dust them off, turn them over, and inquire respectfully about their origins. I did this quite literally one time in the old palace where a former Indian prime minister, Vishwanath Pratap Singh, was reared. I arrived without an appointment, and the guard responded by ushering a tour in which he climbed ladders to pull down old sepia family photographs from the walls. He then used the pictures as exhibits while recounting all the scurrilous gossip he could remember about the family of a man who was at that moment India's most powerful politician. The guard wasn't mean-spirited or disrespectful or politically motivated. It's just that they were such good stories, and really, he seemed to feel, there was no reason not to share them with a welcome guest from abroad. This was hardly an unusual attitude. Revolutionary guerrilla commanders, religious gurus, indentured laborers, nuclear scientists, charismatic national politicians, spies, criminals—everyone, it seemed, was more than happy to take time out for tea and an extended chat, even if they intended to lie boldly throughout.

This book is the ultimate consequence of those travels and those conversations. It is intended as a piece of journalism, in the traditional sense. It is meant to be accessible, idiosyncratic, entertaining, and serious, though I don't mean to insist that it actually turned out that way. My point is that there are a few things this book is not meant to be. It is not meant to tell South Asians what to think about themselves or to compare South Asia's present problems with the equally formidable challenges facing the West. It is not a work of scholarship, as will be obvious, but it does attempt to describe and explain questions that South Asian governments and outside specialists are wrestling with today. These include political violence, separatist and religious rebellion, social conflict, the corruption of public officials, the decay and abuse of state power, and the ongoing attempt on the subcontinent to construct, in a fast-changing global environment, a transition from socialism to capitalism. What these

conundrums now have in common, it seems to me, is their relationship to epochal change in the region that once was Britain's Indian empire. The sources of this change are the end of the cold war, the advanced erosion of the socialist states built by South Asian independence leaders after World War II, and the urgent need of a new generation on the subcontinent to build something of their own, without reversing what progress they have inherited.

You will find here, then, if I have succeeded at all, a sense of what these challenges amount to, where they arise from, why they matter—and, mainly, an account of what this change and conflict looks and feels like on the streets of South Asia today. There, in a variety of ways, the collective future of roughly one billion people too often ignored in the West is currently being decided.

STATES

OF

FLUX

1

Sound and Fury

We who have grown up on a diet of honor and shame can still grasp what must seem unthinkable to peoples living in the aftermath of the death of God and of tragedy.

—*Salman Rushdie*

During three years in South Asia, I shook hands with several men who subsequently exploded. There was no reason to suspect causality in this statistic. But the explosions were instants of intimate violence, and through their intimacy they demanded exploration.

One place to begin is Trincomalee, Sri Lanka, on March 24, 1990, in the sultry morning sun on a concrete jetty beside China Bay. Sweat drawn by the equatorial heat ran like tap water from the pores of those assembled. Three frigates had arrived to take home the last two thousand or so men of the Indian Peacekeeping Force, the dubiously named army dispatched by Rajiv Gandhi in 1987 to rescue the island nation of Sri Lanka from its years of gruesome fratricidal war between ethnic Sinhalese and ethnic Tamils. The army had failed in its mission and had achieved the improbable effect of making Sri Lanka's problems even worse than before. Now the Sri Lankan government had arranged a celebration to mark the final departure of the Indian troops. Hostile civility filled the air. A ragged naval band with brass and bagpipes lined the dock. Sri Lankan honor guards in pressed olive uniforms and pink scarves pointed the way to the departing ships. Turbaned Indian soldiers with the Seventh Sikh Light Infantry stood gamely at attention, melting before our eyes as they waited for the ceremony to end. From unseen loudspeakers came a

medley of popular songs, such as "Oh, What a Feeling" and "We're Going to Have a Party Tonight." Whether these lyrics were meant as a message from the Sri Lankans to the Indians or vice versa was not clear.

On the dock beside the last frigate stood Ranjan Wijeratne, Sri Lanka's minister of state for defense, reputed leader of the island's notorious death squads and all-around hero of his country's counterrevolutions. Dressed in flowing white *khadi*, and with a fine mane of silver hair, he looked nearly biblical that morning. Wijeratne was both a chilling and an entertaining figure as a cabinet minister. He managed vast tea plantations in the island's interior and donned unapologetically the airs of a nineteenth-century colonial master. After rising through planters' and landowners' organizations into politics, he was placed in charge of Sri Lanka's official and unofficial armed forces and directed the beleaguered government's several counterinsurgency programs. That March morning, paramilitary pro-government death squads, which many on the island believed reported to Wijeratne, were winding up a months-long campaign of slaughter that had killed somewhere between twenty thousand and sixty thousand Sri Lankans suspected of involvement with the People's Liberation Front, a Maoist guerrilla group. It was difficult to keep count of the victims. The death squads drove around the island's lush jungles in green Mitsubishi Pajero jeeps, plucked suspects from their homes in the night, and dumped their smoldering corpses on pristine beaches in the morning. Wijeratne never admitted that he controlled the squads, despite considerable evidence that he sanctioned and perhaps even organized them. But he boasted of his sympathies. In his capacity as state defense minister Wijeratne met the press each week in a cool conference room in Colombo, Sri Lanka's seaside capital. At these meetings he tried to exceed his previous achievements in murderous witticism. Once he called the International Committee of the Red Cross a "terrorist organization." He offered to "wring the necks" of demonstrators with the Mothers' Front, an organization of relatives of victims who had disappeared in the night. Threatening to attack the Jaffna peninsula on the north of the island, he advised an estimated one million civilians to vacate the area or "good luck to them." Luck was a favorite theme with Wijeratne. One day in the conference room, he challenged any of the several guerrilla groups he was attempting to crush to go ahead and kill him if they didn't like his policies. He wished these guerrillas, too, "good luck."

Wijeratne wanted the Indian Peacekeeping Force off his island. The

reasons were complicated but one compulsion was that he wished to press more freely his own attacks on the country's various insurgents. He had come to Trincomalee that March morning to wave the Indian soldiers off. As the Sikh infantry marched up the gangway, I asked him how it felt to see them go.

"They had a trying time. They came on a peace mission, but then something untoward happened," Wijeratne said in a patrician tone, referring to the combat deaths of twelve hundred Indian soldiers during their stay in Sri Lanka. "They got bogged down."

We followed the troops up the plank for a last round of speeches aboard the frigate. The Indian ambassador told the dripping soldiers that history would record their achievements "in golden print" and that a "proud and grateful nation awaits your arrival in India," assertions that must have seemed ridiculous to all but the most patriotic infantrymen.

Wijeratne took the microphone. "You have made a great sacrifice, there's no doubt about that," he said. Then he offered this benediction: "Those who sacrifice their lives will be born again as good men in a future world."

The bomb that killed him eleven months later blew a thirty-six-square-foot crater in the asphalt of Havelock Road in Colombo. It was eight-thirty in the morning, rush hour on a busy thoroughfare. Wijeratne was on his way to the office from the airport, where he had seen his son off on a flight back to college in the United States. (Often a bond between counterrevolutionaries and revolutionaries in South Asia is the ambition that their children study hard in America to be doctors and engineers.) The minister rode in a Land Rover flanked by escort vehicles. When the assassin punched the car bomb detonator he or she set off a bang so loud it echoed in Colombo's outskirts miles away. Who pushed the detonator remains a mystery, although guerrillas with the Liberation Tigers of Tamil Eelam head a list of suspects more numerous than any cast summoned to the drawing room at the end of an Agatha Christie novel. In any case, they were thorough. Pieces of flesh turned up 150 yards from Havelock Road. Besides Wijeratne, at least sixteen people died in the explosion and dozens of others were hurt. It took hours to pull the minister's body from his jeep. Buildings throughout the posh palm-lined neighborhood were damaged. Vehicles lay strewn in mangled heaps. One of the smashed cars bore a windshield sticker that said, "Unite to Fight Terrorism."

The Sri Lankan government promoted Wijeratne posthumously to the

rank of general and put on a state funeral at Independence Square, a Colombo memorial to the end of the British Empire in South Asia. Army officers drew the minister's body through the streets on a gun carriage. Sri Lankan honor guards surrounded the square. Buddhist priests eulogized Wijeratne's accomplishments in service to the state. Soldiers fired a twenty-one-gun salute.

One day after the funeral, the weekly security briefing went on as usual in the appointed Colombo conference room. General Cyril Ranatunge, Wijeratne's immediate successor, insisted on two minutes of silence in honor of the departed minister. Then he remarked that the detonation that killed Wijeratne was "the most powerful bomb exploded in the country up to now," as if this were a final tribute to the departed minister's stature.

Somebody asked if Wijeratne's violent end would lead the government to alter or soften in any way its gun-blazing approach to counterinsurgency.

"There will be no change in plans," Ranatunge answered. "We know what the minister wanted."

———

Political assassination in South Asia is an advanced art characterized by grandiose themes of betrayal, revenge, and collective struggle. As in America, murders of beloved leaders hang over the culture, and the spinning of assassination conspiracy theories is a vibrant cottage industry. One of the hottest videotape rentals in New Delhi in the summer of 1992 was Oliver Stone's JFK. As they talked about the movie, many urban Indians, including some in high government office, seemed to find the depth of Stone's paranoia oddly reassuring.

Scan recent instances of violent political change in the subcontinental region bound for two centuries by British influence—India, Pakistan, Bangladesh, Sri Lanka, Nepal, Afghanistan—and you will find the spectacle peppered with overloud explosions and exaggerated gunfire. One feature common to many of the political murders is the excess force employed by the killers. This may be partially explained by the imprecise technologies available to South Asian assassins. But there is another factor: violence of feeling. Political killers in modern South Asia often stalk their victims with fanatical commitment. They are willing to kill themselves and uncounted others in pursuit of their ends. They are men

and women of determination, engaged in grand dramas played out in the murky extremities of social conflict and political change.

They are also participants in mainstream politics. Sometimes, years after their work is complete, their supporters propose to erect statues to their memory, as occurred recently in India with Nathuram Godse, assassin of Mohandas K. Gandhi. Other times, they or their relatives become local heros and are nominated for political office, as has happened with nearly every Sikh in Punjab who has conspired to kill Rajiv or Indira Gandhi, the political (but not the familial) heirs to Mohandas. And of course, there are the more pedestrian cases of assassins committing or organizing murder to obtain office from a rival. Successful practitioners of this career strategy include such well-known names of recent South Asian politics as General Hussein Mohammed Ershad, president of Bangladesh for most of the 1980s; Babrak Karmal, who ushered the Soviet tanks into Afghanistan; and, at least in the view of some Pakistanis, the late cold warrior and military dictator General Zia ul-Haq, who ordered the hanging of the rival he overthrew, Zulfikar Ali Bhutto, the father of Benazir Bhutto.

There is in the details of these stories such genuine pathos as would embarrass even a producer of the most egregious Bombay *masala* cinema. Recall, as one example, Sikh subinspectors Beant Singh and Satwant Singh, bodyguards of former Indian prime minister Indira Gandhi, who stepped from their sentry posts by a wicket gate behind the prime minister's New Delhi residence on the morning of October 31, 1984, to take revenge for a military assault against the Golden Temple, the holiest shrine in the Sikh religion. The bodyguards approached Gandhi as she walked across the lawn in a peach sari, the prime minister's chief aide later recalled. Beant Singh blocked the prime minister's path, silently pulled a service revolver from his jacket, and aimed it at her.

"What are you doing?" Indira Gandhi asked.

The two assailants shot her twenty-nine times. They dropped their weapons and waited for nearby commandos to reach them. "We have done what we wanted to. Now you can do what you want to," Beant Singh said grandly to his captors.

In the aftermath, investigators found a note on Indira Gandhi's desk, apparently written four months before her murder. "If I die a violent death as people have been plotting, I know the [assassination] will be in the thought and action of the assassin, not in the dying," the prime minister

scribbled to herself. "No hate is dark enough to overshadow the extent of my love for my people and my country, no force is strong enough to divert me from my purpose."

Another of South Asia's modern empresses, Benazir Bhutto, echoed Gandhi's tone several years later while recalling in an autobiography one of her last meetings with her doomed father, which occurred in a prison in Rawalpindi, Pakistan, in 1978:

> We sit in the courtyard for a precious hour, our heads close together so that the three jailers under orders to listen to us cannot. But they are sympathetic this time and do not press in on us.
> "You are twenty-five now," my father jokes, "and eligible to stand for office. Now Zia will never hold elections."
> "Oh, Papa," I say.
> We laugh. How do we manage it? Somewhere in the jail stand the hangman's gallows which shadow our lives.

Interspersed with such melodrama there is farce. Consider the tale recorded by Raja Anwar, a former Pakistani leftist jailed for several years in Afghanistan's Pul-i-Charki prison. During conversations with fellow political inmates, Anwar claimed to have pieced together the story of the murder of Hafizullah Amin, the Afghan revolutionary leader who died when Soviet troops invaded Afghanistan in December 1979. Amin had taken power several months before the invasion by directing thugs in his employ to murder the country's president, Noor Mohammed Taraki, by choking him to death with a pillow, or by shooting him in the head, or by some other means (there are several versions). One way or another, the task was accomplished and Amin moved into a grand palace on the southern outskirts of Kabul, Afghanistan's mud-rock capital, from where he evidently expected to direct his country's Bolshevik revolution for many years. Soviet military planners and rivals in Amin's tiny band of leftist revolutionaries, however, wanted the new Afghan president out of the way. As their agents, by Anwar's account (which some Afghans regard as credible, and some regard as incredible), the coup makers selected two Soviet cooks and a Soviet food taster whom Amin employed in his palace because he feared Afghan chefs might poison him.

On December 27, 1979, the day tens of thousands of Soviet troops moved to seize power in Afghanistan, Amin, his children, his daughter-in-law, and two guests sat down for lunch in the palace. According to the

account later provided to Anwar by Amin's widow and surviving children, they all ate food prepared by the Russian cooks. No sooner were they finished than they fell over unconscious as a result of poisoning. The family members and guests remained stricken. Amin, however, awoke and blinked his eyes about two hours later. The reason, his relatives said later, was that the night before, Amin's cooks had unintentionally given him a bout of dysentery, and because of this Amin had only nibbled at his lunch. Grumbling, the nauseated but alert Afghan president was taken to his bedroom. A general from the Soviet army medical corps soon arrived. According to Anwar's account, translated from the original Urdu:

The [Soviet] general must have been disappointed to see that the "patient" was well enough to greet him. Expressing his pleasure at Amin's recovery, he left . . . According to the Amin family, the first tank shell hit [the palace] at exactly six o'clock in the evening. . . . At 6:45 P.M., the invading force was in front of Amin's residence. The resistance being offered by his guards was petering out. Amin ordered his [military aide] to extinguish all the lights, then turning to his wife he said, "Don't worry, the Soviet army should be coming to our rescue any minute." . . . Suddenly, there were men outside shouting: "Amin, where are you? We have come to your help." Abdul Rahman ran down the stairs screaming, "This way, come this way. This is where Amin is." He [Rahman] was shot dead on the lower veranda. Amin's youngest son and Mrs. Shah Wali [one of the lunch guests] were killed while they were still unconscious. One of Amin's daughters was shot in the leg, but she survived, only to become a prisoner. . . . When they entered Amin's office they found him in his chair, his head resting on the table with blood flowing from his temple. They are not sure if he had received a stray bullet or committed suicide.

It might seem obvious to suggest that nations whose politics are shaped by violent, pathological dramas such as these are profoundly unstable, destined to career between dangerous crises. To a degree, this is the impression of South Asia held today in the West, particularly in the United States: one billion riotous and unfathomable poor people best left alone, disarmed if possible. In response to this characterization, some South Asians have evolved a shrill and defensive outlook in which they see themselves as simultaneously victims and conquerors of Western imperialism—the imperialism of history, perpetrated mainly by the British between the eighteenth and twentieth centuries, and the imperialism of culture, supposedly pursued today by the dominant if increasingly amorphous West. Those of us Westerners who move through this debate

learn to recognize its caricatures: the white man haranguing locals because the phones don't work and the planes don't fly on time; the corrupt *babu* who blathers on about Western decadence, then segues into a rapturous account of his last trip to Disney World; the glassy-eyed Western hippie traipsing through the countryside in search of oriental enlightenment; the slick banker in Bombay or Karachi who predicts the imminent collapse of his society over a glass of black-market whiskey.

Often, the specific reference points of this debate about South Asia's past and future are the instances of its sound and fury: its explosions. The themes are what this sound and fury signifies, where it arises from, and where it will lead.

Out of professional obligation and personal curiosity, I wandered for several years across this landscape and this debate, drawn by the needs of the home office disproportionately to the sites of the sound and fury. There was time, too, for sojourns in quieter corners. One of the great privileges of this ultimately circular journey was the ability to cross national borders freely. That is something South Asians, despite common languages and threads of history, can now do only rarely, and even then, what they see of each other frequently seems limited by blinders of enmity, suspicion, and prejudice.

It would be ridiculous to argue that the individual destinies of India, Pakistan, Afghanistan, Bangladesh, Nepal, and Sri Lanka are bound by what they have in common. Since even before the end of World War II, when Lord Mountbatten drew lines on the map of Britain's collapsing Indian empire and scurried home from the subcontinent, these nations have defined and pursued their independence along sharply different paths, and with distinctive results. Yet forty-five years after the empire, South Asians remain in many ways a single people, united by history, culture, geography, and poverty. One of the most obvious features of South Asia's sound and fury is that it often arises from conflicts in which the combatants know each other too well for their collective good. It is easier to make mischief with an intimate enemy. Not only the region's assassinations but also its ideological revolutions, counterrevolutions, covert wars, ethnic conflicts, class confrontations, and religious riots often contain a destructive abandonment possible only in a family feud.

Some students of South Asia argue that the outside world ought not to be alarmed by this surface noise. They make their case most plausibly with reference to India, South Asia's unwieldy, chaotic, but oddly stabiliz-

ing geographical anchor and the region's longest-lived constitutional democracy. Philip Oldenburg, an American scholar, wrote in 1991, "The surface of Indian life is indeed chaotic, often violent, connected to the surge of deeper changes that move at a slower pace. Yet the surface chaos also indicates that the system can bend and be molded by those forces, and that the whole need not explode or crack up because of the rigidity of institutions or a powerful ruling class. There is no sense in which one can call the country stagnant. India's very size and diversity and even lack of discipline ensure that its paths to the future are many. . . . India's 'dark future' may well be an ever-receding image."

During my journey there were many ways in which I came to embrace the strength of this argument and similar ones, not only about India but about South Asia as a whole. Yet there are also reasons to be wary. While they "need not explode or crack up," and while they have achieved much about which they are justly proud, South Asia's indigenous governing elites have also demonstrated ample mendacity, foolishness, and brutality since achieving independence. The intellectuals among them have played a destructively disproportionate role in defining from above the purpose and structure of the postimperial state. Their extraordinary privileges arise from the ways in which the hierarchies of South Asia's ancient feudal societies have been preserved and sanctified by twentieth-century state-dominated "mixed" socialist ideology, the model expounded by Jawahar-lal Nehru during the 1940s and 1950s and implemented in varying forms in India, Pakistan, and Sri Lanka.* From their perches atop society these elites often express self-satisfaction. But states whose very legitimacy is continually challenged by armed insurgents can hardly afford to be complacent about their own righteous viability. This is especially true when, as now, South Asian governments are attempting to revise their basic structure—their stated reasons for being—by shifting rapidly from planned, state-dominated socialism to an as-yet-undefined version of market capitalism.

As the region's elites make this turn, dissenters bark at them noisily from the left and right and sometimes set off the explosions that rattle

---

*"Feudalism," strictly defined, refers to a specific set of political, economic, and social relationships between lords and vassals in medieval and late-medieval Europe. Here and elsewhere I use "feudal" in a broader sense, covering both hierarchical social attitudes and land-based, stratified economic relationships similar to, but not strictly the same as, European feudalism.

South Asia's surface. In Pakistan and Bangladesh, the insurgents include Islamic radicals and secessionists who rail against the whiskey-and-soda set that has managed and mismanaged national affairs since independence. In India, they are Hindu revivalists, unrepentant Communists, campaigners for caste justice, radical separatists, and cranky, idiosyncratic right-wingers. In Sri Lanka, they are fanatical revolutionaries who live in the jungles and communicate through pamphlets. What they have in common is contempt for the status-quo elites, even elites that are attempting to reform themselves.

One of South Asia's most interesting dissidents is Arun Shourie, a much despised and much admired Indian newspaper editor, neoconservative writer, investigative reporter, and religious nationalist. Shourie is a detached, soft-spoken man with a Hitlerian mustache and a penchant for repeating accounts of his early encounters with Robert F. Kennedy during the early 1960s. I sometimes visited him in his air-conditioned office and asked him to identify the ways in which South Asia's elites have helped to fuel the sound and fury they sometimes seem to want to explain away. In response, he spoke of Nehruvian socialism as if it were Soviet bolshevism.

"We have converted socialism into just a device for centralizing patronage," Shourie said one afternoon toward the end of my stay. "The state became those who occupy offices of the state at the moment—it became their private property. We have yet good time to change, and the people will be the great allies. They are the ones who suffer every day from the inefficiency of the state and its owners. . . . These few persons in the elite have become so weak and so illegitimate, even in their own eyes, that . . . they are always in dread that the testimonials on which they survived will be taken away."

One point the elites and the iconoclasts agree on is that the explosions and gunfire erupting across the surface of South Asia today are symptoms and auguries of profound change. Faster than ever before, under immense and varied pressures, South Asia is shedding its past and groping for its future. One side of the debate sees modern India, and to a lesser degree its neighbors, as responsive to these forces of change and capable of withstanding and absorbing them. The other side blames the ruling elites of South Asia for fostering violence and predicts that they will not mend their ways in time to prevent swelling, convulsive bloodshed.

As I wandered through the subcontinent, reporting on slum riots, insurgencies, assassinations, border wars, revolutions, and counterrevolutions, it did not often seem necessary to choose between these analyses or dwell at length on their forecasts. Out on the mud streets and in the villages, the struggle for change, emancipation, social and economic opportunity, power, and revenge—the struggle for possession of the future—seemed filled with such energy that trying to predict the outcome would inevitably be risky. But the faces, the voices, the pathos, helped point the way from the noise along the surface to the pressures rising underneath.

———

Here is one face: dark-skinned, bespectacled, young, white teeth protruding from an overbite. She wore a green scarf and an orange *salwar kameez,* a draping gown. That morning, she had tied her tangled black hair behind her neck; it now fell below her shoulders. Clenched in her hands at chest level was a garland of white flowers attached to a sandalwood rod. She stood in a crowd next to a makeshift corridor built from logs and rope. Beside her was a young Tamil girl who held a sheet of paper containing verses of Hindi poetry composed in honor of Rajiv Gandhi, the former prime minister of India. The young poet planned to read the verses to Gandhi, who was approaching along the corridor dressed in white khadi and Western jogging shoes, smiling amid the commotion, chants, and shouts of joy that routinely greeted his orchestrated public appearances.

Later, millions of Indians concentrated their imaginations on this freeze-frame: The bespectacled dark-skinned woman's mouth was slightly agape and she seemed serene, respectful. She was memorialized at this moment by a photographer, so it was possible afterward to revisit the image again and again. By then, of course, scrutiny was enhanced by the knowledge that beneath the woman's orange salwar lay a Velcro belt intricately wired to a nitroglycerine-based explosive, and that a moment after the picture was snapped, as the little girl prepared to read her poem, the bespectacled woman handed her sandalwood garland to Rajiv Gandhi, bent to touch his feet in respect, pushed a detonator on her Velcro belt, and set off a bomb that ripped her own body in half, obliterated most of Gandhi's head, and killed the little poet and a dozen others standing nearby.

The bespectacled woman's nom de guerre was Dhanu. She was

twenty-four, a Sri Lankan Tamil from Batticaloa, a picturesque city situated beside sandy beaches on the Indian Ocean. Her father was described by Indian investigators as an ideological mentor of the Liberation Tigers of Tamil Eelam, the radical separatist group also blamed by many for the assassination bombing of Ranjan Wijeratne, the Sri Lankan minister of state for defense. Little else could be discovered about Dhanu. She had a sister living in Paris. She had finished junior high school. She may or may not have been raped by Indian soldiers in Sri Lanka. Beyond this, what led her to Rajiv Gandhi's political rally in Sriperumbudur on May 21, 1991, what may have passed through her mind as she stood with her garland beside the child-poet, is not known. A year after the assassination, *India Today*, the country's leading news magazine, could muster only a three-paragraph biography of Dhanu. "An enigma," the magazine called her.

In some ways, Gandhi's funeral was no less mysterious, because by the time it was held in New Delhi three days later, hardly anyone seemed moved by it, other than his immediate family and the thuggish politicians who dominate the rank and file of Gandhi's Congress Party political machine. When Rajiv's mother, Indira Gandhi, died at the hands of her Sikh bodyguards in 1984, organized mobs poured through New Delhi's streets, burning Sikhs alive at taxi stands and apartment houses, slaughtering at least several thousand of them in revenge. Fury begat fury begat fury. But in the aftermath of Dhanu's explosion, fury evaporated. During those three tense days between the assassination and Rajiv Gandhi's funeral, people speculated about why interest in the event was ebbing. Some said it was because Rajiv, unlike his mother, died as a spent political force—nobody cared about him enough to seek serious revenge. Others said it was because Tamils, Dhanu's ethnic group, were less identifiable than the turbaned, bearded Sikhs and thus less easy to isolate and kill in street revenge attacks. Others said the quietude was encouraged by appeals for calm from Congress leaders, which only proved that the 1984 attacks on Sikhs had been an active conspiracy carried out by certain Congress politicians. Perhaps there was something to each of these theories. But in the streets of Delhi that Friday in May, when they pulled Rajiv Gandhi's body along vacant avenues in blistering heat, what seemed palpable was a collective sense of paralyzing shock—at the severed torsos and bloody faces photographed at Sriperumbudur and

splashed across the newspapers, and at the strange audacity of a twenty-four-year-old woman willing to destroy herself and all around her in a political act.

The Congress Party thugs brought in a few thousand peasant farmers and laborers. They packed them into trucks, unloaded them in the center of the capital, and told them to chant slogans on the streets of New Delhi during the three days Gandhi's remains lay in state at Teen Murti House, the official residence of his grandfather, Jawaharlal Nehru. But these professional mourners—Congress street "cadres" like those who burned Sikhs alive in 1984—seemed a little confused about who they were supposed to blame for Gandhi's death and how angry they were supposed to get about it. Around the grassy circle outside Teen Murti and along the tree-lined avenues nearby, the Congress-supplied crowds reached back initially to the old slogans of imperialism, in which foreigners are responsible for most things wrong in India. "The white people are eating away at India!" they yelled, and then beat up Western photographers and reporters who came to see the "grieving" thousands at Teen Murti. After a couple of days, however, this xenophobic theme dissipated, in part because some of the politicians who organized the Teen Murti crowds wanted Rajiv's Italian-born widow, Sonia Gandhi, to take over leadership of the party and the country, and it occurred to them that stirring up hatred of white people might hinder the way to Sonia's rule. By then, evidence from the assassination site made it appear all but certain that the Liberation Tigers of Tamil Eelam had been involved. But while there was tension on the streets, nobody was yet prepared to hold Indian Tamils directly responsible for the transgressions of their Sri Lankan brethren. So after a few days the rabble climbed back onto their trucks and went home, still shouting "Long live Rajiv Gandhi!," only now with less conviction than before.

Everybody was talking about what it meant to lose Gandhi, the last plausible heir to the Nehru-Gandhi family dynasty that had towered over Indian politics since independence from Britain in 1947. Gandhi struck many as a decent man but a lousy politician, prone to autocracy, political cowardice, and outright stupidity. But he was also in some ways a young progressive, enamored of modernity and technology, an internationalist who symbolized the bridge between India's past and future. To lose him to an anonymous young woman with a bomb wrapped around her waist

seemed to many Indians an event of overwhelming hopelessness, a moment when South Asia's collective strength and purpose was subsumed by an incomprehensible, self-destructive anger.

One afternoon before the funeral, after wrestling with the thugs outside Teen Murti, I telephoned O. V. Vijayan, a South Indian author of strange stories and novels about village and city life. Vijayan suffered from Parkinson's disease and lived cooped up in a dark New Delhi apartment. Yet his writing displayed a lively imagination. I asked how he felt about Gandhi's assassination. "It shows how fragile our institutions are," he answered. "I'm not prepared to say that we are going to fall apart, but I think it will be very difficult to reconcile [our differences]. . . . What's happening in India is very murky. The whole thing. The intelligentsia somehow is unable to face the challenge. They seem to be giving in to chauvinism. It's a very ominous thing." And then: "Hope and despair are like a sandwich for us. We have been living on it."

For the march to the cremation ground they brought out squads of Black Cats, elite commandos who wore black jumpsuits and black berets, carried black Sten guns, sported thick black mustaches, and tried to look tough, which they did well. We mingled for several hours with these morose soldiers at the main entrance to Teen Murti, waiting for the funeral organizers to load Gandhi's coffin onto a gun carriage. Garlanded portraits of Gandhi were posted all around. Besides the Black Cats, the turbaned Punjab 26th Regiment stood at attention in the blazing sun. Periodically a helicopter flew overhead and dropped fluttering rose petals on the Teen Murti grounds. Beneath the helicopter, black crows and carrion birds circled.

When the body was finally ready, a professional rabble of a few thousand joined the long march. Along Rajpath, the wide, majestic avenue that leads from the president's palace to India Gate, barricades had been erected to hold back the expected throngs of mourners. But the baking lawns along the avenue were empty. At the cremation ground, whose name translates roughly as "Where Power Rests," the crowds were respectable in number but subdued. We gathered around a raised brick platform where the funeral pyre had been built. Soldiers carried Gandhi's body up to the platform and placed it in the wood. The corpse was wrapped in a white shroud. Singers and priests sat cross-legged, crooning mournful ragas and reading passages from the Bhagavad Gita, the Koran, and the Bible. To one side was the VIP section, a few dozen folding chairs

propped on a dirt slope and cordoned off with logs and rope. The assemblage of political personalities drawn by Gandhi's murder and now forced to sit together on a dusty lot in 101-degree heat looked something like a cartoon from *Mad Magazine:* Dan and Marilyn Quayle in dark suits, Yasser Arafat in his checkered headdress, Prince Charles of England laden with medals, President Najibullah of Afghanistan in his Bolshevik business suit, Benazir Bhutto draped in designer-princess gowns, the King of Bhutan in ceremonial hat and interlocking threads. We reporters were separated from them like cattle in our own pen, so all we could do was speculate irreverently about what this disparate group of Very Important Persons could possibly be saying to one another to pass the time.

As Hindu priests chanted, Rajiv's son Rahul, a Harvard student, walked seven times around the funeral pyre with a burning torch and then set the wood alight. Soldiers fired three volleys of firearms. Bugles blew. Two vultures circled overhead. And then it was finished. Not many cried.

About a week later, I was in Amritsar, the capital of the Sikh religion, covering the last leg of the national election disrupted by Gandhi's assassination. Radical Sikh separatists had already assassinated more than twenty candidates in ambushes and bomb attacks. I went with a colleague to see a Sikh professor of political science, Surjeet Singh Narang, at Guru Nanak Dev University. It turned out that while Narang drew his salary from the government of India and spent his days teaching young minds about the nature and conduct of politics, he was openly enthusiastic about the murder of election candidates because it was an expression of Sikh resistance to Indian rule. We asked what he thought about the assassination of Rajiv Gandhi.

"The feeling is good riddance," he answered. "The assassination of Rajiv Gandhi is an inspiration." Then he meditated for a little while on Dhanu, the Tamil assassin. He was impressed with her cunning. "We never thought of a human bomb," he said. "We thought of other bombs but never a human bomb."

We left the professor in this state of contemplation. So much yet to do, his wistful voice seemed to be saying, so much yet to learn.

In some ways, the problem with bombers in South Asia, whether professorial or proletarian, is not the actual damage they cause but the sheer noise they make—they drown out so much else that matters. Desperate for effect, the bombers ignite public crises and generate swells of political momentum that wash across a broader, more stable, and more

progressive political economy on the subcontinent. This, in fact, is the bombers' goal: to tranform the immediate chaos of a violent explosion into a sustained wave of political revolution or upheaval. Yet the bombers fail more often than not because for all their smoke, they cannot finally obscure South Asia's quiet accumulation of ordinary change and ordinary achievement beneath the surface—the slow buildup of forward-looking middle classes, for example, or the countless negotiations within and between families and clans and castes to achieve peaceful social and economic change across generations. The bombers touch and even influence this slower, familiar change in South Asia. And they are abetted by the failures of South Asia's political institutions and governing classes. But so far, after forty-five years of independence, they have found it maddeningly difficult to actually achieve violent or sudden political revolution in South Asia. So much incremental nonviolent revolution is taking place away from the sound and fury that it is in fact the bombers, and not the great "masses" they seek to stir, who often find it hard to keep up.

This, at least, is what a dour man named Bhajan Singh impressed on me one sultry week in the autumn of 1989 when we climbed into his garishly decorated ten-ton monster truck and set out across the northern Indian heartland for Calcutta, aiming simply to deliver a few piles of Punjabi cloth to a modest clutch of Bengali merchants some nine hundred miles away.

2

The Grand Trunk Road

A line of stalls selling very simple food and tobacco, a stack of
firewood, a police station, a well, a horse-trough, a few trees, and,
under them, some trampled ground dotted with the black ashes of
old fires, are all that mark a parao on the Grand Trunk. . . . The
police are thieves and extortioners but at least they do not suffer
any rivals.

—*Rudyard Kipling*

After tramping through mud and pools of oil, we found Bhajan Singh
asleep in a mosquito-infested back room beside his trucking company's East Delhi office. He was a long, bony, bearded Sikh. A soiled
white turban draped his eyes. Rousted from his nap, he led us wordlessly
through the fetid night smoke spewed by East Delhi's factories.

He climbed into the ten-ton Tata truck that was his home. He seemed
less than overjoyed about my plan, concocted upon arrival in South Asia
in the summer of 1989 and partially appropriated from Kipling, to satu-
rate myself with India by taking a nine-hundred-mile truck journey from
New Delhi to Calcutta along the Grand Trunk Road, which spans the
breadth of northern India. Later, Bhajan Singh grumbled to my translator,
a portly high-caste Brahmin with a waxed mustache who I will refer to
here as Vinod, that prior to our departure the trucking company boss had
pronounced it essential that we reach Calcutta uninjured, and that further-
more, if this was not achieved, Singh would lose his job. It was hard to
tell whether the demand ticked Singh off because he thought it an
unreasonable expectation or because it meant that to keep up appearances
along the way, he could not drink as much whiskey or smoke as much
opium while driving as he might otherwise do.

"These drivers—Muslims, Jats, Sikhs—are very rough, very rude,"

Vinod explained in a condescending tone that night. "They are subjugated by everyone—bosses, financiers, police, tax authorities. So they fight back."

Anyone who has weaved through the chaos and carnage of South Asia's phantasmagoric intercity roads might reasonably be nervous about riding shotgun in a Tata truck—a two-axle, six-wheel, top-heavy steel box that looks to drivers of oncoming cars like one of those carnivorous contraptions from the *Mad Max* movies. But after I climbed into the cab, the butterflies subsided. Looking down through the panoramic windshield decorated with swirling stickers depicting Sikh gurus, roses, and fish, I suddenly realized: It was not *we* who should be nervous about careening down the highway in this metal monster. It was everybody else on the road who should be worried about us.

Singh jammed his gears and pulled out from the mud lot, weaving down the night road through dust and diesel smoke, blasting his horn to overtake cows, taxis, camel carts, bicycles, motorcycles, three-wheeled motorized rickshaws, water buffalo, dogs, zippy Maruti economy cars, and pedestrians. The animals, objects, and people meandered backward, forward, and sideways in what seemed a continuous choreographed dance of near-miss. Singh did his bit and managed not to hit anyone.

The unlit, unlined, undivided road fell in small receding patches beneath the Tata's headlights. Tall stands of eucalyptus trees flanked the highway on the flat stretches. Roadside restaurants with illicit bars and brothels attached flashed past. Chimneyed brick kilns loomed in the moonlight. To the sides, we could sometimes see sleeping villages nestled in the shadows. Not only did the truck have no seat belts, it had no doors, so we leaned to and fro in the rushing air, gripping our seats on the heavy bends. Eucalyptus, industrial effluent, burning dung, spices and incense assaulted our nostrils. Horns—ours, theirs, everybody's—blasted all around.

On South Asian roads, where the chance of being accidentally blindsided is high, horn-honking is an act of courtesy. Should it ever become an Olympic event, the Indians would have a leg up for technical prowess, but the Pakistanis, who like to wire snippets from Western popular songs into their steering columns, would score well for creativity. Once, stuck at the Khyber Pass, I listened to a Pakistani truck driver push his way through a traffic jam leading into Afghanistan by using a horn that played at deafening volume the refrain from *Never on Sunday*. Cars and trucks

peeled out of his way just so they wouldn't have to listen to the damned tune anymore.

Inside our spacious Tata cab, Singh kept his distance and projected a hard, lonely demeanor. He deferred to Vinod and myself and worried about our comfort. At the same time he bullied his assistant driver, a poor Bihari named Santosh, unmercifully. This seemed to reflect the unspoken hierarchy of our traveling party, with myself at the top by virtue of being a foreign guest, Vinod next by virtue of his Brahmin birth, which he advertised at every opportunity, then Singh, and at the bottom Santosh, who was of a caste similar to his boss's but earned one tenth his salary and suffered in apprenticeship. Whether one chose to see this hierarchy in terms of old identities such as caste or new identities such as economic status, there was no denying its palpable presence inside our truck. Among my three companions, groveling deference from below and spiteful bullying from above seemed to be the guiding principles.

Hunched with hooded eyes over the steering wheel, Singh spoke laconically about his past. He said he was born as a Jat Sikh, an unruly subset of India's minority Sikh religious group, whose male members traditionally wear turbans and never cut their hair. (Jats are a peasant farming caste group that can be either Sikh or Hindu.) On the small farm in rural Punjab where Singh grew up, his status was ordained by tradition but his opportunities were defined by modernity. His ancestors had been farmers and soldiers, but after dropping out of high school, he took to trucking because the money was good. Now he was independent, even upwardly mobile. He wore a shiny gold watch and said he sent one hundred rupees a month home to Punjab to his wife, whom he wed in an arranged marriage in 1984. Those he left behind in the village were trapped now in the Sikh separatist insurgency, in which more than five thousand people, mostly Sikhs, die in shootouts, bomb explosions, and police killings each year. In any event, apart from the war, farming bored him, Singh said. He preferred to be on the move. "I'll drive until my body quits."

Or until the road kills him. Daring and reckless behind the wheels of their massive vehicles, India's truck drivers are modern heirs to the traders, conquerors, robbers, and religious seers who have traveled the Grand Trunk Road for centuries. Several hundred years before the birth of Christ, Mauryan emperors laid the first tombstone-shaped mileage markers between Kabul and Calcutta. In some ways, not much has

changed on the highway since then. As ever, the road is vividly dangerous. More than one thousand truck drivers, passengers, and pedestrians
die in accidents along the highway each year. Its shoulders reveal an
almost surreal display of wreckage: trucks lying smashed and upside
down in ditches every thirty to thirty-five miles, buses wrapped around
trees, vans hanging from bridges, cars squashed like bugs. Sections of the
road are controlled by bandits who hijack trucks several times a month,
sometimes killing the drivers. Corrupt policemen demand bribes at every
checkpoint and throw drivers in jail if they don't oblige. And in rural
areas, if a cow or pedestrian is run over, mobs of villagers attack, burn
trucks, and lynch drivers in revenge—a peril of which Bhajan Singh
would twice be reminded on the road ahead.

In some ways, the Grand Trunk depicts what is unsettled and unfinished in South Asia. The road is the backbone of commerce in the
northern subcontinent, and commerce is perhaps the most powerful force
churning up change in the region these days—raising expectations, dash-
ing expectations, rearranging old caste, class, political, and religious orders. V. S. Naipaul traveled around India recently and described what he
saw and heard as "a million mutinies now." At least half a million of them
concern money.

We paid our first bribe almost immediately. An inspector waved us
down and demanded tax papers. In India's Nehruvian, "mixed socialist"
economy, taxes on commercial goods are supposed to be paid by truckers
at every state and city border. The system is partly a legacy of the old
European feudal idea, carried abroad by the European colonialists, that
whoever controls the road—bandit, prince, thug, foreign imperialist—
takes his tribute. In India, the tax goes back to the nineteenth century.
More recently, the Nehruvian state has claimed authority but has shared
its booty with the bandits and thugs, some of whom are in its employ,
others of whom just rush in where the state has left a void. Modern
truckers, like the traders of old, have adapted nicely to the system,
foraging inexorably toward profit wherever it can be found. Since following the official rules and paying all the official taxes would bankrupt most
transporters and bring commerce to a halt, the trucking companies have
developed an intricate, shifting system of bribes paid to bureaucrats and
police to keep the wheels turning. Private tribute has been substituted for
public tribute. The Nehruvian state may be going broke as a consequence,
but its employees and their allies are doing rather well.

Our first inspector glanced at the truck's papers and asked for a modest five rupees. Santosh, the assistant driver, slipped him the note while leaning out the doorless cab into the enveloping darkness. Bhajan Singh didn't even bother to slow the truck as Santosh handed out the cash.

Some miles on, a policeman waved us down with a flashlight. Singh leaned out and shouted the name of his trucking company, whereupon the policeman stepped aside and waved us through. "The boss pays him eight hundred rupees per month for all vehicles," Singh explained, driving on. "If you are a newcomer, it would cost one hundred rupees—for nothing, just so he will not inspect."

Vinod elaborated. "The trucking companies all pay about forty thousand to fifty thousand rupees to the police per month, handled from the home office, so they do not check for sales tax. He pays because he can't afford not to. There are massive systemic bribes to avoid sales-tax checks. That's why we're waved through. . . . A friend of mine in Agra has become a multimillionaire mostly because his savings are on sales tax. Bogus permits let you save. That is where the money lies. Freight is nothing."

Besides keeping an eye on me and translating, Vinod had another purpose in traveling to Calcutta. His regular job was as a repo man who chased down truck drivers who defaulted on loan payments. If a driver "absconded," in the Indian phraseology, Vinod tracked him down and tried to get the truck back. Two absconders were believed to be hiding out somewhere in Calcutta and Vinod intended to find them. Normally a few threats and shoves were enough to get the job done, he said. But sometimes he had to go to court. He explained his craft, telling a story about a repo man he knew, whom I will refer to here as Rajiv. Once, traveling by rail to a provincial capital where two repossessed trucks were tied up in seemingly endless litigation, Rajiv found himself by chance in a first-class compartment with two senior judges from the relevant court. Sensing opportunity, he broke out a bottle of whiskey, poured generously, and then explained his legal predicament, gently asking the esteemed judges if they had any advice for a man in his position. The judges cited a few vague statutes. Later, asleep, Rajiv felt himself being shaken awake by one of them, who summoned him to the corridor. The judge handed Rajiv a slip of paper containing the name of an attorney in the provincial capital and told him to contact the lawyer. Within a week, he had funneled a fifty-thousand-rupee payment through the lawyer to the judge and he had his trucks.

While office mavens like Vinod handle the systemic bribes, Singh takes care of the petty cash out on the highway. Throughout any journey small bribes must be paid to uninitiated tax inspectors and policeman encountered at random. Singh said he works on an incentive-bonus plan. His regular monthly salary is two thousand rupees, or about seventy dollars at present exchange rates. But at the start of each trip, the boss hands over an estimated bribe allotment of about two hundred to three hundred rupees, depending on the going rates. Then, it is up to Singh to make it to Calcutta without spending more than this allotment on actual bribes. Whatever he doesn't pay out to police and bureaucrats, he keeps. Some months, he said, he earns an additional one thousand rupees this way, plus more for fees charged to hitchhiking passengers and kickbacks from truck repairmen.

Shortly after midnight Singh paused to rest at a bustling *dhaba*, or truck stop, beside the moonlit highway. Santosh jumped down quickly and began to dig mud from the truck's tires with a stick. Two dozen or so Tatas surrounded us in the pale light. Boy waiters wandered among the trucks carrying clear glasses filled with milky tea. Singh took a glass, stretched his legs, and pulled out a flask of whiskey.

"We can't live without it," he said, dumping the tea and filling his glass with malt. "The time is short—so I like to drink the whole bottle at once."

As he did, I asked about life on the road. He said he spent much of it sitting in truck stops. "These places are run by the powerful people of the area—*goondas* [thugs]. You have to be a powerful goonda to handle these truck drivers. You will find drugs, liquor, opium. Everything is available. . . . Generally, everyone is available on the road. Calcutta is famous for prostitution. In Bengal [the state surrounding Calcutta], a beetle is more expensive than a prostitute. Drivers are homosexual. They enjoy each other, prostitutes, whiskey, drugs, and beer. Before I got married, I did the same thing."

The difficulty, he continued, is that "there's no respect from the police, no respect from the drivers. At least in Bengal they respect the driver and call him 'sir.' You can drive the whole state and pay one rupee. In other areas, even if the papers are all right, they will arrest me without a bribe. We pay on the spot, officially and unofficially, so I've never been arrested. But there are bandits, too, working with the police, and sometimes those people try to find a way to stop the truck. But I find a way out. The fleet owners and drivers travel in convoys in some areas. Bihar is notorious.

There are night robbers. Even here. If we wanted to go past Etah tonight, we would have to drive in a convoy."

Criminal gangs, some of whose leaders are prominent elected politicians, have risen in the last two decades to dominate commerce across northern India, as the Nehruvian state has faltered under bankruptcy and self-interested leadership. For ambitious members of lower and middle castes in the north, the gangs provide a rapid means of social and economic mobility. To achieve influence, the leaders drape themselves with the flags of the major political parties—the long-dominant Congress Party, the leftist Janata Dal, and the Hindu revivalist Bharatiya Janata Party—and sometimes they put their electoral services up for bids. One of the most notorious mafias runs the coal fields. Others dominate road building and public housing construction. P. R. Rajgopal, a retired senior Indian police officer, cites an estimate that half of the senior officers of the public-sector trading companies in northern Uttar Pradesh, India's largest and most populous state, are involved in corruption. There are, of course, many Indian civil servants, perhaps even a majority, who struggle against great odds and temptations to remain honest—their moral courage is all the more remarkable because it goes unrewarded by the system. But there can be no doubt that corruption within the Indian bureaucracy is extensive, even systemic. Officers at nationalized banks routinely demand kickbacks of up to 25 percent before disbursing loans. Since, in the Nehruvian model, government dominates the economy, access to government office is the key to acquiring wealth. Bureaucrats, judges, elected politicians—nearly everybody has the chance to skim at least a little from the public till. It's just that in the northern states, the skimmers tend to be better organized and better armed, which occasionally leads to conflicts between rival gangs battling for control of particular regions and industries. Kidnapping industrialists for ransom is a booming business these days. The man who was my travel agent in New Delhi for two years disappeared one afternoon after a squad of Uttar Pradesh goondas showed up in his office and asked for a meeting. A passerby found the man's poisoned corpse dumped on a roadside near the Grand Trunk Road in Etah.

Singh runs this gauntlet in his Tata truck six times each month—five days down to Calcutta from Delhi, five days back, three round trips per month. No holidays, no sick pay, no overtime. Yet he feels in some ways a privileged man. "The road is my house," he said that night in the truck

cab, belting down his whiskey. And then, smiling and gesturing to the trucks parked around him in the dark: "We are the road kings."

———

At dawn the countryside awoke. Bullock carts and horses rattled down the road. Goats wandered through the dirt courtyard where the trucks were parked. The air was heavy with mist, dung, and spice. Even before the sun struck the treetops, men and women trudged by the dozens from nearby villages to the surrounding fields and back, bent under the weight of wheat, sugar cane, and corn. Purple *bahya* flowers rose in a pond across the highway. Cranes and herons bathed among them.

Singh lay passed out on an exposed wooden cot, sedated by his whiskey. Beside him a Muslim truck driver filled bucket after bucket of water at a well, carried the buckets to his truck, hoisted them by rope to the top of his trailer, and dumped the water into the bin. I watched this for half an hour, sipping milky tea, before finally asking Vinod to inquire why the driver seemed so determined to fill his truck with water. The Muslim explained that he was carrying coal from Calcutta to Delhi and wanted to add some weight to his load before he arrived. He gets credit for the extra weight on delivery, he said. On the Grand Trunk Road, everybody has an angle.

Impudent goats woke Singh, who shouted abuse at Santosh, who scrambled to bring tea and hustled to wipe off the driver's seat inside the truck. Soon we were rumbling east again. On a five-kilometer stretch, we honked our way past the following: one small boy hitchhiking, a bullock cart out of control, two cows running amok, bicyclists toting heavy burlap sacks, a horse-drawn rickshaw carrying a smartly dressed family, nine cows and two boys swimming in a muddy water hole, a bullock cart carrying a load of sticks, one behind it carrying a family, three men sleeping at the roadside with their heads protruding onto the asphalt, a herd of goats grazing on the road, a herd of cows crossing, dogs, pigs, bicycle rickshaws, and camels.

A police constable flagged us down, climbed in, and demanded a free ride to the office. As we rumbled along, I asked why all the cops we met wanted a handout. "It should not be that way," he said sheepishly. "But they only pay us eight hundred rupees a month and we have to work twenty-four hours a day. That is not enough money."

As we weaved ahead, Santosh leaned out of the cab, waving to other

drivers to move aside. Sometimes they did. The policemen fell asleep and began to snore. When we reached his office, Santosh shook him awake and helped him down.

The partnership between Santosh and Singh was uneasy. Most of the drivers and assistants on the Grand Trunk Road are Sikhs or Muslims—outsiders to mainstream Indian society. But Santosh is a Hindu. He was raised in Bihar state, a poor region traversed by the highway, where banditry is endemic. Fleet owners sometimes hire Biharis as assistants in the hope that their local knowledge will lessen the risk of hijacking. For this, and his ability to pry mud from truck tires with a stick, Santosh earned about seven dollars per month. When we had parked that afternoon at a truck stop called Hotel the Great Papa, whose shabby sign bore the motto "Love Is Sweet Poison," Santosh said that he was worried that his boss, whose friends and colleagues are mainly Sikhs, might never teach him how to drive the truck, and that he would be stuck as a poorly paid assistant for years to come. "My main motivation is to be a driver," he said, glancing nervously at Singh, who was asleep on a cot below him. "If he won't give me a chance, I will go someplace else. A good driver must have sympathy with his assistant, must give him a chance and teach him."

Santosh, eighteen, also confessed to a series of romantic entanglements not unlike those of truck drivers celebrated in American country music. Two years ago his family arranged a marriage to a thirteen-year-old girl in his Bihar village. But he said he had not seen his wife since the wedding—she was too young to consummate the relationship. Meanwhile, Santosh said, he had been having an affair with a fourteen-year-old who had recently been forced into marriage with a fifty-five-year-old Calcutta man. He said he saw the girl on his three-day stopovers. "She needs me," he remarked.

No matter what, he said, he would never return to village life or to the small farm tended by his family. With all its risks and hardships, the road was a better living. "Some day," he mused, "I know that I will die in a truck."

Shortly after Santosh made this forecast, a truck passed us going in the opposite direction. Its entire front end and windshield had been ripped away but for the driver's seat and the steering column poking up from the engine. The truck seemed to be running fine, bound for New Delhi with a full load.

We slept in a roadside dhaba managed by a white-bearded Sikh who approached me as I lay stretched on a wooden cot to announce that he had just ingested a large amount of opium. Thereupon, he sat down and volunteered his life's story in manic, singsong English, occasionally rising to career around the dirt courtyard at points of emphasis. He had been a sailor on a Greek cargo ship and had traveled to Germany, Holland, and America, where he had been particularly impressed by New Orleans, Seattle, and the "great city" of Norwalk, Connecticut. "I loved the sea, but it brought me nothing—only this little hotel," he shouted. If he liked the traveling life, why not become a truck driver? "I thought about becoming a driver, but now I would like to stay in one place. I have seen most of the world, but now I am in India. When in India, it is better not to think of other places."

We bathed each morning at the outdoor public wells, stripped to our underwear beside the main highway, soaping ourselves into great froths of lather. Evidently short on entertainment, large crowds of local villagers gathered to watch the white man wash himself. There seemed to be much amusement over whether, in leaning awkwardly across the well on the slippery bricks, I would fall in. Fellow bathers gestured and offered suggestions, whether helpful or devious I could not make out since I lack fluent Hindi and it seemed a ridiculous time to insist on translation. Singh lounged on rope cots with other Sikh drivers and tried to explain me to them. "He is telling them that you say that in America they have trucks that make ours look like pullcarts," Vinod reported. But I had said no such thing. "He is only trying to win influence with his friends," Vinod said.

On the third afternoon, passing two mangled trucks just west of Varanasi, the sprawling metropolis that is the holiest city in Hinduism, we asked Singh gently about the matter of all these road accidents we kept passing. In twelve years, he said indifferently, he has had only one, resulting in a minor shoulder injury. But there are certain risks, he added.

"If you run over a person, the best thing to do is to run away—drive to the nearest police station and turn yourself in, lock yourself into the jail," he explained. "If you stay at the scene of an accident, the people will burn the truck and beat you to death, especially if it is a child that has been hit. If you strike a cow, they might or might not attack. That depends on whether you are a Muslim. As for pigs and dogs, nobody bothers. You might have to pay some compensation."

The risks are especially acute for Sikhs adhering to religious tradition,

since their turbans and beards make them readily identifiable targets for any excited Hindu mob. Ever since Indira Gandhi's 1984 assassination by Sikh bodyguards and the subsequent anti-Sikh riots, Sikh drivers on the Grand Trunk Road have traveled in convoys. On our trip, Singh stopped only at dhabas owned or managed by fellow Sikhs. "After 1984, we feel unsafe," he said. "I don't believe that the Sikhs will ever become a part of India again. It is not possible." After parking in a ditch along the road, Singh mulled the question over with other Sikh drivers in his ragged, shifting convoy. They all blamed the Gandhis, Indira and Rajiv, for stupidity and mendacity. And they said the situation was getting worse, not better.

"Today the life has become very dangerous," said one driver with a tattoo of Sikh visionary Guru Nanak emblazoned on his hand. "Now I would never advise anyone to become a driver, especially not a Sikh. When you travel the roads alone, it is not safe."

The point was made that evening. Forty miles east of Varanasi, as a pink sun fell over fields of sugar cane, Singh slammed on his brakes, sending us sprawling around the cab. To the left was a truck smashed against a tree. Around it had gathered a large group of villagers, some of whom were milling in the road, slowing traffic. Singh drove several hundred yards farther on and parked under a tree, out of sight. He said it looked as if a small child had been killed by the smashed truck. He thought it would be unwise for him to investigate.

Vinod flagged a bicycle rickshaw and we rolled silently back to the accident site. There we found farmer Ram Prashad, his face streaked with tears. His six-year-old daughter, Lakshmi Devi, had been squatting by the side of the road, relieving herself, when a speeding truck swerved to avoid a bicycle and hit her, killing her instantly. (Public roadsides are sometimes the only available bathrooms for the Indian landless, who in some cases can face severe reprisals if they trespass or relieve themselves on the land of upper-caste neighbors. Children of all classes find the roadside a convenient toilet.) The girl's body lay wrapped in a cloth sack, covered with flies. The truck driver involved had run to the police for protection and had been arrested. But the villagers were restless.

"What was my mistake? Why did the gods penalize me?" Prashad shouted. "God and this driver have killed her. That bloody bastard—I want to kill him!"

With that, the crowd surged toward the smashed truck. A lone police

constable carrying a single-shot rifle tried to hold them back and urged us to leave the scene quickly. Simultaneously pushing and cajoling, the policeman managed to hold the mob back.

Minutes later, after we returned to the truck, Singh rolled us back onto the highway while Santosh lit two sticks of incense for evening prayers. Singh folded his hands toward the pictures of Sikh gurus pasted on his windshield, no easy feat while trying to drive. Santosh climbed onto the dashboard and twirled incense in circles around Singh, the steering wheel, and the gearbox on the floor.

"Our life is in his hands," said Singh, gesturing to the image of Guru Gobind Singh, the tenth and last of the Sikh gurus.

"We must worship the gods for our safety, and for the safety of trucks," said Santosh.

———

Beneath a full moon several hundred trucks stood parked in congested lines at the Bihar state border, halted before a police barrier where goods are inspected, taxes imposed, and the wheels of commerce lubricated. Diesel exhaust and smoke from coal fires clouded the air. Vendors of juice and nuts called out prices from beneath kerosene lamps. A bearded medicine man wandered by, offering a bottled cure for eczema from his suitcase.

Tardip Kumar of Supreme Commission Agents, which operates from a roadside wooden stand, climbed into the cab, asked for our papers, and said he would try to clear us across the border within an hour. His fee was twenty rupees, of which he said half would be paid in bribes and the rest pocketed by his agency. Small change, but despite his promises we were stuck in place for nearly four hours. Impatient, Vinod and I wandered around looking for somebody to bribe. We were told that the officers in charge were taking a dinner-and-nap break and could not be disturbed. That night I slept on top of the truck and tried to drift off while listening to Van Halen full blast on my Walkman. It had become clear that to sleep at truck stops, you needed something loud to drown out all the competing tapes of screeching Hindi film songs wherein damsels sing of love and honor and revenge.

The next afternoon we pushed into the jungles of central Bihar, where the roads have been ripped away by floods and hijackers are said to rule the mountains. Singh rounded a bend and spotted a truck lying upside

down in a pit, wheels in the air, as if in a state of rigor mortis. Beside the wreck three men sat before a pup tent, cooking lunch on an open fire. Singh honked and waved as he drove past. "Those are the drivers of the truck," he said of the men outside the tent. "They've been living there for a month. They're waiting for a crane."

All along the road we saw the carcasses of crashed vehicles, resting like fossils in the exact position in which their accidents left them. Repairing smashed trucks can take a long time. Often, drivers refuse to leave their vehicles unattended, fearing that bandits or corrupt police will loot the cargo. So the wreckage sits, week after week.

From the jungle hills the road fell slowly into coal country, heartland of Bihar's organized crime syndicates, a region of strip mines choked in black smoke. At brick depots along the highway, shirtless laborers hoisted large bowls of coal on their backs and carried them up ramps to load fleets of Tata trucks, which poured onto the road. Traffic slowed to a crawl.

At last, shortly after dawn on the fifth day, the coal towns yielded to cool, green rice fields on the western edge of the Ganges delta. In hours Singh would reach the outskirts of Calcutta's urban chaos. He would deliver his crates of cloth and garments to the office. Vinod would search for his absconding truck drivers. Santosh would visit his fourteen-year-old mistress.

Then a mob attacked us. It happened in an instant. Driving close behind an unfamiliar truck with Bihar license plates, Singh turned into Memari village, a tiny hamlet of grass-topped huts thirty miles or so west of the Calcutta city line. Suddenly villagers were all around us, banging on the doors, pounding on the engine, shouting for us to stop. Somebody called for vengeance and smacked the door of the truck with his fist. Shouts went up. Somebody yelled that there had been a traffic accident and they wanted Singh to carry a wounded man to the hospital. Most of the crowd seemed furious, however, and some blocked the truck's path. Singh pointed at me in the center of the cab and shouted, *"Sahib hai! Sahib hai!,"* which means roughly, "There is a white man, an officer, here!" Confused, the crowd fell back slightly. Singh jammed the gearshift and roared ahead. Some villagers chased the truck briefly but let us go.

"I don't know what happened," Singh said a few minutes later, after snapping his fingers for some chewing tobacco from Santosh. "There must have been an accident. Something had gone wrong, though."

Singh himself appeared unconcerned—about himself, his truck, the

allegedly wounded man, or the village mob. Twenty minutes later he saw a driver from his company coming down the highway from Calcutta, carrying a load to New Delhi. Singh flagged the man down and the two talked for half an hour, gossiping about a driver in trouble with the boss, another who had left his suitcase in Calcutta, and about conditions on the road. Singh never mentioned the incident in Memari.

An hour later, as we finally reached the Calcutta line, I asked him why he hadn't told his friend about the crowd that attacked him in the village.

Singh laughed at me. "Oh, that was a minor thing," he said. "Happens all the time."

3

The Gravy Train

Long years ago we made a tryst with destiny. And now the time
comes when we shall redeem our pledge, not wholly or in full
measure, but very substantially.

—*Jawaharlal Nehru*

The headlines in South Asia today splash news of the ongoing attempt to reform, reconstitute, resuscitate, redeem, and otherwise
rescue-before-it-is-too-late the Nehruvian state, an entity that surely exists but is not so easy to define or explain. Poor Nehru—for being
eloquent and historic, he gets blamed for many things he had nothing to
do with. Pakistan, Bangladesh, and Sri Lanka, for example, have constructed, between independence and the present day, political economies
that in many ways can be called Nehruvian, but Nehru himself contributed little to them directly. Jinnah, Ayub, Bhutto, Mujib, Ershad, Zia,
Bandaranaike, Jayewardene—these are some of the leaders who deserve
credit and blame for what is happening today on the geographical rim of
Britain's former subcontinental empire. Even in the heartland of independent India, Nehru's home turf, much of what is now referred to as the
Nehruvian state consists of structures, policies, and attitudes inherited
from the British colonies and the indigenous feudals and babus through
whom the British sometimes ruled. Also, what Nehru built upon as India's
first and most important prime minister has been undermined by politicians who came to power after his death in 1964, including Nehru's direct
political and familial heirs, his daughter, Indira Gandhi, and her sons,
Sanjay and Rajiv. Yet as the dominant, defining South Asian statesman of

his time, and as the man who stood in a New Delhi assembly hall at the "midnight hour" of independence on August 14, 1947, promising in stirring rhetoric to "redeem our pledge" after decades of struggle for freedom, Nehru is the individual most commonly and most justly memorialized as the architect of the modern South Asian state.

The Nehruvian state is what Bhajan Singh drives through in his ten-ton Tata truck several times each month. It is what he and some other Sikhs in Punjab—not to mention dozens of other South Asian separatist communities—aspire to break free from, though no doubt they would replicate many of its features if they did. It is what Sri Lankan revolutionaries wish to overthrow, what Indian Hindu revivalists wish to reinvent, what Pakistani Muslim radicals wish to replace with an Islamic theocracy. Indeed, what matters most about the state in South Asia these days is that it is under assault and looking none too stalwart—badly indebted, overextended, systematically abused, demonstrably unjust and inequitable, threatening at times to fall down of its own weight.

As the mild-mannered, bookish cousin of the domineering Bolshevik state, the Nehruvian state has been deeply unnerved by its relative's sudden and spectacular death—and just when cousin Bolshevik appeared to be striding along with such vim and vigor. Yet the death of bolshevism has had a salutary effect on the subcontinent. Stimulated by fears of mortality and revolution, the Nehruvian state's various keepers have undertaken late-in-life fitness regimens, slimming down and toughening up in reluctant recognition that self-discipline may be necessary to avoid their cousin's cataclysmic end. Whether or to what degree the region's elites can succeed with this reform, economically and politically, is an overarching question about South Asia's future.

———

How the South Asian state formed, swelled, creaked, split, recovered, and fought to protect itself from challengers in the four decades after 1947 is a story too long and complex to be recounted fully here. In the present debate over what to do about its decrepit condition, however, one important theme concerns historiography. There are two basic schools of thought about the state's rise and decline. One holds that the Nehruvian ideal was sound, inspired, humane, and appropriate for its time, and therefore any adjustment ought to be a matter of tinkering and adaptation to changed circumstances. This is what most members of the South Asian

elites believe. The opposing view, calibrated in different ways by various dissenters, is that the state was fundamentally flawed and unjust in the first place, and that saving it will require radical, even revolutionary measures.

Jawaharlal Nehru would be appalled to hear this discussion. An upper-caste lawyer whose ancestors emigrated from Kashmir and settled in the Gangetic heartland along the Grand Trunk Road, Nehru helped for three decades to lead the independence-seeking Indian National Congress, predecessor of the Congress Party. He then served continuously as prime minister of independent India for seventeen years, longer than any other national leader in modern South Asian history. The state that bears his name—best thought of as an ideological model, rather than a particular government at a particular time—took form during the 1950s and early 1960s, the coldest years of the cold war. Like Egypt's Nasser, Nehru saw himself as a historic cold war statesman treading a neutralist, balancing "middle way" between communism and capitalism. In international affairs, his neutrality was less consequential than he believed. But in domestic affairs his outlook shaped the lives of many millions.

His model is a prescription for constitutional democracy, social advancement, and economic growth for poor, exploited, preindustrial societies. Its principles include federalism, socialism, parliamentary democracy, ethnic and linguistic pluralism, and rapid industrialization to be led by a strong central government. In arguing that extensive government planning was essential to take a backward society like India's rapidly into the industrial twentieth century, Nehru borrowed from Stalin. He even appropriated Stalin's impressive-sounding idea of government-led five-year plans, the first of which Nehru announced for India in 1951. Unlike Stalin, Nehru did not seek to achieve industrialization and improved agricultural efficiency through coercion or violence. He was a genuine democrat and strengthened institutions such as parliament and state government at the expense of his own power. It is certainly arguable that his emphasis on the omnipotence and benevolent wisdom of an elite class of federal bureaucrats and planners, who controlled the state's meager resources and directed the economy from commanding heights, was from the beginning a prescription for injustice and corruption. It also must be recalled that in the 1950s, when this system was erected, sanctified, and taken over by the South Asian elites, the superiority of a "mixed socialist" approach to Third World development was a tenet of the conventional wisdom; the

theory was being implemented in various forms across Western Europe and the neocolonial countries, and was nearly as popular, for example, on some American university campuses as theories about capitalist "shock therapy" are today.

The institutional by-products of these ideas everywhere dot the South Asian landscape. One feature of the great bureaucracies and "public-sector enterprises," as the hundreds of largely money-losing state-owned industries are known, is their enthusiasm for sign-painting. All along the highways and back roads are signs pointing this way and that to such obscure-sounding entities as the "Haryana Co-Operative Scheme for Sugar Warehousing" or the "Sind Regional Development Authority's Public Service Building Society Housing Scheme Part IV." The signs tend to be in better repair than the facilities they advertise, which often consist of water-streaked concrete hallways reeking of mildew, and acres upon acres of dimly lit desks manned by armies of the gratefully—but not gainfully—employed. At least half of the public-sector enterprises in India and Pakistan lost money in 1990, the last year for which statistics were available, contributing to budget deficits considerably larger in relative terms than the enormous one in the United States. The national-ized banks have been forced to dole out so many bad loans to political cronies or unworthy public-sector businesses that a number of the banks would be insolvent if subjected to rigorous accounting. Laying off work-ers, which might improve the prospects of some of these "sick" compa-nies, as they are called, is politically and often legally forbidden, even in the recent reform climate. *The Economist* noted in an influential 1991 survey of India's economy, which it dubbed a "caged tiger," that the Indian bureaucracy's rules and regulations had become so duplicative and impenetrable that extreme violence would have to be committed on them simply for the capitalist economy underneath to glimpse the light of day.

The Nehruvian state fit well over South Asia's colonial inheritance. In service of the empire, the British had constructed a vast hierarchical administrative apparatus, which Nehru and his colleagues converted to their own, initially idealistic, ends. For the socially privileged leaders of the independence movements, the conversion was convenient because it left in power much of the elite colonial class the British had used for several centuries to control their territory and earn their riches. The variously nationalist, leftist, and Gandhian rhetoric of South Asia's several independence movements suggested that the colonial structure would be

torn down and replaced with an egalitarian model. Attempts of this sort were indeed made after independence and some of them succeeded, but in such crucial areas as land reform, higher education, caste, and access to English—the language of power—not enough changed, compared with what was promised. In India, this was in part because of the evolutionary, tolerant, democratic character of the Nehruvian ideal, which rejected purges. It was also because the indigenous elites used for centuries by the British had the wisdom to switch sides during the independence struggle and then claimed the mantle of victory when independence arrived. Some of the old princes and local aristocrats had to give up their country estates, but many of them moved straight over to the rapidly expanding federal ministries to get on with the business of building "socialism," effectively trading one sort of fiefdom for another.

South Asians themselves often use the term "elite" in broadbrush fashion to encompass strata of the socially or economically privileged who may have little in common or even be in fierce competition with one another. No single approach to defining or understanding the elites is satisfactory. There are, for example, millions of impoverished high-caste Brahmins in India and a significant number of millionaire "untouchables" made rich by the state's various affirmative action plans. At the same time, wealth alone by no means guarantees status, except perhaps within the narrow band of one's own community. One of the richest men in my New Delhi neighborhood earned a fortune by selling tobacco while squatting in a wooden booth. Yet it would be impossible to consider him part of the elite; few of the less wealthy Nehruvian bureaucrats who bought his wares would consider sharing a meal with him. There are many such contradictions within the elites that span South Asia. The equations vary from region to region, from caste alignment to caste alignment, from nation to nation. In Pakistan, a rising if narrow middle class uses the cloak of Islam or the army or multinational business to challenge the landed feudal and tribal leaders. In Bangladesh, the army and the trading families carve up the state's scant resources and collaborate against competitors. In northern India, leaders of the new coal and labor and caste mafias compete with the old land barons. Across South Asia, some elements of the elite are challenging the status quo, others are defending it, still others are sitting on the fence, wetting their fingers and lifting them to the wind. The political economy is defined by dynamism, struggle, and change.

And yet despite this complexity and swirling momentum, there is in

fact a grouping of elites in South Asia that continues to share and protect the colonial inheritance. These elites have in common the centralized, sprawling, suffocating state, and they defend this franchise—even while competing for its spoils—against hundreds of millions of dispossessed. What Simon Schama wrote recently about the pluralist revolution of the French privilegentsia under Louis XVI, just prior to the French Revolution, applies in some ways to the present South Asian elites. The problem, he wrote of the French elites, was partly "a matter of attitude. Just because privileges were so widely available and no longer at all synonymous with birth or class, those who stood to lose status as well as cash constituted an ever-broadening coalition." Nehruvian club membership may be dynamic, but for four decades in South Asia its purpose and uses have been largely static.

Besides special access to the state or the lucrative licenses the state confers, South Asia's pluralist elites also tend to have in common the English language, which they use to define the terms of internal competition and exclude national majorities. Despite much genuflection since independence to the idea of linguistic pluralism, English remains the ultimate language of control in New Delhi, Bombay, Islamabad, Karachi, Colombo, and Dhaka. Some among the political classes who nourish themselves in various ways on the wealth generated by the state urge the unwashed masses to return to their linguistic roots—while they ensure that their own children are fluent in English and are thus prepared for international opportunity and domestic political inheritance.

Measuring the successes and failures of these reconstituted South Asian elites between 1947 and the present is a tricky, complicated business. My own view, in brief, is that there were many successes but more failures, and that some of the failures were catastrophic.

South Asia's ever-expanding socialist bureaucracies, stretching their tentacles into far corners of the subcontinental hinterlands left to rot by the British, managed some improvements in literacy, health care, life expectancy, and agriculture. In a few places, such as the Indian state of Kerala and Sri Lanka, these improvements were spectacular. Literacy and life expectancy rates soared to become the highest in the world among comparably impoverished countries. But in most parts of the subcontinent the plans came to little, as slothful bureaucrats and abusive politicians siphoned off money or watched programs decay from neglect. Agricultural advances eliminated the threat of famine, which still gnawed at the

subcontinent as recently as the early 1970s. But productivity growth was slower than in some other developing areas and was unbalanced. In India employment expanded with the new five-year plans, but the planners tended to direct resources into factories and power plants and sugar mills controlled by members of their own families, castes, and clans, so the pattern of development was sometimes duplicative. At least the factories were built. Private enterprise, forced to adapt and mutate in order to survive amid the strangulating public sector, nonetheless grew and sometimes even flourished. In contrast to what happened in some African and Latin American countries during the 1970s and 1980s—and despite excessive spending, absurd subsidies, great legions of unproductive public-sector employees, and the overall creep of corruption and rot—the bloated state did not implode. It kept on chugging, generating economic growth rates that varied between pathetic and adequate, but that contrasted with the shrinking economies of some Third World countries that had stood with British India at the postcolonial starting line following World War II.

On the whole, independent India did better than its South Asian neighbors, in part because it preserved its constitutional democracy, and thus its elite was more able to creak and bend and respond in a constitutional, evolutionary way to the injustices and stupidities and competing claims inherent in the new form of feudal, neocolonial socialism. The conventional wisdom these days in Pakistan, the Islamic state carved from Hindu-majority India in the bloody horror following the 1947 partition, is that Pakistan might have done just as well if its founder, Mohammed Ali Jinnah, had lived as long as Nehru did. It is certainly true that Nehru laid crucial democratic foundations for India between 1947 and 1964. It is also true that the successors in Pakistan to Jinnah, a lawyer and secular democrat who fell ill and died shortly after independence, botched things badly, leading to a series of military coups from which the country has yet to fully recover. The catastrophe of 1971, in which Pakistan split in two and the new nation of Bangladesh was formed in the midst of war and natural disaster, is the most gruesome testimony to the sometimes extreme mendacity of the Pakistani elite that took charge after Jinnah's death. Sri Lanka's feudal socialists did no better, bequeathing to their tiny island paradise one of the century's most brutal civil wars, in considerable part because they hoarded the proceeds of the postcolonial state for themselves. The Indian elite has tended to look down its nose at the

collection of militarists, plantation owners, and corrupt industrialists running the nations on its borders, but this attitude can be difficult to justify, especially if you wander through Kashmir or Punjab or the northern urban slums. Nonetheless, one remarkable thing about the state across all of South Asia has been its resiliency. Even amid catastrophes such as the ones in Sri Lanka and Pakistan, the bureaucracy and the political class have rebounded and reasserted themselves with impressive ability, strengthened not so much by the righteousness of their politics as by their positions of social privilege, whether inherited, acquired by force, or bought with money siphoned from or granted by the state.

The Nehruvian state's present crisis, which has produced so much talk of radical economic reform along democratic-capitalist lines in India, Pakistan, Bangladesh, and Sri Lanka, flows from several accumulated failures. After decades of egalitarian socialist rhetoric, the South Asian elites have failed to eliminate or even seriously reduce poverty or economic inequality. Per capita income remains pitiful, in the range of $350 to $700 per year across the region. Several hundred million people—a minority, but a large one—live in dire squalor. The South Asian economies have fallen badly behind Third World economies that tilted to capitalism earlier, even unwieldy and oppressive ones such as Communist China, not to mention the East Asian tigers of Hong Kong, Singapore, Taiwan, Korea, Malaysia, Indonesia, and Thailand, which lately have been racking up annual growth rates nearing 10 percent. As their neighbors to the east raced on, the bloated South Asian governments fell so badly into debt internally and externally that they eventually found they had little choice but to slim down and tighten up. And of course, the socialist ideas that so animated Nehru and other South Asian leaders forty years ago have fallen into disrepute. Theorists such as India's Prem Shankar Jha, who argues that the socialist elites in South Asia deliberately created shortages in their economies to enhance the profitability of controlling their governments, are helping, directly and indirectly, to write the reform agendas. It is a remarkable turnabout, although the elites are anxious to present it more as a form of continuity so as not to discredit themselves and the history they have made.

In India, and to a lesser degree in Pakistan and Sri Lanka, the impetus for capitalist reform is also rising from what has been arguably the state's most important success: the creation of an expanding middle class. In Pakistan and Sri Lanka, the questions of what the middle class is and

whether it has real strength are problematic. In Bangladesh, Nepal, and Afghanistan the middle class barely exists, although there are relatively small urban classes that sometimes wrestle for power with the old elite. But in India nowadays the middle class—one hundred million to two hundred million people who earn incomes large enough to permit savings, families who organize themselves around familiar Western concerns such as planning for college, providing for children, acquiring creature comforts—is broad, deep, simultaneously a bedrock of social conservatism and a vehicle for revolutionary social mobility and progressive change. What successful political economies exist in the world today—in the West, in Asia, and now the tentative embryos in Latin America and elsewhere—were erected atop the middle classes. To see India at the threshold of a similar achievement cannot help but inspire hope in anyone who feels sympathy for South Asia's centuries of suffering. The Indian neocolonial elite likes to take credit for the middle class that swelled beneath it during the 1980s—15 to 25 percent of the population, depending on how you measure it. But truly, this was in many ways an involuntary and painful birth. And now the Indian middle class is showing the same ingratitude to its feudal parents that middle classes throughout history and around the world have done. The Indian middle class by and large wants opportunity, stability, a level social and economic playing field, and a share of power in a clean, forward-looking government, which these days means an orientation toward the internationally ascendant free market. It wants the corrupt neocolonial elite, Nehru's wayward children, to step aside. This has not, so far, been a stark confrontation, like that in Tiananmen Square between the Chinese middle class and the Maoist old guard, or in central Bangkok between the Thai middle class and their corrupt generals. Because India has clung stubbornly to its electoral democracy, its politicians, however mendacious or corrupt as a group, have been forced to take into account the middle class's aspirations in order to win elections and garner campaign funds. Sometimes the middle class's demands have seemed dangerous products of manipulation or anger or confusion, as in the Hindu revivalist movement or the Punjab insurgency. But its energy has been inescapable. And it is threatening to derail what has been the most precious, profitable creation of the old guardians of the state—the great South Asian socialist gravy train.

———

As it happens, train stations are not a bad place to sniff the fumes of the decomposing Nehruvian state.

South Asia's railways are much romanticized by Westerners, and with reason. They certainly do better than the mobile torture chambers collectively referred to as Indian Airlines. Mark Tully, for seventeen years the British Broadcasting Corporation's correspondent in South Asia, writes that the railways reveal a "talent for developing the modern without destroying the ancient." The Indian railways do move many people and much freight cheaply, and they manage to earn a profit, which is a lot more than most subsections of the Nehruvian state can claim. Whether they represent an ideal marriage of the ancient and the modern is another matter. As a social enterprise and a microcosm of the state's public hierarchy, the railways exemplify the ways the state has both failed and succeeded in India since 1947. These days, down in the bowels of the railway ministry lies an anxious culture of 1.6 million sinecured employees who suspect that their best days may be behind them.

Wander through the Old Delhi station and the first thing you notice are all the signs carved in English and Hindi on polished wood, swinging neatly from their hinges, indicating the offices of the station superintendent, deputy station superintendent, ticket collector, deputy ticket collector, personal secretaries, security supervisors, and on down the line to the peons in their oil-stained T-shirts who rate no signs but seem to do much of the actual work. Once, on a thirty-six-hour ride from Delhi to Madras in the south, I brought my notebook along and talked to dozens of employees about their lives and work. It was like wandering through a living Victorian museum, but the anxiety shared by the employees arose distinctly from the pressures buffeting the South Asian state in the late twentieth century.

The first man I met was Chandra Mohan Soli, a deputy station superintendent in Delhi who sat in a dim office with a concrete floor, clacking manual typewriters, and piles of carbon papers attached to forms printed on the coarse, soft paper common to the Indian bureaucracy. I asked him about his railway career. He explained the rigorous exams he had taken thirty years before and then described the benefits: subsidized housing for himself and his family in the "railway colonies" scattered across India, free medical care from the dispensary in the colony, hospitalization at the railway clinic, a pension, sick days, personal leave, holidays. If he dies in an accident on the job, the railway is required to give his son a career

position as compensation. Seniority determines who gets the promotions, the larger houses, the air coolers and air conditioners in the offices. Since he was a senior employee, the system seemed fair enough to him—he had an air conditioner, at least. I asked what he thought about all this recent talk of privatization and capitalism. His answer was direct. "This is safer," he said. "If it is privatized, then the big guy of the company can fire you any time, according to his whims and fancies. Here, nobody is going to get fired."

As he spoke, a radio set beside him crackled and he began barking into it urgently, ordering subordinates around his desk this way and that. He paused, exasperated. "VIPs on the trains are a daily affair," he sighed. "We give them the front seats and we meet them on the platforms." He shuffled through piles of forms on his desk. In South Asia, VIPs throw their weight around in ways unfathomable to anyone raised amid the nominal egalitarianism of the West. The VIP definition covers anyone with enough power within the state to command patronage. VIPs go immediately to the front of the line, harass lowly government servants with impunity, and demand special treatment for the most ordinary services. A common way for a VIP to assert his status is to be late for an Indian Airlines flight and demand that the plane wait for him on the tarmac. The station manager holds the flight or faces the risk of transfer to a godforsaken hinterlands outpost as retaliation. Soli seemed animated by a similar concern. "The VIPs arriving today are a railway officer, an adviser for planning on the railway board, an Uttar Pradesh state railway minister, an Uttar Pradesh party minister, the executive director of the railway board, the union minister of petroleum, and a former union finance minister and minister of defense," he said, shuffling hurriedly through his pile of forms. "Actually, this last one might be a special VIP, a VVIP. If it's a VVIP, then the senior superintendent of the station attends to it. That would be the prime minister or the chairman of the railway board. . . . Half of my job is watching after the VIPs."

A deputy stepped into the office and told Soli that a state minister was pulling into the station. Soli jumped up and buttoned his wool coat to the top. He grabbed a telephone and cranked the old-fashioned handle. "Which train is he in?" Soli demanded. "There's no air-conditioning in that train? How can he travel in that train?" And then he was off, marching briskly through the swarms of passengers, tobacco sellers, porters, dogs, and hangers-on congregated on the platforms.

Aboard the train I introduced myself to the superintendent, P. Kadiresan, a thin, dark-skinned southerner with oiled hair who sat in a small compartment filled with passengers making elaborate complaints about lost baggage. Kadiresan diverted them with forms and carbon paper and then sat back to narrate the story of his career. His was a tale of how the Nehruvian state built the Indian middle class and how it was running out of ways to sustain its achievement into the next generation.

Kadiresan was born as a shunned untouchable in an impoverished Tamil Nadu village prior to independence. His father was a coolie, illiterate and overworked, paid day wages when he could find a job. He pushed his son to stay in school, and when Kadiresan graduated, he won a position as a government clerk through a postindependence affirmative action program for untouchables. In 1954 he sat for the railway exam and passed. Kadiresan said he never considered looking for a job anywhere but with the government—as an untouchable, he had only one other realistic option, to replicate his father's life as a landless laborer. So for twenty-nine years he worked his way slowly up the railway ladder, eventually earning a middle-class salary and—just as important—respect. He put his sons through college or engineering school and they did well, but not one of them had been able to find a job. The railway, like nearly all of the bloated federal ministries, had stopped hiring. Untouchables find it difficult to enter the management ranks at private companies. Kadiresan sounded genuinely puzzled and frustrated by his sons' predicament. But he was sure of one thing: Capitalism was not the answer.

Private employers "will extract more work," he said in lilting English. "Under this system, there is some leniency. I mean, they don't extract so much work from us. According to the rules and regulations, they don't extract so much. They give job security. If anything goes wrong, the family gets a compassionate job. After joining in railways, I never fear anything. After coming to my duty, I am arriving, working very loyally without any fear. I never care about my family. I only care about my passengers and my train. This is the mentality of Indian people. Railways is the way. The rules and regulations are very much known. Without knowing the rules and regulations, nobody can come and work here."

In the second-class carriages I found S. M. Mahule, a thirty-three-year veteran of the railway service. He was a ticket collector and wore a yellow-and-red cloth armband. He talked about the extraordinary benefits of government service—forty-five days of paid vacation each year, a

dozen government holidays, and up to one hundred twenty sick days each year, paid and unpaid. Mahule said he took two months off the previous year for what he described as irregular blood pressure and said he planned another extended leave soon. "Most of our employees, they are sick," he said wryly. He, too, lamented that the socialist gravy train was running out of steam. He had six children, all college graduates, all unemployed. He was more sanguine than some of his colleagues about a future dominated by the private sector, but he was worried. "In my time government service was more important," he said. "Not anymore. Direct recruitment from the service commission has been stopped. If they privatize, that would be better. They pay more attention in the private sector than in the government because they are getting the benefits to their own pockets. They are choosing candidates according to their caliber and ability. In government, seniority is all." He mentioned a son who had twice taken the railway exam but had not yet found a place. I asked why his son wanted a government job. "He's not so much brilliant or extraordinary. He is an ordinary boy. That is why he wants a government job."

Mahule punched the ticket of N. Ramesh, a well-dressed twenty-five-year-old returning to Madras from New Delhi. I asked Ramesh what he and the younger friends he went to college with thought about government service. "Most of my friends want to go on their own," he answered. "They want to work. They don't want to sit idle in government. If you want to learn, you have to work. Most of those who are skilled don't have an interest in government work. With my skills I know I can always find something. If you have an invention you can surely make a go of it. You can work for a few years to learn what the work is about, then you go on your own. That is everybody's idea. I personally want to start my own company in computers in a few years."

If reform of the Nehruvian state succeeds, then Ramesh and his generation will be the ones to lead and define the new order. The impressive number of Indians who have succeeded after emigrating to the West suggests this generation ought to do well if they have the chance. But what worries the generation of Ramesh's parents—the middle class built by the state after independence and steeped in its values—is that something essential may be lost in the transition.

At the head of the train was H. N. Sharma, a driver for thirty-three years and a former member of India's national field hockey team. His gray hair was neatly coiffed and he wore black spectacles and a pressed gray

uniform. As he rolled down the tracks, punching buttons and waving to passersby, he said he felt that in the present rush to reform and repudiate the Nehruvian tradition, the younger generation might lead India in dangerous directions. "If a boy is twenty-three or twenty-four or twenty-five and he's earning a lot of money, he may spoil his habits," Sharma said. "Young people today are not so interested in government service. They are busy making money. I could have made money. Money is a criterion, no doubt, but side by side you've got to see your reputation. Men who are fortunately born, they become train drivers. It is a hardworking job with a lot of responsibility and respect." It had provided him a good business, a well-constructed house and a garden, a good life for his family. Here, he implied, was the spine of Indian democracy. What similar stability could this next, impatient, money-hungry young generation construct?

———

The most important architects of South Asia's economic and social reforms have been Nawaz Sharif, the prime minister of Pakistan, who came to power in October 1990; P. V. Narasimha Rao, the prime minister of India, who took office in June 1991 following the assassination of Rajiv Gandhi; and Rao's finance minister, Manmohan Singh, a Sikh and a longtime bureaucrat and socialist who very recently embraced the neo-conservative creed with a convert's enthusiasm. All three have attempted to reform radically the establishment apparatus that gave birth to and nurtured their careers, by reducing the state's relative power throughout the political economy. They see themselves in political positions comparable to Gorbachev's in the late 1980s. Indeed, one of Rao's first mistakes was his spontaneous pronouncement during the first days of the August 1991 coup attempt against Gorbachev that the event was a lesson to reformers everywhere that they must proceed cautiously. When Yeltsin prevailed, Rao was roundly denounced for implicitly backing the wrong side in the Soviet coup and for suggesting that spinelessness was the solution to his own political predicament.

Much of the publicity about reform of the socialist bureaucracy in South Asia has centered on India, but actually it was Sharif who moved first and who has been the boldest. (Sri Lanka's elite moved sharply to the right during the late 1970s, but hardly anyone paid attention because the reforms were subsumed by civil war.) In time, it may be judged that

the greatest significance of Sharif's move was not that he saved Pakistan, whose politics are so fractured and whose key state institutions, such as the police, are so decayed that they may be immune to a prime minister's policies. Rather, by announcing his embrace of the free market, Sharif provided the only stimulus capable of moving his lethargic rivals in the Indian elite. The motivating power of the hatred and rivalry between India and Pakistan is difficult to overestimate. Throughout the late 1980s, Westerners and cranky right-wingers in the Indian elite, including the leadership of the rising Hindu nationalist movement, had been urging reform of the tottering Nehruvian behemoth. Many of India's brethren in the leftist nonaligned movement were already well down the path to free market reform: Malaysia, Indonesia, Mexico, Brazil, Chile, China, even Yugoslavia. Yet the New Delhi bureaucrats stood firm. India was not like any other country, they insisted again and again. It required guidance, protection, nurturing from above. Even when it became clear that the reformers had gained ascendancy in the Soviet Union, the most important source of subsidies for the Nehruvian state, the elite was unmoved. But when Pakistan—Pakistan!—started talking about free market reform as the key to higher economic growth rates, wider prosperity, national strength and self-reliance in the new world order, well, the New Delhi elite took notice. One of the most important intellectual events in India's sudden move toward capitalist reform was an interview Nawaz Sharif gave to the accomplished Indian journalist Shekhar Gupta early in 1991. Sharif used the forum to explain how he intended to turn Pakistan into a new Asian economic tiger, freeing capital and human energy for economic growth and then using the proceeds of that growth to strengthen the welfare state. Gupta hurled at Sharif the usual tenets of the old feudal socialist order: What about the downtrodden out in the villages? What about the poor? Sharif knocked the questions down. What the poor need are jobs, he said. The only viable way to create jobs is through business. The state is broke, unsalvageable. Businesses require a free market, and Pakistan will give it to them. After the interview was published, it was all anybody in New Delhi government and media circles could talk about. It was as if the Pakistan cricket team had announced the discovery of a new bowling technique guaranteed to baffle Indian batters. There was a sense, as so often arises in the relationship between India and Pakistan, that India was not to be outdone.

Sharif pressed ahead to redeem his pledges but his quest appeared

increasingly quixotic. Pakistanis are divided, as they so frequently are, about how much blame Sharif himself deserves for the difficulties he encountered. One problem is that Sharif had poor credentials as a reformer-from-within because politically he is a creature of one of the Pakistani establishment's most divisive incarnations, the long period of martial law led by General Zia ul-Haq during the 1980s. Sharif was Zia's martial-law governor in Punjab province, and so his credentials as a plain-speaking businessman are undermined by his history of rank political opportunism. The family industries Sharif built were constructed during a period of oppression and corruption. In person, he comes off as a bit befuddled. Despite these and other limitations, as well as the chronic maladies of Pakistan's divided polity, the economy has kicked out briskly under Sharif's spur. The prime minister abolished foreign exchange controls and many customs restrictions and he proudly declared that Pakistan should now be considered one giant airport green channel. The country's well-developed class of heroin smugglers and gunrunners, among others, are responding vigorously. "Our policy today is whoever wants to invest in Pakistan, whether Pakistani or foreigner, doesn't have to seek permission from the government. He can do what he likes wherever in Pakistan, no matter how much money he brings into Pakistan in dollars or other foreign currency—no questions asked," Sharif explained one morning over breakfast at the governor's mansion in Lahore, glancing at a prepared stack of note cards he kept in his lap. "Of course, we want to have minimum contact of the government with the people to eliminate corruption, and, of course, exploitation." Exploitation of the people by the government? For years, that idea languished.

India's top-down reformers are more credible politically than Sharif but less enthusiastic about the actual matter of capitalism. Prime Minister Rao and Finance Minister Singh both spent their long careers as public servants in the heart of the Nehruvian bureaucracy. Compared with their peers in the elite, they possess the rare virtue of not being corrupt. But both were for long years Nehruvian true believers and Rao, particularly, now in his early seventies, sometimes talks as if it is painful to let go of the old ideas. At the least, his understanding of how one might strive for a fair and just free market that would consolidate the Indian middle class seems limited.

In the spring of 1991, after Rajiv Gandhi's assassination, I spoke with

Rao at length on a train rumbling across northern India. The train bore Gandhi's ashes for immersion in the Ganges River near the Nehru family's Allahabad home. It was a strange setting—the assassination had thrown the country into political chaos in the midst of an election. The headless Congress Party was wrestling with the succession, and while it seemed that the longtime loyalist Rao would prevail, the situation was volatile, not least because so many rank-and-file party thugs, pushed by a clique of Gandhi loyalists, kept clamoring for the nomination of Sonia Gandhi, Rajiv's Italian-born widow. At stations along the whistle-stop train tour, mobs of paid Congress workers surged toward a garlanded car at the center of the train where some of Rajiv's ashes were being kept in an urn. Sonia and her children, engulfed in grief, sat cross-legged on the carriage's floor. Behind the urn most of the party leadership rode in an air-conditioned coach with curtained windows. When I wandered in during the middle of the afternoon, with Mark Fineman of the *Los Angeles Times*, to look for Rao, the car was as dark as night and the Congress pols—mainly fat men wrapped in great robes of white khadi—lay flopped on their first-class bunks, asleep, snoring. Bending and peering in search of familiar faces, we could not help thinking that we had stumbled abruptly into the land of the dinosaurs.

Fortunately for India, Rao is different—gentle, scholarly, fluent in nine languages, seemingly possessed of many of the virtues and few of the vices of his generation and class. Boldness, however, is not in his character. As we rumbled along, I asked what he had in mind for India, should he come to power in the weeks ahead. The government was nearly bankrupt, in danger of defaulting on more than $70 billion in foreign debt—a figure that the World Bank later estimated would rise to $93 billion by the mid-1990s, requiring India to come up with $10 billion annually to pay interest and principal and to finance export imbalances. The previous administration, a brief farce led by the sweet-tempered socialist Chandra Shekhar, had been forced to pawn off confiscated gold to make its loan payments. In reply, Rao talked of change as if it were something a minister had ordered and which he, the senior civil servant, was now about to implement.

"Rajiv had set up a cell to deal with this, the economy," he said. "Their papers are there. The cell is there. There has been interaction. He [Rajiv] has [*sic*] been talking to vast numbers of economists in the last six months.

He has given the lead." Rao conceded that he had long believed in Nehruvian socialism, but "we have been compelled to revise and at least rethink our own beliefs."

If this was not the talk of a capitalist revolutionary, perhaps it was because that afternoon Rao had other things on his mind. The leaderless Congress Party lay in fragments. The Hindu revivalists were clamoring for power. Staring out the train window at the blistering summer heat that shimmered in waves across the parched brown countryside, Rao spoke mainly about Nehru's political inheritance, which he felt had to be some-how stitched back together if India was to have the opportunity to change. He said with conviction that the party would not split, but at the same time preventing catastrophe would be no small matter. "Right now, we feel it as the greatest challenge," he said. "To lose a leader in the middle of an election, that has never happened before." Still, the adhesive of the Nehruvian state arose from one fact, he continued: "This party is where power is available. This is the source of political power in India. There will be claimants and claims, people who get it and don't. Rivalry will remain but the party will not break. We know when to stop the fight." He rhapsodized about the Nehruvian elite, its long struggle for independence and nation-building. "This is a one-hundred-six-year-old party, four or five generations. We have lots of families in India where the head of the family is not the most brilliant or able but still the family continues because of the loyalty. The party has always thrown up leader-ship that is good enough to keep the party together. I stand for what they stood for. All the ideas are there. The whole case is there but we have to marshal it." And then, referring to the impending vote, he added, "We have three days."

In the election and its aftermath, Rao squeaked in, and the man he appointed to marshal was Manmohan Singh, the Sikh finance minister. Quickly Singh announced the first phase of free market reform—a cur-rency devaluation, tax cuts, reduced regulations. It was perhaps not enough but it was a beginning. And Singh seemed the one man in India with the courage of his convictions. He accused the entrenched bureau-cracy of "selling poverty" to hold on to their positions. In a ground-breaking budget speech on the floor of the *lok sabha*, or lower house of parliament, he intoned that India could not be held "permanent captive to a fear of the East India Company," by which he meant that it was time

to stop using old fears of the colonial powers to block integration with a fast-moving international capitalist economy. Politicians of many stripes who had been feeding at the state's protected trough for several generations were, of course, outraged. So were the public-sector unions, including the railway workers. But the urban, young, business-oriented middle class cheered, and it seemed immediately that they would provide the political support—backed up by the implicit promise of campaign money should another election be required—to push the reforms along. Shortly after he took office, I went to see Singh in his spacious office to talk about what he had begun. He spoke like a neoconservative—one who embraces socialist or social democratic ends, but who insists that capitalist means are necessary to achieve them.

"These reforms are not about enriching the rich people, as some people say," Singh said. "Their purpose is to release the creative energy of our people, to accelerate the rate of growth of our economy, to accelerate the growth of the public revenues, which we can then plow back into those sectors of our society, of our economy, which market forces by themselves cannot look after. And this is education, more emphasis on health care, safe drinking water, rural roads, agricultural research . . ." and on down the list of goals that the Nehruvian state had set for itself and failed to achieve. "We have to do a great deal in educating public opinion," Singh conceded. "So I do not minimize the enormity of the task. But I believe that among thinking segments of the population there is already an awareness. . . . Now it is true, [to translate] admission in private [that the Nehruvian state is failing] into a broad, mass-based program is going to take a lot of time, a lot of energy, a lot of faith, a lot of courage, a lot of stamina. Only time can tell us. But I do believe, I think our country will have that strength."

But in a society where a large and powerful class, including most of its politicians, has been enriched and entrenched by the state, how does a lone finance minister go about detaching so many people from their privileges?

"Many of our intellectuals, our social scientists, our people, have been brought up in the whole belief that somehow an overcentralized command economy provided all the answers to the problems," he replied. "For a period of time, even the people in the United States were mesmerized by the high growth rates of the Soviet Union. . . . So I think we were

not the only ones who believed at that time that somehow the Communist world had found an answer to solve problems of poverty and underdevelopment that no other society had found. A lot of people were brought up in that tradition. Now experience has shown that is a god that has not worked."

4

Village on a Hill

I regard the growth of cities as an evil thing, unfortunate for
England and certainly unfortunate for India.

—*Mohandas K. Gandhi*

From Chopta, you can see China. It rises beyond the stripped Himalayan foothills, a few jagged peaks dimly visible in the haze that slips
over the Garwal on summer evenings. You can stare at China while
sitting on the slate wall in front of the Chopta village chief's stone house.
The villagers talked of China as if it were somewhere over the rainbow,
not so much a paradise as an unfathomable place far, far different from
their own. If you turned around and looked hard at Chopta, the useful-
ness of this imagined China became obvious. To live and die here in the
late twentieth century, you would need something strange and vivid to
dream about.

When we first arrived, we could not help but notice the dead trees—
thousands and thousands of barren saplings lying on Chopta's patios and
narrow hillside fields. Most of the dead seedlings were still wrapped in
plastic casings supplied by the World Bank and the government of India
as part of a reforestation and poverty-alleviation program. On and off
over two years, my researcher, Rama Lakshmi, and I came to Chopta,
trying to sort out why the trees were dead. To do that, we had to try to
unravel the relationship, in a single village, between rural poverty and
urban-based government. It was no easy matter.

Chopta is a cluster of hewn-stone houses that rests on a mountain ridge

in the corner of the Himalayas where India, China, and Nepal meet. For centuries, its residents have survived—barely—by farming small, terraced plots of wheat and rice. They have no electricity or running water. They do have flies. The flies buzz in black swarms through homes choked with smoke from cooking fires. They congregate on piles of threshed wheat stacked on porches and in doorways. They flit from face to face and arm to arm, creating a buzzing drone behind the odd burst of village noise: the clanging bells of wandering cows, curses shouted at wayward chickens by scythe-waving women, flutes blown by preteen goatkeepers on the rocky slopes above the village. In the evening, the flies retreat and their drone is superseded by tinny Garwali folk songs from Chopta's lone cassette player, which is usually propped up near the slate wall by the village chief's house.

About three quarters of South Asians still live in the countryside. Chopta's 235 residents are among the poorest of South Asia's poor, physically isolated on their steep ridge from the socialist bureaucracy. Measuring poverty in South Asia is not easy, since by Western standards there is so much of it. India's government has set its poverty line at about 90 rupees per capita per month, a monthly income at present equivalent to about three dollars. The government estimates that 35 percent of the population live below this line; the World Bank puts the number somewhat higher. In Pakistan and Sri Lanka the unofficial percentages are a little better. In Bangladesh and Nepal they are markedly worse. Afghanistan has been so decimated by war that it doesn't even have statistics anymore. In any case, what reliable regional statistics there are describe about half a billion people living in destitution, mostly in the countryside. Alan Heston, looking for a way to compare South Asian poverty with that in the West, has noted that in the United States, less than 0.5 percent of the population survive on five dollars a day or less. Yet an equivalent income in rupees would place an Indian or Pakistani firmly in the middle class. The poorest of South Asia's poor live at a level of poverty that cannot be found in the West.

You can find it in Chopta, where poverty is the daily arbiter of life and death. Bacteria and viruses course through the village, felling residents at random. Women give birth in cowsheds or dirt basements. They and their children often die in the process. The nearest road is a mile's walk down a rock path. The nearest doctor lives about three miles off. Reaching the closest hospital requires a seven-mile hike along a dirt track and then a

sixty-mile, four-hour ride in a hired jeep. Even the dirt road is relatively new; before it arrived about a decade ago, the villagers had rarely seen a bus up close. They refer to an automobile, an even more recent arrival, as "son of a bus." Medical problems are addressed through a vague faith in injections and pills administered by local, untrained quacks on the one hand and on the other a somewhat firmer belief in spirits and bad luck. A crippled girl is said by her mother to have been frozen by a cold wind. A teenager with seizures is said to be plagued by bad dreams. A mother whose two newborn infants died is said to be the victim of an evil gaze. In the still, moonlit nights, the villagers huddle in their cramped homes, afraid to wander alone among the ghosts and wild beasts that are said to roam the mountainside.

The women are preoccupied by work and procreation. They rise at five in the morning in a clatter of gossip and banging pots, cook breakfast, feed and dress the children, milk the cows, fetch water from drying springs, grind grain, work the fields, cook lunch, grind more grain, march off to gather firewood, clean the house, work the fields again, cook dinner, wash the dishes, and put the children to bed. The women manage the grain stocks and the harvests. They spend long hours squatting on the straw mats in their kitchens, which are filled with smoke from cooking fires. "Indoor air pollution," the environmental scientists in New Delhi call it, as if it were a symptom of faulty valves. The women usually fall asleep around eleven at night and rise again at dawn to do it all again, seven days a week.

Their husbands help them out by getting them pregnant with great frequency. The cycle plays out like a game of Russian roulette. Just before our first arrival, Rameshwari Devi, the wife of a determinedly cheerful villager named Than Singh, lost out on the twisting dirt road that leads from the village to the jeep stand seven miles away. Ramesh Singh, an enterprising untouchable carpenter who lives just below the village chief's house on the ridge, described the scene: Devi lay on a handmade wooden stretcher fashioned from logs and rope, shouldered by four village men, who walked rapidly through the dust. She had been in labor for two days—the baby's hand was protruding—but she could not give birth. The men decided to carry her on foot to a jeep that would take her to the hospital. "We kept giving her water and sugar," recalled Ramesh Singh, one of the bearers. "She was awake. She kept saying, 'I'm all right. I'm okay.' When we got to the bridge, nearing it, we said, 'Look, there's

your jeep.' She suddenly seemed to get very frightened. She said, 'I feel heavy. My throat is heavy.' And then she closed her eyes and died. . . . We carried her body up the mountain, into the woods to the cremation ground, and burned her."

Many of the men in the village are unemployed high school drop-outs—the Nehruvian state provided schools but not jobs. They sit around on chairs and benches during the day, talking. The only agricultural work deemed appropriate for them is plowing, and this they do infrequently. Some of them are hangers-on at the local offices of the state and federal bureaucracies, which run a few permanent outposts in the valleys below Chopta's ridge. The bureaucracies recently have built a few more outposts with the World Bank's money. In the evenings the village men gather on the slate wall outside the chief's house and gossip about the day's events beneath the ridge. Their wives and daughters trudge by with pots of water and great piles of wheat on their heads. The elected village chief, known as the *pradhan*, the last member of the Brahmin Dhondiyal family still resident in Chopta, works about fifteen hours a week at a post office several miles off. These duties appear to weigh heavily on him. His wife, as best we could count, works about 105 hours a week running his house, tilling his fields, and raising his children. At one point during the period of our coming and going, she nearly died in labor with a stillborn child. Nobody was paying attention—she was out in the fields cutting wheat when she began screaming in pain. "Oh God! Oh God!" Several women ran to her. One rubbed oil on her stomach. Another reached in crudely and pulled out the dead child. The mother rested a few days and then went back to work in the fields. If she didn't nobody would.

Shortly afterward, her husband, the pradhan, turned up at my office in New Delhi. He was in the city on unspecified business. Rama asked about his wife.

"She is better now," the pradhan answered laconically.

"What happened, exactly?" Rama pressed him.

"Problems. But now she is better."

"Was it a boy or a girl?"

"Dead child," he answered.

Ranjana Kumari, who has written an extensive study of households headed by women in rural India, wrote that the men she saw in the villages she studied were "totally irresponsible toward their household affairs [but] they do extract enough money from activities like negotiating

in land conflicts or campaigning during elections to manage their personal expenditures." In some cases, these expenditures included "drinking liquor, going to films and to the market centres where they spent lavishly on different kinds of consumer goods. . . . Due to their unfinished education and in the process imbibing strong urban values they consider agricultural activities as undesirable." This is the way it is, by and large, in Chopta. The Nehruvian state, by providing a partial education and no gainful local employment, taught the Chopta village men just enough to ensure the misery of their wives and daughters. Of course, wives and daughters in Chopta were no doubt miserable hundreds of years ago as well, long before the modern socialist state came along. The difference today is that on both sides of the gender divide, villagers move about in an atmosphere of self-conscious resentment about their lack of opportunity in the modern world. The creation of this atmosphere seemed to be the Indian state's principal achievement in Chopta.

Those in Chopta with any ambition—some of the younger men and nearly all of the women—said they primarily wanted one thing: to get out. Nearly a quarter of the village's families have already done so, migrating to Delhi or other cities to take jobs as factory workers or domestic servants. The conditions may be difficult in the cities, but at least there is some money to be had. Most of the able-bodied young men have already left to chase it. This strain of ambition could be measured in part by the frequency with which Chopta villagers turned up at my office once our reporting project began. They would sit around in the wicker chairs, patiently answering questions about their lives and families before politely inquiring whether we knew of any jobs that would permit them to migrate to Delhi. Back in Chopta, sitting on the slate village walls or squatting out in the fields with the women while they threshed and gathered, we would hear the same themes.

"There isn't much respect for people working here," explained Madan Singh, seventeen, a green-eyed boy typical of Chopta's younger generation. "Look how much respect they give to the ones working in factories. You should see how people surround them when they come back from Delhi. I want them to respect me too. I will do anything in Delhi, even wash dishes, be a servant. At least I will be in a big place."

One afternoon on the terraced hillside, Kesari Devi, a member of the Rajput caste and a mother of six, whose husband did more work than most, confided that her son had found a job filling water coolers in New

Delhi's federal parliament building. "What is the point of keeping anyone here?" she asked, gesturing toward her plots of wheat and rice, and beyond them, to China. "Slowly and slowly [my son] will take everybody with him. What is there in these villages? Useless. Finished. . . . My son comes and says there is nothing here. He is right."

We found Birendra Singh, Kesari Devi's son, on a rainy day back in the capital. With parliament out of session, and thus no watercoolers to fill, he had found a temporary job as a watchman at a carpet showroom in Hauz Khas, a funky, chic shopping area for the South Delhi rich that has deliberately been made to look like the rural village it once was. This pleases wealthy urban shoppers who have left their villages behind but hold them in romantic memory. As the rain fell in sheets, Singh talked to my researcher, Rama, about what he had learned in the big city. "People here are cunning," he said. "They are very smart. Even little boys can ride cycles and scooters. Looking at them, I feel Garwalis [hill people] are so simple. In fact, we Garwalis are nothing. When I first began working in parliament, I would get very scared when people spoke to me. I could never go near an officer without getting nervous. I kept to myself all the time. . . . It's not the same anymore. I am opening up," he concluded, smiling shyly.

——————

What Birendra Singh calls "opening up," replicated countless times among the millions and millions of South Asians who have migrated from villages to cities and towns in search of better lives, sometimes makes the urban elites uncomfortable. They wish to protect the masses from themselves. They restrict public advertising of consumer goods so as not to whet the appetites of the poor. They impose some of the world's highest tariff rates to protect domestic monopolists and to ensure that only those with serious money can afford the best of modern Western technology. They look out on the sprawling tar-paper slums of Delhi, Bombay, Calcutta, and Karachi, review the appalling labor conditions in the city factories (which the elite families generally own), assess the limited spaces available at the best schools and universities, and pronounce that the villagers would be better off staying at home in their villages.

South Asian governments have compelling reasons to invest in their one million villages. The cities are overburdened, sometimes virtually crushed by mass migration from the villages. The state has failed to create

industrial employment sufficient to match population growth, so for a time at least it must generate work in rural areas. Above all, South Asian governments need prosperous, efficient farms to feed their people. In East Asia, poor countries that have grown rich have proven that you cannot get from poverty to prosperity without enriching the countryside, the villages. Yet in South Asia the form of rural investment has too often been patriarchal, patronizing, and counterproductive. This is partly because rural policy emanates from the spiritual independence philosophy of Gandhi, whose courage and genius still influence South Asian politics, but whose xenophobia and mystical reverence for timeless village life are sometimes used by the entrenched urban elites to protect themselves from challengers. It is also a consequence of a hackneyed leftist syllogism: The enlightened elite must serve the masses; the masses are in the villages; therefore the elite—and the central government it controls— should be the primary font of village improvement. By this logic, those who control the government not only do what is ideologically correct, they expand their power and access to the state trough as well. This produces corruption and leaves tens of millions in the villages beholden to patronage and bereft of resources.

Beyond all this, in South Asia the villages matter because there is a powerful feeling of rootedness that none of the recent political econo-mies, leftist or imperialist, has yet eroded. And at the base of every man's or woman's sense of self is his or her village. In the West, people speak of being "from" somewhere, a word that implies that home has been left behind. In South Asia, you are not from a village, you "belong to" it, even if you have never lived there.

This idea throws light on the views of Bivekanand Dhondiyal, Chopta's patriarch. He talked of Chopta as if it were a shining Village on a Hill, a beacon of the ideal. He had never lived there, however. He had mainly dreamed about the place.

Before climbing up the ridge to his ancestral village, I went to see Dhondiyal, a thin articulate man approaching sixty, in his expansive office at the federal parliament, where he worked at the time as a member of the Indian Administrative Service, the supreme branch of the Nehruvian civil service. Like many in the South Asian upper classes, he was thoughtful, gentle, well-meaning. He seemed a little perplexed that the reforestation and antipoverty plan he had helped to develop with the World Bank and the Indian government was not working too well in Chopta.

"My grandfather came out from that village," he explained. "My first visit to my village was in 1948, after high school. Later, at the Planning Commission in 1985, I was in charge of the hilly areas. I visited that area as part of my official duties. The World Bank had a project [but] they were fed up with it. I persuaded them to continue and to include new villages, including a miniproject around Chopta." The idea, he said, was to improve agriculture, the environment, and local incomes by providing support for traditional forms of agriculture. "This is the holistic thinking they have tried to bring into their planning. . . . [It] is the answer because it is a holistic approach. It restores the forests and the capacity of the soil. If we set up modern industry in that area, whatever the capacity of that fragile environment, it will be exceeded. This whole area is seismically very active. There are landslides. You cannot bring modern industry. Your development strategy has to take into account the fragility of the ecology."

And yet, he acknowledged, "there was a problem of getting the cooperation of the people. Most of the able-bodied males have migrated. The initiative is very low." But wasn't migration to the cities a sign of initiative? The Dhondiyals had migrated years ago. Anyone with the means to do it would want to get off that ridge, wouldn't they? Why not spend the World Bank's money to help them, rather than to keep them there, trapped in the ninth century? "The problem is that most of them come to Delhi as domestics," he answered. "They're exploited. Unfortunately, I've been unable to persuade the government to give them training—train them as chefs, try to give them some protection and verify their character. Imagine a twelve-year-old boy coming to Delhi. He almost becomes a bonded slave here." Urban labor conditions were indeed horrible. But who was responsible for that? Anyway, Dhondiyal went on to talk about how he was optimistic that, in time, government support would generate enough rural income in the hills so that villagers who had migrated to Delhi would want to go back. "Maybe I will take a summer home there," he said wistfully of Chopta.

Of course, the Dhondiyals keep their New Delhi house full of domestic servants, as does everyone of their station. Some of their servants are from Chopta.

Chopta's villagers treated the Dhondiyals with both fealty and resentment. Once, Rama and Vinita Dhondiyal, Bivekanand Dhondiyal's daughter, were huffing and puffing up the ridge to the village when a local

named Pooran Singh shouted down at them, "So! You are Bivekanand Dhondiyal's daughter! When people from the hills go to the big cities and become such big officers and do not even look back at us, this is what happens to them! They can't climb back to their homes. That's your punishment, girl."

In its attitudes and strategies, the World Bank–funded forestry and development program in Chopta reflected the failed patronage of the Dhondiyal family. One of the program's purposes was to provide resources that would encourage villagers to stay where they are and farm the terraced land as they have always done—but with new, environmentally sound technologies that would turn the land green again and raise agricultural output. The technologies included solar lights, biogas stoves that convert cow dung into cooking gas, special grasses to prevent erosion, superior bulls and cows for breeding, and hundreds of thousands of apple and walnut trees that would allow villagers to earn extra cash from horticulture, apart from their centuries-old subsistence farming of wheat and rice. Together, the donations had the impact of a Gandhian version of the welfare state: charity without sustainable market incentives or follow-through, and patronizing charity at that. For Dhondiyal and other planners, the pastoral village ideal of their romantic memory echoed what Gandhi once said of the spinning wheel. The medieval wheel was a "work of art," Gandhi said, that "typifies the use of machinery on a universal scale. It is machinery reduced to the terms of the masses." It is one thing to countenance this approach from Gandhi, who led by example. It is another to accept it from "big officers" whose lives are made comfortable by machinery such as cars, air conditioners, televisions, and electric lights which they consider inappropriate for the masses.

One afternoon in Chopta, climbing the hillside with Dilbur Singh, a barefoot villager with matted hair who earns about twenty dollars a month looking after "superior bulls" supplied by the World Bank, I asked him what he thought was the objective of the program in Chopta. He hesitated and then replied, "Their objective is to keep us here. But everyone wants to go out. To keep us here, you'd have to give us a lot. But that's not the program. It's a kind of sop to keep us here and it isn't working."

Villagers blame the government for the program's failings. They say many of the trees supplied to them were dumped on valley roads by delivery trucks and were half dead by the time they were planted. They

say many others died because project supervisors were too lazy to climb the mountain regularly and check on how the trees were doing. And, they add, maintaining the trees required techniques they were never taught. Neither of the two solar lights installed in Chopta works. The one biogas stove does not function—specialists say the stoves generally do not work at elevations above six thousand feet, but one was installed in the village anyway, despite its higher elevation. Cement tanks built around existing natural springs are cracked and leaking and villagers say their water supply has declined as a result. Three big cement buildings constructed to house the superior breeding bulls sit unoccupied most of the year because villagers say, their interiors are too cold for the bulls. "They came and made tanks in our fields—didn't ask our permission, didn't give us money for this. Now there's no water," complained Sudeshi Devi, the women's cooperative leader, when we asked her on our last visit what she thought had gone wrong. "People come here with different programs, eat the money, and go away. What do we get out of it?"

The government blames the villagers. "They don't think about the future," complained S. K. Kala, a frustrated state bureaucrat who lives in one of the new concrete houses built with World Bank funds at the base of the ridge. "The problem with people here is they're too concerned with what they're doing today. They don't worry about what will happen in the next five or ten years when all the trees are gone. They don't even think about it. If you don't have the people's cooperation, it won't succeed. Where we have had the people's cooperation, we have had some success. Without it, they just go on cutting trees and letting their animals run. They have no idea what we are doing."

"They're right—we haven't cooperated with them," replied Kamla Devi, the pradhan's wife, when I climbed up from Kala's office and reported his comments. "But how can we cooperate with them? We don't even trust those people. . . . The biogas stove, the tanks, the smokeless chimneys—none of it worked. The trees died. If they had gotten one thing right, maybe we would have worked with them."

In nearly all of the villages immediately surrounding Chopta, the story is the same: The vast majority of the trees supplied have died and most of the "appropriate technologies" are not working. But in one relatively prosperous village at the base of the ridge, Gurfali, the program has made more progress. There, only about half the trees have died and about six biogas stoves work, reducing the need to cut trees for firewood. Gurfali

villagers complain about the same failures of government implementation as do those in Chopta. But they say proudly that they have done somewhat better than their neighbors because they are better educated. "Half the people in Chopta don't even understand the word 'environment,' " said Bahidhar Dhondiyal, a member of the region's Brahmin clan. One afternoon, I sat in the fly-infested house of the Gurfali village chief, Sultan Singh, and asked him and Dhondiyal to tell me what they would do if the World Bank gave them $30 million to improve the quality of life in the area. Without hesitation, they outlined a sweeping vision of improved horticulture, spreading agricultural technology, new roads and markets, and light industrialization. Their informal plan emphasized technical education, factory jobs, and cash crops simultaneously. In its detailed grasp of the region's needs and limitations, it sounded impressive. But of course, the Gurfali leaders said, nobody in the Indian government or the World Bank has ever asked them for their ideas. "They think they know better," Sultan Singh said. "Obviously, they don't."

After I published a long story in the *Post* about Chopta, its conditions, and the failed World Bank program, I got a lot of mail. Some of it expressed shock at the conditions in which the Chopta villagers live. Some writers complained that while I had described a series of compelling problems, I had offered no solutions. Dissidents at the World Bank said the lesson to be learned in Chopta was that development planning required close interaction at the local level. That would certainly help. But none of the writers seized upon what I thought of as the main points: that the Chopta villagers wanted mainly to define their own lives, that they shared a universal ambition to move themselves forward economically as quickly as possible, that many of them were willing to work unbelievably hard to achieve their goals, that they recognized injustice when they saw it—and that because of all this, governments and World Bank planners ought to concentrate on creating opportunities for them comparable to those enjoyed by the urban elite, rather than trying to keep them down on the farm with Gandhian welfare schemes.

The leftist South Asian elites have rejected such obvious market solutions on the grounds that capitalism was the form of historic exploitation on the subcontinent and would exaggerate the discrepancies in income and opportunity contained in the colonial inheritance. In many ways, this argument has been turned upside down since independence to justify a new form of exploitation. At the same time, it is clear that in the midst

of dire poverty, market economics by itself is no magic pill, and that the feared consequences of a widening gap between rich and poor are serious indeed. To have capitalism, you need enough capital to go around; otherwise, those in power horde scarce capital for themselves. Rightist governments in Pakistan, Bangladesh, and Sri Lanka that came to power during the 1980s used the controlled introduction of market mechanisms to reinforce military or elite dominance of the Nehruvian state and its meager resources. Spurred by market energies, their economies grew, and the rich got richer. That provoked those left behind to revolt. The revolts confirmed the worst fears of the governing socialists. They saw what happened in the Soviet Union. They feel the rumblings on their own doorstep, the clamorings of Kamla Devi and Birendra Singh for an "opening up," for change. It may be difficult to stage a revolution when you are chronically malnourished, but still, the socialists worry: *Après nous, le déluge.*

———

The deepest depths of rural poverty in South Asia are plumbed not so much in India as in its severed limb, Bangladesh. A nation born in war and mismanaged since then by corrupt revolutionaries and generals, Bangladesh is seen by the West as the epitome of pathetic South Asian wretchedness. The head of an international relief mission in Dhaka once told me cynically that at least Bangladesh is a popular basket case, which makes for good fund-raising. "Among the donors there is a general bewilderment at how many emergencies Bangladesh faces," he said. "There is a profound misunderstanding of the country, but a profound sympathy." I suppose that is better than profound misunderstanding accompanied by profound lack of interest, but not by much. And there are plenty of thoughtful Bangladeshis who would prefer the lack of interest, believing that Western aid only helps to reinforce their corrupt government. As in Chopta, in Bangladesh I found myself torn between disgust at the political economy that produced and reinforced the country's rural poverty and awe at the ability of impoverished Bangladeshis to find their way forward despite the obstacles.

Bangladesh flashes periodically onto Western television screens when it is in the throes of calamity. The catastrophe on my tour occurred in the spring of 1991, when a cyclone rushed up the Bay of Bengal, swept onto the bay's heavily populated sea islands, and killed upwards of one hun-

dred thousand people overnight. I was caught in Afghanistan when it happened, so another reporter was sent in initially. By the time I got back from Kabul, Western interest in the Bangladesh story was ebbing with the swollen tides. The Dhaka government tried to keep the story alive by inflating the casualty figures, announcing higher numbers each afternoon at a five-star hotel in the capital. But there is only so long that you can sustain interest in pictures of bloated corpses. I decided to take a long trip down to the sea islands, which had been made generally inaccessible by flooded roads and rough waters, to write about why and how so many people lived where the killer cyclones blew. Anita Pratap, a reporter with *Time* magazine, found a stalwart van driver and translator, and so we headed south from Dhaka in the smoky quiet just after midnight.

It took sixteen bone-rattling hours over pitted two-lane roads and by ferries to reach Cox's Bazaar, the fishing port at the far southern tip of Bangladesh, where the country bleeds into the green hills of Burma. Along the way we passed through Chittagong, second to Dhaka in population and certainly one of the grimmest cities in South Asia. The streets were flooded with water, mud, and oil slicks. Diesel smoke choked the air. Fires burned in trash bins. Hordes of bicycle rickshaws clattered about, powered by thin Bengali men who stood as they pedaled, leaning all their weight from side to side to force the pedals down. These are the cities to which South Asian villagers like the ones on Chopta ridge aspire. The money had better be good, because in the worst of the cities just about everything else looks like hell. In fact, the problem in Chittagong is that compared with Delhi or Bombay or Karachi—relatively prosperous urban centers—jobs and money are scarce. To quote one of the boilerplate lines from Bangladesh-disaster newspaper stories, the country has one hundred million people jammed into an area the size of Wisconsin. That is a lot of people looking for the same patronage and opportunity.

Chugging on a rickety wooden sloop through the gray-green waters of the Bay of Bengal on our way to Moheshkhali Island, where some eleven thousand farmers and fishermen reportedly had died in the cyclone, you could sense immediately why a Bangladeshi with few alternatives would risk the occasional murderous storms to live free along the sea, rather than scraping for some handout job from a prosperous thug in the city. Better to die on Moheshkhali than live in Chittagong, I thought. There was sky out here—air, space, sunlight. And in the water,

fish. Shrimp. Protein. I talked to the passengers on the boat, islanders returning from Cox's Bazaar. A student named Ashish Kumar Dey sidled over between the sacks of food and belongings stacked in the boat. "My father was born on the island. I was, too," he said. "There are three ways to make a living other than fishing—farming, betel leaves [a product like tobacco], and salt. I've seen three cyclones in my lifetime. Now, what we have over here, even if we sell it, we won't be able to buy land on the mainland. There just isn't any land to buy. It's extremely expensive. Here we've started something of our own, something we can claim. That's the main thing."

A local relief volunteer on the boat, Binoy Krishna Biswas, like Dey a member of Bangladesh's small Hindu religious minority, said pride and stoicism had contributed to Moheshkhali's high death toll during the cyclone. Accustomed to lashing storms and swollen tides, the islanders refused to leave their villages for prefabricated shelters even when the government broadcast its highest possible cyclone warning by radio and loudspeaker. "The police had to beat them with sticks to bring them in," Biswas said. "They never paid heed to the signal. They're too proud of their courage. Fighting with the ocean and the cyclones—they think that's their life."

On the island we found scenes of devastation and resilience. We rode toward the interior on a three-wheel rickshaw, then walked when the roads ran out. On a dirt path we passed an accident involving a bicycle rickshaw loaded with hay and a cart carrying sacks of rice. Children rushed out and scooped up handfuls of rice from the ground and scurried away. Every family, it seemed, had lost something—a chicken, stores of rice, grains, seeds, livestock, houses, money, relatives. Corpses lay in the marshes. Collapsed thatched homes dotted the landscape. Entire villages had fallen in on themselves. Survivors had built tree houses for their children on the sites of their wrecked homes. Throughout, we saw no tears, no paralysis of mourning. Everybody seemed busy.

At dusk we stopped at a tin lean-to occupied by the family of Nural Islam, a fisherman who had lost his house and several relatives. I asked about the apparent mood of calm determination on the island. "If one person had died, the others would have consoled," he said. "But we have all been afflicted with the same calamity. We are stunned. The response has been a mixture of families caring for orphans, community relief, social organizations helping, and then some people looting. We

have the courage and strength to work in the sea. The children are hungry and crying but getting by. The fishermen are ready to go back to the sea as soon as the trawler owners say so. The ocean is never an enemy, only a friend. We have a phrase in Bengali, 'The ocean always gives back what it takes.' "

I asked what the ocean gives back in a good month. Islam said his boats sometimes earned two hundred thousand takas (about five thousand dollars) in a month. In Bangladesh, that is a lot of giving back. Absentee landlords, protected on the mainland by the Dhaka government, take most of the cash, and the fishermen and the farmers get the worst of the bargain. But they make a living, they live free, and they have something of their own to claim.

I pitched a tent in the sand outside the lean-to and zipped in for the night. Monsoon clouds gathered into a torrential storm. Lightning flashed continually, illuminating the surrounding paddy fields in an eerie glow. Thunder rumbled in the distance and crashed nearby. Rain poured down as if shot from a fire hose. Figuring that I wouldn't recognize a tidal wave if I saw one, I decided to rejoin Anita and Nural Islam's family in the lean-to. I showed up at the entrance waving my flashlight and drenched to the bone. Anita and our translator were awake, watching the fireworks. Everybody else was asleep, snoring soundly. In the morning, they explained that it was just a normal storm. The cyclone was a little like that, they said, only the wind was much stronger, and in the middle of it all, a twenty-foot tidal surge crashed through an embankment and washed many from their homes. They talked about it as if it were just one of those things.

We ate a few bananas and hiked back across the island to hire a boat for the day. After much bargaining, in which the islanders took us for all we were worth, we found a captain of a motor sloop willing to ride through the marshy channels and visit a few more islands. Churning through the muddy waters, you could tell when you were approaching the worst places because the trees suddenly disappeared and the air filled with the thick stench of decomposing bodies. The initial relief effort had been botched, and thousands of the poorest had trekked to local centers to wait for biscuits, rice, and rehydration pills that had not yet arrived. We filled our notebooks with the usual grim quotes.

On the way back, we stopped at the Moheshkhali jetty to drop off a local guide. Dozens of islanders jumped uninvited into our boat. The

captain shouted at them, putting on a show for our benefit, then pulled away and began collecting money for fares. Fifteen minutes later, in choppy high seas, the sloop's motor quit. The passengers all stood up and shuffled from side to side on the deck, nearly tipping us over. They flagged down two passing trawlers, whose captains each in turn pulled alongside, sized up the situation, waved sheepishly, and pulled off at full bore. Adrift, we were knocked around by the waves and it looked as if we might go over. The shore was a couple of miles off but I thought I could make it if the tide was with us. I pointed out some floating driftwood and suggested to Anita that if we capsized, we should meet at the driftwood and swim in together. Unflappable as ever, she chose this moment to mention that she could not swim. The panicked passengers did not look like Olympic champions, either. I remembered what they taught us in junior lifesaving about what drowning people do to those who think they can swim. With renewed self-interest we watched our captain as he dove from the stern and swam beneath the boat, trying to fix something. He was made of muscle and swam like a fish, clad only in a sarong wrapped tightly to his thighs. He was utterly calm. Of course, he had nothing to worry about—he probably swam five miles each morning to fetch his breakfast. Finally, he climbed aboard, pulled a rope, and the motor roared. We bounced on the waves and chugged into the harbor at Cox's Bazaar. At the harbor's mouth we passed one of the two trawlers that had passed us up. It was stuck now on a sand bar. Passengers on both boats jeered and cursed one another as we went by.

The West feels pity for these people. If it values courage and determination, what it ought to feel is respect. If South Asia's rural poor received from their political leadership one tenth of the opportunity they deserve, they might do a lot more than survive.

Back in Dhaka, feeling oddly bullish about Bangladesh in the midst of this catastrophe, I went around to talk to Bangladeshi friends and acquaintances active in rural development. One was Mohammed Yunus, a remarkable man who founded something called the Grameen Bank, which lends money to rural women, and which seems to have found a niche somewhere between market mechanisms and the Gandhian ideal, the Village on a Hill. I asked him whether he was optimistic or pessimistic about the future.

"There's a tremendous amount of strength in the people," he answered. "Among the young, they're willing to make any sacrifice. There's enough

of everything but there's a lack of information and management structure in the society. We have enough things but we don't know how to make use of them. . . . In some ways we are moving forward and in some ways backward. In terms of development we're going backward because we are stuck with the same old approaches and ideas.

"What is the difference between here and Florida?" he continued. "The difference is poverty. The basic fault is not on the developed countries, not on the West. It is on us. Why should we glow year after year in the sympathy of the West? If you squander what is coming, that is the tragedy. . . . We have tremendous potential together as a people. Our only problem is our stupidity as a nation."

STATES

OF

MIND

5

Enemies

These brave warriors will think you have withdrawn from battle
out of fear, and those who formerly esteemed you will treat you
with disrespect. Your enemies will ridicule your strength and
say things that should not be said. What could be more painful
than this?

—*The Hindu god Krishna, to Arjuna,*
in the Bhagavad Gita

In the fall of 1990, Pakistan had an election. The campaign was filled with
egregious lies, distortions, vilifications, exaggerations, and corruption,
but at least it was an election campaign and not martial law or revolution,
which in Pakistan meant there was some reason to be optimistic. On polling
day the question was whether or not the vote would be stolen by the
government, so those foreigners who were around fanned out to the cities
and the countryside looking for malfeasance. As it turned out, what
malfeasance occurred was generally difficult to see, so mostly we scurried
from polling place to polling place and watched large numbers of Pakistanis
stand in line. Late in the day, in Rawalpindi, a gray-brown urban sprawl just
south of the capital of Islamabad, I wound up in an elementary school that
was being used as a polling booth. The lone classroom was dim and bare. A
single naked lightbulb glared above concrete floors and chipped green
walls. Anatomy posters of human skeletons and organs loomed over rows
of old wooden desks, the kind with holes for ink pots. Bored with the voting,
which was proceeding smoothly, I wandered around the classroom and
looked carefully at the teaching materials, some of them in Urdu, some in
English. Taped to the wall in front of the little desks was a fable in English
scrawled by a felt marker.

"The Wolf and the Lamb" was its title. It went this way:

Once a hungry wolf was drinking water at a stream. He saw a lamb also drinking water there. He became very happy. He wanted to kill him and eat him up. He went near the lamb and said to him, "Why are you making the water muddy?" The poor lamb replied that the water was flowing from his, the wolf's side, to his, the lamb's side. So he was not making the water muddy. The wolf said angrily, "Why did you call me a name last year?" The lamb replied that he must he must be mistaken because he, the lamb, was then only six months old. The wolf said that it must be his, the lamb's, elder, so he jumped on the poor lamb and killed him.

Such is the peril faced by South Asia's lambs, such is the disingenuousness of its wolves, and such are the lessons about each conveyed to young minds. In the jumble of codes, ancient and modern, that coexist uneasily on the subcontinent—legal codes, democratic codes, feudal codes, tribal codes, revenge codes, caste codes, family codes, religious codes—there are many possible routes of appeal and many possible justifications for pouncing and eating.

The overarching political struggle in South Asia late in the twentieth century can be seen as an attempt to squeeze an ungainly, unruly feudal body into a neatly pressed, imported democratic suit of clothes. The fitting is as yet incomplete. Part of the trouble is, you can try to import democratic or socialist or capitalist structures, but you cannot so easily import or impose an egalitarian state of mind. This is not because South Asians are inherently or culturally antidemocratic. Rather, modern democratic ideas and identities must compete with older, better-established ones such as tribe or caste or religion. In Western Europe a version of this competition took place over a span of centuries—and even today the struggle to reconcile hierarchies remains unfinished. In South Asia the effort has been compressed into decades, not so much because the region's internal social evolution demanded such acceleration, but because the subcontinent suddenly found itself sucked into a newly interdependent twentieth-century "global village," where all sorts of ideas and identities splashed freely across national boundaries that were themselves artificial. Many new nations have had to cope with this tide and backwash since World War II and a few have been destroyed by the pressures. In South Asia, the result has been occasionally catastrophic but more often merely peculiar.

You see this tension in the obscurantist leaders who tried to build their movements with the most modern Western technology, such as the

turbaned Islamic radicals in Pakistan who traveled with cellular telephones or the saffron-robed Hindu revivalists in India who spread their message with mobile video vans. Some people are alarmed by this appropriation of modern technology for potentially repressive ends, but in these cases, at least, I figured that in time the machines might win out over their proprietors, in the sense that movements built with such dazzling technology would ultimately have to find a way to deliver the same technology equitably to the faithful; otherwise, the movements would fail. A more disturbing question, it seemed, was how high the costs might be in human lives and liberty before this process worked itself out one way or the other.

Where the old and the new often blend most dangerously in South Asia is around the idea of the enemy. Every South Asian is born with potential enemies—members of rival families, rival tribes, rival castes, rival ethnic groups, rival religions. As an individual, you cannot easily opt out of these conflicts because you cannot escape your identity. It is there in your name, or in answers to the inevitable questions about what place your family "belongs to." Even in the loose, chaotic cities, ethnic and caste and tribal clans reassemble and protect their members. Clan leaders graft themselves to the Nehruvian state and acquire power through patronage, setting the stage for wider conflict if the leaders compete for power on the national stage. Even South Asians who migrate abroad cannot completely escape their enemies. In England, expatriate Hindus and Muslims have fought battles in the streets occasionally, and rival factions of Sikh separatists have struggled violently for control of Sikh temples. Westerners impressed by the recent glories of the nation-state tend to view this fratricidal factionalism as evidence of a sort of unfathomable preindustrial chaos, a view reflected in newspaper boilerplate phrases about South Asia such as "centuries-old ethnic feuding" or "Afghanistan's internecine tribal rivalries." But clan identities in South Asia represent continuity rather than chaos; they are the identifies that have survived all the shifting empires and the failed emperors. National citizenship, however essential in the present world of global interdependence, is a new idea on the subcontinent—and it is the idea that has tended to stimulate the worst spasms of bloody chaos.

In the accelerated struggle to define South Asia's political economies, ancient codes of identity, violence, and honor are mustered and melded in the service of modern ideology, such as separatist nationalism or leftist

revolution. At the same time the codes are mustered and melded in service of old ideology, such as religion. Leaders reach back to old myths in order to whip up extreme feeling—and to produce extreme actions—sufficient to challenge the practical power of their opponents and the more ephemeral power of the ascendant national, democratic-pluralist idea. In reaction, those playing defense appeal to the same old codes, employ the same language of extremity. In this way rivals are confirmed as enemies and conflicts that might have been resolved through negotiation are settled in blood. And once the blood flows, the old codes are doubly confirmed.

The public manipulation and exploitation of feeling and tradition in this way can be both dangerous and absurd. It becomes necessary to see opponents not just as bad or misguided but as evil incarnate, evil in the face of which there can be no compromise.

One example from my time is what happened to Salman Rushdie, a Bombay-born Muslim whose family emigrated to Pakistan before Rushdie went on to settle in the West. As is well known, Rushdie ran afoul of Ayatollah Khomeini for writing the novel *The Satanic Verses*, which some Muslims found blasphemous. Khomeini then issued a *fatwah*, or religious edict, condemning Rushdie to death and forcing the author into hiding. That such an edict would emanate from the puritan terrorism of the Iranian revolution did not seem entirely surprising. But what was mind-boggling was the way Rushdie was treated in the land of his birth. India's nominally democratic and pluralistic government, fearful of rioting and political blackmail provoked by local Muslim politicians, banned the novel. In Pakistan, a sporadic campaign of vilification culminated in a hit movie, *International Guerrillas*, in which Rushdie is portrayed as the decadent and evil leader of a worldwide Jewish conspiracy against Islam. More than a million people saw this movie, its producers said. Many went back to the theater two or three times.

At the height of the film's popularity I was in Karachi and forced my friend and colleague Kamran Khan to go out and rent a videotaped copy and to translate the dialogue while we watched it on his VCR. He kept a remote control device handy to fast-forward through the song-and-dance numbers. This proved a brilliant stroke because, for a movie supposedly dedicated to the defense of Islam against its greatest living enemy, there was much shaking of flesh and crooning of passionate lament.

The movie opens with a Koran, the Islamic holy book, towering on a pedestal. There is a meeting of Jews who have decided to destroy Islam. Rushdie wears pince-nez and a white leisure suit. (In real life, in case there is any confusion, Rushdie is neither Jewish nor a wearer of white leisure suits.) The Jewish conspirators drink champagne and liquor with women in short skirts. They discuss who will go to war with Pakistan, the "fortress of Islam."

We cut to the fortress. Various male heroes and their brothers and their cousins are introduced. These movies always have a few cousins and other lesser relatives because family is a bedrock cultural organizing principle yet somebody's got to die before the hero kills the villain. Various episodes of gun-fighting and song-and-dance follow—in the dance numbers, plump and scantily clad Pakistani actresses lip-sync to love songs, gyrate, and jiggle themselves thoroughly. A corrupt police chief unjustly shoots a few people, including the niece of our hero. She lifts her head from a pool of blood and says, "That dog Salman Rushdie must die." Then she collapses.

"This is the first sacrifice in our holy mission," says the hero. Zoom! Reaction close-up shot of the hero. Zoom! Zoom! Zoom! Reaction close-ups of all the brave Islamic guerrilla fighters who will soon track down Rushdie at his tropical island headquarters and attempt to kill him.

On the island, we find Rushdie amusing himself by tying some captured Arab fighters to wooden crosses, cutting their throats with a long, curved sword, and inhaling the blood of his enemies. He breathes in the fragrance of one dead Arab's shirt and says delightedly, "This is the blood of the lovers of Mohammed," as if impressed by a seductive perfume. Rushdie's island security detail, led by a former commando of the Israeli army, nods in agreement. Rushdie retires to his extensive glass house to order weapons and liquor on a cordless telephone.

To Rushdie, our heroes vow, "Even the grave will not accept you! You ridiculed Mohammed with your tongue! We will cut your tongue into pieces!"

Three of the Pakistani guerrillas dress up as Batman with black capes and bat insignias to try to penetrate Rushdie's security wall. It doesn't work.

Rushdie kidnaps the wife of one of the guerrillas and tortures her by reading aloud sections of *The Satanic Verses*.

At the end, Rushdie hurls a few hand grenades, blasts away with a

machine gun, captures the heroic Muslim guerrillas, and ties them to wooden crosses to crucify them. On the crosses, our heroes sing about the Koran. Lightning bolts free them. Rushdie's former girlfriend converts to Islam, war breaks out again, and a deep voice booms from the sky to say, "The Holy Book is the most powerful. This is the Book about which there is no doubt. The Koran's protector is God himself." We see the Koran on its pedestal again. It zaps Rushdie with a laser beam and he burns into nothing.

Now, it is arguable that the difference between this cultural fantasy and, say, an American vigilante-revenge-on-the-criminals movie boils down to a gap in cinematic production values. But the contexts are different. The West is not yet prepared to organize its political economies around revenge fantasy, the death penalty in the United States notwithstanding. In South Asia, the political economies are still forming, and the dialogue of the Rushdie movie reflects what too often passes for political speech in the region.

After watching more than three hours of this egregious schlock in Kamran's flat, we drove over to a movie theater where *International Guerrillas* was in the midst of its record-breaking Pakistani run. In the lobby, at the end of a show, we collared some young men who turned out to be Pakistani air force recruits. One of them had seen the film three times. All were impressed by the force of its message. "We want to see what is the end of somebody who ridicules Islam," said Mohammed Ismail, an eighteen-year-old mechanic. "Whoever sees this movie praises it highly. We haven't seen such a good movie ever—and it's also Islamic," he concluded. This appreciation seemed appropriate for a young man entering an air force whose generals in Islamabad like to boast privately that they have recruited suicide pilots willing to fly F-16s laden with nuclear bombs right into the apartment blocks of downtown Bombay, should nuclear war with India ever become necessary.

We arranged an interview in Karachi with the movie's director, Jan Mohammed. We found him in the mildewed upstairs offices of a Karachi film production company. He was a plump man squeezed into a kaleidoscopic polyester shirt that opened to his belly button and revealed much curly chest hair and—yes—gold chains. He was a bad imitation of a bad imitation of a Hollywood director, but there was something a little bit endearing about his being so self-consciously hip and nouveau riche. As

we talked, it seemed obvious that he was in over his head with this whole Islam thing.

"It's made about a million rupees so far," he said of his film. "All of them are big hits that we've made, but this one has gained fame world-wide. The earlier ones were only commercial films. There was nothing meaningful in the ones before. There was something which was lacking. People would say they were hits, but there's no thematic value. We were searching for something which would be meaningful—something entertaining which would be meaningful as well. The important thing was that it shouldn't have been taken as a documentary because then people wouldn't go to the cinema. . . . If we had not had all of these dancers and all of that, then people would not go as much to the movie and they wouldn't have absorbed so much. A film is an attraction. I've been making entertaining films, but I always put in a holy bit or a miracle at the end of the reels. People say I repeat myself, but I try to do it every time."

I asked about the propaganda aspect of the movie, its endorsement of the murder of Salman Rushdie, whose life had been ruined by a campaign in which the director's film was perhaps now the most popular component. Mohammed paused for a while, seemed to struggle for his answer, then offered an entertainer's utilitarian defense of murder. "I am not a religious man, or, I mean I am not a religious leader," he replied, seeming to revise his thought in contemplation of the mullahs. "I want that everybody will be happy. If Salman Rushdie is killed, everybody will be happy."

Islam, with its theory of martyrdom and its present international strain of expansionist fervor, is one movement on the subcontinent in which leaders and propagandists continually vilify their opponents for tactical reasons, whether to seek political office or reap box office receipts. But Islam is only one example. The uses of the abstract, exaggerated enemy are many—in politics, in business, in revolution. Lest the West should convince itself that it has somehow evolved beyond all this, the carnage in Yugoslavia is a reminder that when the nation-state weakens or collapses, prenational identities and enmities fill the void. In South Asia, the state has never grown strong enough to suppress these ancient enmities, so they rise more easily to the surface.

In the tribal areas of western Pakistan and Afghanistan, for example, various nation builders have tried for the last 250 years to impose new

codes on top of the old tribalism—codes of imperialism, democracy, communism—but they have failed so completely that the conventional wisdom these days is that it is a waste of time and effort to even try. Under Pakistan's constitution, there are areas of Baluchistan and the Northwest Frontier provinces that are officially designated "tribal areas," meaning that ordinary Pakistani laws and political processes simply do not apply. Tribal leaders are free to govern by their own traditional rules, which in effect means they are free to kill each other with impunity and stifle progress at will, if they have the strength. The system was explained to me one afternoon in Quetta, a mud-rock Pakistani mountain city that is the provincial capital of Baluchistan province, by Nawab Bugti, then the provincial chief minister, a longtime Baluch nationalist and a member of the local tribal royalty who grew up in imperial style during the days of British colonialism. Bugti's political problems that afternoon were considerable—shifting tribal relations, the legacy of leftist revolutionary movements, the resurgence of Islam, ethnic troubles with neighboring Pakistani and Afghan groups. But the chief, with his long, dignified white beard and flowing white Baluch turban, talked of his province like the fictional Godfather casually dismissing a few recent troubles in the family. As he spoke from behind his large desk, a turbaned servant brought him a glass of water on a tray, delivered it, waited for Bugti to finish, then placed the glass back on the tray and walked briskly off.

"The crime rate has gone up," Bugti said. "There's car theft, kidnapping, highway robbery, murder. Now we are trying to impress upon tribal elders the need to change. Generally, law and order is better than in other provinces, but we have the normal thing—tribal feuds, blood feuds, and vendettas.... Going about armed, that is the traditional way. It is a man's ornament. He feels naked without a weapon on his shoulder. That is one reason why we have proper law and order. Everyone has weapons. The mutual fear keeps people in their places."

I asked him when, under tribal law, it was justifiable for a man to kill his enemy. "It just depends on why A killed B," he answered. "Was it a justifiable murder? If B owed a life to A, one could call it justified because B had previously killed A's father or uncle and had not made restitution according to the tribal code. Adultery or fornication—the punishment is death, to be meted out by the person concerned, the father or the brother or so on. You kill both if it's a case of adultery—the man and the woman, although sometimes the man will escape."

"How often does this happen?" I inquired, meaning killings for adultery, not the men escaping.

"That depends on desires," Bugti answered. "It happens very often. If anyone kills for black work, which is what we call adultery or fornication, everyone will say, 'Well done, very good. You have washed the situation clean.' We have one honorable member of the provincial assembly who killed his own brother, the chief of the tribe, so he could become chief. That whole family, they have been killing each other for ages. None of them has ever died a natural death."

Bugti spoke in a tone of light amusement about all of this, playing it up for the effect, and it was easy to share his jocularity. You could laugh with a guy like Bugti, or even the film director Jan Mohammed—until you remembered that there are a whole lot of ordinary South Asians who don't get the joke. They don't get it because the joke's on them.

You think, for example, about the twelve- and thirteen-year-old Tamil boys patrolling the jungle roads in northern Sri Lanka these days with AK-47 assault rifles cradled in their arms and capsules of cyanide poison tied around their necks. Of all the dozens and dozens of guerrilla movements in South Asia founded in one way or another on ethnic or tribal identities, the Liberation Tigers of Tamil Eelam, or LTTE, represents perhaps the most horrifying melding of old codes and new ideology. The Tigers began little more than a decade ago as a liberation movement representing the legitimate aspirations of Sri Lanka's Tamils—a besieged ethnic, religious, and linguistic minority—against the island's dominant Sinhalese group. Nurtured by Sinhalese racism, by a brutal civil war, and by the megalomania of a fanatical leader, Villaphallai Prabhakaran, the LTTE has grown into a grotesque cult of suicide and murder organized around the manipulation of hatred, the depersonalization of the enemy, and the desire of children who don't know any better to die as heroes.

After Dhanu, the bespectacled Tamil girl, blew up herself and Rajiv Gandhi, I traveled with Mark Fineman of the *Los Angeles Times* back to the jungles of northern Sri Lanka to write again about the LTTE's suicide culture and its growing isolation from ordinary Tamils. We found ourselves one afternoon in a Sri Lankan army bunker at the edge of an abandoned stretch of military no-man's-land with a captain named Randu Hathnuada. He wore a nine-millimeter pistol at his waist, a crescent scar on his forehead, and a black T-shirt emblazoned with the slogan "Another Elephant Pass Hero," which referred to a thirty-day siege-battle he had

fought against the Tigers at a fort just north of his present bunker. Peering out through the slits of his bunker, he talked about what it was like to fight against the Tigers. What impressed him was the vivid recklessness of their assaults, the suicide charges. They come in the night in waves, boys and girls no older than fifteen, in shorts and flip-flop sandals, attacking with assault rifles, armored cars, antiaircraft guns, bulldozers with explosives rigged to the blades. "They charged," Hathnuada recalled of a particular attack at Elephant Pass. "We are shooting. As soon as they are hit, they are eating cyanide. Small children, even small girls. I have seen it so many times. They vomit and die."

The Tigers communicate with their Sinhalese enemies through propaganda letters tacked onto trees around the army camps or smuggled into barracks by local Tamil servants. One of them, addressed to "the Sinhala Soldier," was published by LTTE partisan Satchi Ponnambalam:

We see you riding down the streets of Tamil Eelam, khaki-clad and armed. The care of an old mother or father, or a sister, maybe, compels you to carry arms. While those in the seats of power in Sri Lanka flourish, you fall down as the victims. Very soon, you will stand, turned against your own people, your own class, ordered by this very same class in power. Those in power will use you to crush the revolt of your own people.

We, motivated by an unceasing yearning for national liberation, are forced to oppose you, a puppet of the state. When we meet at the battlefront, you become the sacrificial lamb.

Hathnuada, determined to become nobody's lamb, said this of the Tigers that afternoon as we stood with him in his bunker: "They are crazy. They are motivated. And as fighters, they are very good."

The Tamil journalist N. Ram is one of the few who have spoken at length with Prabhakaran, who lives in the jungle and shifts from bunker to bunker; his whereabouts are shielded by the suicide culture he cultivates, since Tiger cadres nearly always kill themselves before they can be captured and interrogated. "You won't find our people in jail," Prabhakaran once told Ram. "It is this cyanide which has helped us develop our movement very rapidly. . . . In reality, this gives our fighters an extra measure of belief in the cause, a special edge; it has instilled in us a determination to sacrifice our lives and our everything for the cause." He described his struggle as one between the forces of good, his fighters, and the forces of evil, the Sri Lankan state and its army. "The state's army

functions there as a racist, destructive military force; we carry on as a national people's army for the liberation of the Tamil people. . . . We prepared the people for this crisis. . . . We were determined to demonstrate our resistance, our fight in an all-out, foolhardy way. Whatever be the numbers of fighters we lost, we would not give in—that was our decision. . . . Can we afford to be peaceable in our ways in the face of a ruthless enemy? We certainly cannot, that's the truth."

Political ideology, in the ordinary sense, is the least of it. Prabhakaran spoke to Ram vaguely about "socialism and Tamil Eelam," an independent Tamil homeland. In Trincomalee and in the jungles of the north, I questioned various Tiger "political officers" at length about their program. They, too, talked vaguely about socialism and housing, but essentially they had no program. At one stage in 1990, when the Indian Peacekeeping Force withdrew from Sri Lanka, the Tigers possessed uncontested control of the northern island region they designated as part of independent Eelam. Western donors were prepared to funnel nearly $750 million in reconstruction aid to the Tigers if they would begin the transition from guerrilla fighters to political administrators. Autonomy negotiations with the Sinhalese-dominated Sri Lankan government were making progress. But when you talked with the Tiger officers in the battered northern cities during this period, you could feel that they simply could not handle politics. They were itchy and uncomfortable behind their desks with their pistols belted to their fatigues. All these civilians with problems—houses burned down or bombed out, wells dried up, roads unpassable. The Tigers had promised for years to solve these problems, but now, when it was possible to try, they discovered that they lacked the temperament. They wanted to fight. Peace made them edgy. Within three months, they staged incidents to start the war again, kidnapping a few hundred Sinhalese policemen, taking them into the jungle, and massacring them with machine guns. The Sri Lankan army responded with force. The Tigers abandoned the cities and went back to the jungle, back to what they knew.

After half a dozen trips to Sri Lanka and talks with Tigers ranging from preteen patrolmen to senior political leaders, I met S. C. Chandrahasan, a Tamil lawyer who worked closely with Prabhakaran in the early days of the Tiger movement and then broke with him, disillusioned. Now he works with refugees from the northern war. "I find nine- and ten-year-olds who can clean and load a rifle," he said despairingly. "Among the

young people, they were so full of hate. They were just so warped. We tried to introduce them to sports. The Tigers said we were trying to reeducate them." I asked him to analyze the Tiger supremo, as the local newspapers call him. "Prabhakaran's commitment is total," he answered. "But as time went on, he became more and more powerful. He became a fascist. On the military side he is a genius, but other faculties have not been developed. They have not developed political faculties. . . . It's quite clear that they've gone well beyond the limits of a group fighting for liberation. They're going for methods of terrorism only."

Another Tamil leader who knows Prabhakaran said that over the years, the Tiger suicide cult had solidified around two principles. One was that Prabhakaran himself was the reincarnation of Tamil warrior kings of the Middle Ages, particularly the ancient "Raja Chola," a Sri Lankan Tamil ruler during the period of the Chola dynasty who went off to fight in India and China and was renowned for his prowess. The use of these myths, the old codes, to build a personality cult around Prabhakaran was reflected in the Tigers' practice of forcing new recruits, young boys, to swear loyalty to Prabhakaran himself, rather than to the liberation movement or the Tigers. The second principle was to rely on the deep hatred felt by the ethnic Sinhalese for the ethnic Tamils. This racist hatred among the Sinhalese would in time produce actions by the Sri Lankan army or others that would confirm Prabhakaran's most extreme judgments and tactics. Thus the Tigers would be sustained. Prabhakaran relies "on the inherent irrationality of the south, the inherent extremism," this Tamil leader said. And for most of the last decade, Prabhakaran has been fortunate to have Sinhalese enemies he could count on.

The Tigers are a stark example, but elsewhere in the region the same principle operates. A talented leader with credible claims to history and strength in a brutal present can launch the most extreme attacks on his or her enemies, then withdraw and wait for the enemy to confirm that such action was necessary in the first place. This has been true as much in politics as in war.

As the accused murderer of Rajiv Gandhi, Prabhakaran is a complicated case because he developed his military strength through secret training and weapons provided by the government of Gandhi's mother. Later, after Indira was assassinated, Prabhakaran met Rajiv himself in New Delhi. When Gandhi signed the 1987 accord with Sri Lanka's government authorizing the deployment of Indian troops on the island, ostensibly to

secure the Tamil population Prabhakaran wished to "liberate," the Indian government flew the Tiger leader to its capital to explain the deal and urge him to cooperate. Prabhakaran sat in an office with Gandhi for several hours. Evidently flattered by the attention, the LTTE leader flew back to Jaffna and made a public speech praising Gandhi. "The Indian prime minister offered me certain assurances," Prabhakaran told a Tamil audience on August 4, 1987, according to a translation made available by the LTTE to the Indian journalist Mohan Ram. "He offered a guarantee for the safety and protection of our people. I do have faith in the straightforwardness of the Indian prime minister and I do have faith in his assurances." That professed faith did not last long. Prabhakaran broke his agreement and went to war with the Indian army as soon as he was able. In that same Jaffna speech, he offered a hint as to why, a preview of the attitudes that continue to define Sri Lanka's predicament years later.

A peace agreement, Prabhakaran said, "affects the form and shape of our struggle. It also puts a stop to our armed struggle. If the mode of our struggle, brought to this stage over a fifteen-year period through shedding blood, through making sacrifices, through staking achievements, and through offering a great many lives, is to be dissolved or disbanded within a few days, it is naturally something we are unable to digest."

6

Through the Looking Glass

We should take certain measures to bring in a little more sanity into politics.

—*General Zia ul-Haq*

When I arrived in South Asia in 1989, the single most momentous mystery in the region—and there were many—concerned the death of Zia ul-Haq, the middle-class Pakistani general who seized power in a 1977 coup, imposed martial law, and held on to the country's highest office until August 17, 1988, when he died in an unexplained plane crash along with many of his top generals, the U.S. ambassador to Pakistan, and an American general.

One glaring aspect of the mystery was that nobody seemed to want to unravel it. Zia was widely disliked. He was entangled in sensitive, shifting cold war geopolitics. Virtually any explanation of his death other than certification that it was an accident would complicate, if not badly disrupt, contemporary South Asian affairs. There was plenty of speculation. Some said the Americans killed Zia because of the general's rightist Islamic ideology, an explanation which, if true and exposed, would be disastrous for the American government's standing in the region and the world. Some said the Soviets did it in revenge for their defeat in Afghanistan, which, if true, would be disastrous for them but also potentially for the Americans, in part because it would discredit Gorbachev, then still the key figure in the negotiated end of the cold war. Some said the Indians

did it, which, if true, would be particularly dangerous because it could lead to war between India and Pakistan. Some said Benazir Bhutto's relatives and political allies in Pakistan, hardened enemies of Zia, had killed him, which, if true, would mean the end of Benazir politically and bad times for Pakistani democracy. Some said Zia's rivals in the Pakistan army killed him, which, if true, would make everybody very nervous, since arresting a general for murder is not a simple proposition in Pakistan. For all these reasons and others, nobody in power seemed to want to investigate the August 17 plane crash seriously. So I figured that was enough reason for me to do it.

This explains why in April 1991 I found myself standing in the trash-strewn parking lot of a garden-apartment complex in suburban Chicago, Illinois, screaming at an overweight East European building manager who wore great rings of keys on his belt and who kept shouting "Vuck you! Vuck you!"

What else it may explain is not easy to summarize. This is the story in part of a journey into one of South Asia's most introspective, incestuous, and psychologically tangled palace courts: the capital of Pakistan, Islamabad, where lies and whispers are the ordinary language of political discourse, as they have been in subcontinental princely courts for hundreds of years. It is also a detective story in which, time and again, the main puzzle is not who or what or where, but why. Finally, it is a story about what happens when you look in the mirror and see a ghost over your shoulder—a predicament, I think, that plagues South Asian intellectuals and Western newspaper reporters considerably more often than other classes of people.

———

Pakistan is a country that sometimes appears to be organized around the greeting card aphorism "Just because you're paranoid, it doesn't mean they're not out to get you." No nation is more entangled in conspiratorial fantasy. Generals and politicians will pull you aside at cocktail parties and, unprompted, spin elaborate theories about the most mundane national events, suggesting—furtively but vaguely—the moving presence of unseen hands, whether American, Soviet, Indian, or domestic. Nothing occurs in isolation. Everything is connected. The opposition leader flew to Dubai because the Arabs financed the mistress of her dead father, who

lost office when the CIA used the Arabs to persuade the Pakistani military to stage a coup. And so on. Pakistan is like an out-patient who refuses his lithium—functional but deeply strange, trapped in mirrored interiors.

Yet the paradox is that no nation has more cause than Pakistan to believe in conspiracies. For the forty-five years of its existence, Pakistan's destiny has been diverted time and again by small cliques of powerful men, native and foreign, who have plotted in secret. Its army, six hundred thousand strong, has staged several coups against civilian leaders—coups preceded by closely guarded conspiracies and extensive work by domestic intelligence agencies, whose wiretaps and attempted manipulations proliferate so awkwardly even today that anyone who spends time in the country inevitably begins to trip over them.

Moreover, during the cold war, which coincided with the first four decades of the country's independent history, Pakistan became an unusually important bulwark against Soviet expansion for the Americans, particularly during the 1980s, when Pakistan was the staging ground for the semisecret U.S. program of military support for Afghanistan's mujaheddin rebels. During that period, the United States pumped about $2 billion in covert aid through Pakistan's main intelligence agency, ISI, for use by the Afghans. It also provided a similar amount of money directly to the Pakistan army and government, making Pakistan, in financial terms at least, the third-most-important American ally during the 1980s, after Israel and Egypt. Most aspects of this highly sensitive relationship were worked out in secret between American diplomats and spies and their Pakistani counterparts. Evidence of how sensitive Washington considers the relationship can be found in the way it classifies historical national security materials concerning Pakistan. Before I left for South Asia in 1989, mainly out of curiosity, I submitted a dozen or so Freedom of Information Act requests for materials held in Washington about the U.S. relationship with Pakistan. All but the most innocuous were rejected in their entirety for national security reasons. An archivist at the Lyndon Baines Johnson Memorial Library in Austin, Texas, where I dug out a few boxes of material from the 1960s, told me that the U.S. government still refuses to declassify reams of Pakistan-related documents thirty years old or more. He said that in his experience, the only country American classification bureaucrats are more paranoid about is Israel.

Zia's sudden death in the summer of 1988 drew together in a single explosion many strains of American and Pakistani suspicion. Among the

Pakistani elite, everybody had his own conspiracy theory. I don't think I have ever met a Pakistani, elite or not, who believes that Zia died accidentally. What they disagree about is who led the plot and why. When I first began to look into the case in depth in the late autumn of 1989, it became clear that any investigation would be driven as much by this tangled psychology as by material fact. But I underestimated how difficult it would be to separate one from the other.

———

At the beginning, the accessible, undisputed facts were intriguing but inconclusive.

At the time of his death, Zia's power in Pakistan was under challenge as it had not been for some years. In May 1988, Zia had tossed out of office his civilian prime minister, who had been advertised as a significant figure in the transition to democracy. Zia had also cracked down on Pakistan's minority Shia Muslim sect, and he was seen as responsible for the murder of a local Shia party leader, which angered the neighboring revolutionary Shia Muslim government of Iran. He had allowed Benazir Bhutto, the charismatic opposition leader, to return home, and she and her Pakistan People's Party had loudly and convincingly demanded the restoration of democracy. The war in Afghanistan looked to be winding down with a promised Soviet withdrawal, which in turn promised to reduce America's decade-long expedient tolerance of Zia's authoritarianism and pan-Islamic ideology. Zia apparently sensed a potential danger. That summer he rarely left his heavily guarded home and office in Islamabad. He made an exception on August 17, the scheduled date of a U.S.-sponsored special demonstration trial of a battle tank the Americans wanted to sell the Pakistanis as part of the extensive program of arms sales and transfers from Washington to Islamabad. A demonstration of the tank's features would be held in the dusty plains of south-central Punjab province, near the midsized cities of Multan and Bahawalpur.

That morning, Zia boarded in Rawalpindi a camouflaged C-130 transport plane maintained and flown by a special unit of the transport wing of the Pakistani air force. With him were several senior generals in the Pakistan military and various military officers on Zia's personal staff. The passengers sat comfortably in what was called the VVIP capsule, a tube appointed with carpeting, armchairs, and other amenities that could be inserted as needed into the hull of a C-130, a four-engine transport

manufactured by Lockheed Corporation of California. The plane was a proven workhorse of the U.S. Air Force and other militaries around the world. The pilot of Zia's C-130, which was designated Pak One because the president was aboard, was Wing Commander Mashoud Hassan, a transport flyer of distinction and experience. The copilot was a Shia Muslim officer with a similarly impressive career.

The C-130 flew that morning without incident to a military air base at Bahawalpur. Zia and his traveling party boarded helicopters and flew to the site of the tank trial, where they were greeted by the U.S. ambassador to Pakistan, Arnold Raphel, and Brigadier General Herbert Wassom, the chief U.S. military attaché in Islamabad, as well as by other Americans involved in the tank demonstration. This distinguished audience sat in the dusty sunlight and watched the American tank do its thing, which it reportedly did very badly that day, to the embarrassment of the Americans. Afterward, Raphel and Wassom flew back to Bahawalpur in the helicopters with Zia and his officers. They landed before lunch. Raphel went to a local Catholic convent to express condolences for the recent, unsolved murder of a resident American nun. Zia went briefly into town on political business and then joined Raphel and others for lunch at the canteen of the Bahawalpur army base. After lunch, Zia prayed. Shortly after 3:00 P.M. his party headed for the air base to fly back to Rawalpindi. A few presents, purchased for Zia in the area, including a crate of mangos, were placed aboard the C-130, uninspected. Zia invited the Americans, Raphel and Wassom, to join him for the flight home. The Americans had their own small jet available. But they agreed to join Zia. The plane they boarded had been sitting on the Bahawalpur tarmac throughout the day, guarded by mixed and relatively loose contingents of soldiers, airport security paramilitaries, and local police. Nobody had performed any unusual repairs or maintenance, though the flight crew had spent a brief time fixing a jammed cargo door.

At 3:46 P.M., Pak One rolled down the runway and lifted off in clear weather, circling toward Islamabad as it climbed. After a minute, perhaps two, a controller in the Bahawalpur tower asked the plane for its position. The C-130 was now out of sight. "Pak One, stand by," answered the captain, Mashoud. That was the last the tower heard.

About a minute later, unable to make further contact and now alarmed, controllers in the Bahawalpur tower declared Pak One missing. General Aslam Beg, the vice chief of the army staff and one of the few senior

Pakistani generals who did not fly back with Zia, went looking for the C-130 in a small jet, which was to have taken him separately to Rawalpindi after a meeting Beg said he had scheduled at another city. Witnesses on the ground reported seeing Pak One flying exceptionally low to the ground, pitching up and down as a roller-coaster car would. The witnesses said the plane made one last steep climb, then dove straight into the ground at a sixty-degree angle—accounts consistent with later analysis of the wreckage. Just after the crash, General Beg spotted the burning C-130 wreckage in an open field not far from the Bahawalpur air base, ascertained that there could be no survivors, alerted the control tower, and flew on to the capital to convene an emergency meeting of what remained of Pakistan's government.

By nightfall, the crash site had been cordoned off by the Pakistan army. Zia's death was confirmed and announced at about 8:00 P.M. on the state-controlled television network. Beg succeeded Zia as the top man in the army. Back in Bahawalpur, efforts to recover bodies and collect evidence at the crash site continued under the army's direction through the night. Later there were contradictory claims about how the initial forensic evidence was handled, and how much evidence was found in the heaps of fire and metal at the crash site. What is certain is that at least some identifiable bodies or body parts were recovered, since a single autopsy was later performed on the remains of the American general, Herbert Wassom. Also certain is that no autopsies were performed on the remains of the Pak One flight crew, if any such remains were identified. In Washington, a senior team on the White House's National Security Council decided that the Pentagon should take the lead in the U.S. response to the crash. The Federal Bureau of Investigation, the Justice Department's principal criminal investigative agency, was denied permission to have its agents depart for Pakistan, even though the FBI had jurisdiction under American criminal and antiterrorist laws. Exactly why the FBI was denied permission to investigate immediately remains murky, but some in what was then the last vestiges of the Reagan administration later blamed publicly a lone American military officer on the ground in Pakistan for issuing the decisive refusal.

The first extensive investigation of the crash was conducted by a joint American and Pakistani board of inquiry led by Pakistan air commodore Abbas H. Mirza. Nine members, besides Mirza, were named to the board, six of them American air force officers and three of them Pakistani air

force officers. Over a period of months, the board interviewed many witnesses and conducted what it later termed, in a summary of its classified report, "exhaustive laboratory tests regarding the aircraft structure, instruments, engines, propellers and flight controls." These tests included flight simulator analysis produced by Lockheed, the C-130 manufacturer, and technical analysis carried out by military and nonmilitary laboratories in the United States.

In its report, the board of inquiry offered definitive, confident conclusions about a number of matters. It said the C-130's engines and propellers had definitely been functioning at the time of impact. The plane had not disintegrated or broken up before it crashed. There was no evidence of fire before impact or any external explosive or military ordnance, such as a missile or a rocket. The board ruled out pilot error definitively, although here an American reader of the summary report would notice that its language shifted from the recognizable cadence of American military authorship to the recognizable rhythms of Pakistani English, perhaps suggesting that this was a conclusion held more firmly by the Pakistani board members than by their American colleagues.

After ruling out these other factors, the board "studied in great detail," over a period of months, questions concerning "a control problem" within the aircraft. The board worked at length on two hypotheses. One was that the "control problems in the pitching plane could have been caused by a mechanical or a hydraulic fault in the aircraft systems"—in other words, that the crash was an accident. The other hypothesis was that the control problems were "induced by the pilots either voluntarily or involuntarily"—in other words, a suicide dive or some kind of foul play.

On the accident hypothesis, a number of potential mechanical problems with cables and other structures inside the steering system were ruled out. What did seem to intrigue the investigators were "high levels of contamination by nonorganic matter consisting of aluminum and brass particles" discovered in a key area of the steering system. The contaminants greatly exceeded the acceptable level. Tests ruled out the most likely source of such contamination, a failed pump in the system. Investigators checked all the other C-130s in the Pakistan air force to see whether the problem might be generally poor maintenance of Pakistani transport plane hydraulic systems. They found no similar contamination and no dirty filters. Records of the specific C-130 that was designated Pak One on August 17 showed that it had been inspected thirty days prior

to the crash and that the appropriate filters and fluids had been changed.

The board could not, therefore, "with the available evidence," explain the hydraulic contamination. In any event, the experts believed such contamination could cause "excessive wear" but not a total breakdown of pilot control. Such a breakdown could occur only through a combination of valve failures, perhaps influenced by contaminated hydraulic fluid. But tests ruled out such a total valve breakdown—the valves in question were located and found to be in good condition. Thus the worst thing that could have happened because of the steering contamination was "sluggish controls leading to over control but not to an accident." Unstated, but perhaps implied if you were reading the report very closely, was that a panicky pilot might react badly to this presumed "over control" in the elevator steering and cause further difficulties. Yet there was no overt suggestion that this had happened nor any evidence to support the implication.

Lack of definitive or even probable evidence of an accident led the board to consider sabotage. The obvious means of sabotage were ruled out. Deliberate contamination of the steering system was a "very remote" possibility but largely implausible on technical grounds. Physical interference with controls in the cockpit such as a fight between the pilot and the copilot "cannot be considered seriously" because of the way the cockpit controls work. A conventional "incapacitation of the pilots," such as shooting them or hitting them over the head, "would invariably leave obvious telltale signs," of which there were none.

This led the board to speculate about the possible "use of ultra-sophisticated techniques" that would necessarily involve "a specialist organization well-versed with carrying out such tasks and possessing all the means and abilities for its [sic] execution." Here again the report's language begins to sound Pakistani. Yet it is endorsed by the entire membership. "The board feels that a chemical agent may well have been used" to cause the "insidious incapacitation of the flight deck crew" with such simple gases as odorless, colorless carbon monoxide, or with other, "much more efficient [agents that] may well exist." The gas might have been dispersed inside the C-130 by "low intensity explosives" used to fire "pressurized bottles containing poisonous gases." There were unusual quantities of chemicals in the wreckage, including some that are sometimes associated with explosives, but these chemicals could also be traced to other, benign sources, such as fire-fighting agents. So the gas theory

was possible, but you would have to be at the least sympathetic to paranoid thinking to regard it as something other than a descent into the Pakistani hall of mental mirrors. Proper autopsies on the flight deck crew would have cleared up the question. But "unfortunately," the board lamented, no such autopsies were carried out.

In its conclusion, the board of inquiry reported that it was "unable to substantiate a technical reason" for the crash, which of course is different from saying that it had found no evidence at all of a technical cause. The board went on to conclude that in the absence of a technical explanation, the "only other possible cause of the accident" was a "criminal act or sabotage." And the only one of these acts the board considered plausible was the theory of the exploding—but not too violently exploding—undetectable canisters of poisonous gas. I was told later that in the final discussions, the Americans were inclined to see the evidence as pointing toward an accident, while the Pakistanis saw it as pointing toward sabotage. The Pakistani view won out, but the American view was there in the report as well.

———

When I began to investigate the crash, the board of inquiry's report was about nine months old and not much else discernible was going on. The FBI had finally received permission to investigate the case in Pakistan, but many in Pakistan and a few in Washington saw the FBI's efforts as desultory, part of a broader American cover-up. Whatever one's view of this specific charge, it did seem that, at the least, the American government wanted to do something near the minimum necessary to follow up on the crash. Their geopolitical equations in Pakistan were changing rapidly. Benazir Bhutto had become prime minister in late 1988. Democracy had been restored. The Soviets had pulled out of Afghanistan in February 1989. Mikhail Gorbachev was moving ahead with his revolutionary reforms in Moscow. Nobody wanted to wander around the cold war graveyard, digging up corpses. Nobody in the American government wanted even to talk about Zia or the crash. This attitude just made the Pakistanis, and now me, more suspicious.

Early in 1990, I had dinner with some Pakistani acquaintances in the establishment, as the local elite calls itself. I said I wanted to conduct my own investigation, on behalf of the *Post*. I didn't want to get involved with conspiracy theories, I just wanted to stick to the material evidence,

especially the forensic evidence from the crash site, which the joint board of inquiry had implied was mishandled, and which might provide answers to unresolved questions. Since there were a lot of other stories in South Asia that the *Post* expected me to work on at the same time, I told my Pakistani acquaintances that I needed help to get started. I asked whether, through their connections in the Pakistan army, the intelligence agencies, and the national police service, they could obtain the names and addresses of all the Pakistani relatives of those who had died in the crash; the names and current postings of all the army officers on duty at and around Bahawalpur on August 17; and particularly the names of the doctors and technicians at the Bahawalpur army base hospital, where the remains of the victims had been initially collected. My idea was to review the forensic evidence and how it had been handled to see if anything of interest came out of it. Within a few weeks my fax machine in New Delhi began to spew out an extraordinary—and extraordinarily long—list of the names and addresses I had requested.

I flew to Karachi to see Kamran Khan, the *Post's* stringer in Pakistan and easily the country's most accomplished investigative reporter, an occupation that can be exceedingly dangerous for a South Asian, as Kamran would later discover. Kamran is a relentlessly cheerful man who earnestly embraces the revolutionary eighteenth-century ideas about freedom of the press that twentieth-century Americans mainly take for granted, if they don't hold them in contempt. He agreed to start poking around with his Pakistan military and law enforcement sources. I decided to start visiting the relatives of crash victims.

In Karachi, Lahore, and Islamabad, in between the usual scrambling to write news stories, I rumbled around in the backseat of a chauffeured Toyota with my lists of names and addresses, looking more ridiculous than usual in a pin-striped suit, carted out of mothballs, from a previous posting on Wall Street. I figured the suit would lend an air of authority to unscheduled visits with grieving relatives of generals and army officers, but probably it just made me look like some fish from abroad who didn't know how hot it was in Pakistan. I saw perhaps two dozen relatives of victims. Aside from the pathos of grief, the interviews produced a few interesting bits.

One was that on the night of the crash, amid all the chaos sparked by the sudden and mysterious death of a dictator who had ruled the country for eleven years, the Pakistan army had made a clear and firm decision to

get the remains of all the thirty-one dead aboard the C-130 away from the crash site, packed into coffins, and buried as quickly as possible. Relatives around the country, huddled in shock, received quick calls from the army high command asking where they wanted their relatives to be buried. At dawn on the second day, August 18, helicopters and transport planes began flying out of Bahawalpur, carrying coffins to cities and villages scattered around the country. In each case, the army dispatched soldiers and officers to surround the coffins until they were put into the ground. Later, some Pakistan government spokesmen suggested publicly that the hurried burials had been ordered in response to Islamic law that the dead should be buried within twenty-four hours. This seemed a specious rationale. The relatives I interviewed said that while, tradition-ally, Pakistanis buried their dead before the corpses began to rot, there certainly was no twenty-four-hour time limit if autopsies were required. Also, a family typically would wait until relatives and friends traveling from outlying areas could reach the funeral site. In fact, the army itself made such an exception in the case of Zia. It held the president's coffin in Rawalpindi for a couple of days until dignitaries from abroad, including U.S. secretary of state George Shultz, reached Pakistan for the funeral.

It wasn't clear to the relatives whether the army had bothered at all to identify particular remains and pack them separately before dispatching the thirty-one coffins around the country on August 18. The coffins were all nailed shut and none of the relatives were permitted by the escorting soldiers to open them; few of the relatives I spoke to had been inclined to try, having been told that the crash victims had been burned to ashes or horribly disfigured. Some speculated that the coffins had only rocks inside them. Others thought there might have been some remains. The father of Mashoud Hassan, the pilot of Pak One, said he was told nothing officially about the condition of his son's corpse. "The coffin we received was sealed," he told me. "When they took off the flag his name was given, and it [a notice on the coffin] said, 'Not to Be Opened.' I felt there were some remains inside, and I was sitting near the box and I could smell a very weak smell. It was very hot. That gave me the impression that some part of his body was there. An air force officer later told me that he came to know that at least half the upper half of his body was there, was tied with belts and that it was found. In what condition, I don't know."

The suggestion by some Pakistan government spokesmen that the cockpit crew's bodies could not be autopsied was further contradicted

about six months after the crash when Mashoud Hassan's father received an anonymous mailing of four of his son's identity cards. The father said Mashoud usually kept the cards in a zippered pocket in the pants leg of his flight suit. The paper cards had no burn marks on them. One was Mashoud's national identity card, another his military pass to enter VIP enclosures, both of which he presumably would have carried on August 17. Other relatives said they received similar materials—cloth armbands with only slight burn marks, paper identity cards with no damage or slight burn marks, pouches, even a few official papers. Sometimes the materials were turned over officially by the army upon request of the relatives. Other times they arrived unexpectedly in the mail, with no return address on the envelope.

I talked to a few other Pakistani officials who had been present at Bahawalpur on the afternoon of the crash. With one I spent long hours because he was articulate, well placed, had spent years in the West, and spoke about what he saw strictly in terms of material evidence and not in reference to conspiracy theories. I asked him to tell me exactly what he saw. He told me that he reached the crash site within thirty minutes. Some civilian Pakistani officials were present "and a few army officers [who] had moved by helicopter" from Bahawalpur. "There was just ashes, no flames, a little smoke. . . . Some parts of the bodies were recovered. It was just a big lump—a bone, an arm or leg, a bone, a shin. . . . There were just a few things intact. A diary book, some shells, some shells from the tank trials that had been presented as gifts. . . . One assumed the military doctors had done autopsies. One couldn't dream of them not doing it." My informant conducted interviews with witnesses during the next week or two. He remembered particularly talking on the night of the crash to a police constable posted on the bridge above the field where the C-130 crashed. "He told me they [the army] took some things away. They took some things away on the helicopters before anyone got there. There were two helicopters. He [the constable] mentioned boxes. A box or something." There was no reason to believe this meant anything in particular. But by now the story was beginning to pull me in.

A few weeks later, Kamran and I arranged to meet in Lahore and make the long drive to Bahawalpur through the gullied drylands of southern Punjab. We had been refused any appointments at the Bahawalpur army base, but I figured we might be able to bluff our way on. Meantime, we checked into Bahawalpur's finest hotel, a one-star with concrete floors,

green walls, naked light bulbs, and padlocked room doors. We went out to see a few local police officers, which didn't yield much. Late in the afternoon, we stopped by the Catholic convent where the U.S. ambassador, Arnold Raphel, had offered condolences on the day he died. An American nun from New York told us about the murder of Sister Margaret Theresa: She was killed just before the C-130 crash, in an atmosphere of hot Islamic anger in Bahawalpur sparked by the Salman Rushdie affair. She had been walking back to the convent after dinner at a local Chinese restaurant when a man came out of the shadows, said a few angry words, grabbed her shoulder bag, and shot her in the head, according to a Pakistani woman who saw it. Sinister, but so far as anybody knew, irrelevant to our inquiry.

After nightfall we drove to the army base. Soldiers flagged us down at the gate. I rolled down the window in back, flashed various cards in my wallet, mainly credit cards, and spoke in rapid-fire English, as if I knew what I was doing. Kamran sat quietly, trying to look important and impatient. A soldier hesitated and then let us through.

We wound through the grounds, searching for the hospital. As always, I was impressed by the superior amenities the Pakistan army allocates to itself—the trimmed, spacious lawns, the large bungalows, the cinemas and athletic fields. Just goes to show there's a lot you can do in South Asia if you have the money. Stopping periodically to ask directions of soldiers and officers in the streets, we found the hospital. My list of names included the colonel who had been in charge of the hospital on the night of the crash as well as several majors and captains—doctors—who worked below him. I went into the hospital lobby on my own and asked an officer at a reception desk for the colonel. He told me the colonel had been transferred out a year earlier. I pulled out my sheet of paper and tried to pretend that this news was a grave, grave disappointment. I asked about the next man on my list, Major Munir Ahmed. Yes, he was still on the Bahawalpur base, the receptionist was delighted to report.

Was he in the hospital?

No, in his bungalow.

Fine. Where's the bungalow?

He provided the address. He never asked what I was doing on a restricted Pakistani army base flush on the Indian frontier. In fact, he sent along an army private to make sure that I could find the major's address without difficulty.

I rang the major's doorbell. He came out onto the darkened stoop, accepted my business card, didn't look at it, and began to fidget. I said I needed to ask him a few questions about the night of the plane crash. He didn't invite me in, but he didn't shut the door, either. He said he was an anesthesiologist. He was off duty on the afternoon of August 17 but had been called to the hospital after the crash "in case there was a need to resuscitate bodies. Quickly it became apparent that there would be no survivors. We came and went for dinner and so forth. The question of autopsies would be handled by the pathologist." That night, he said, the regular pathologist was on leave, so a major was summoned from nearby Multan. The major drove through the night and arrived around midnight. The hospital was equipped "only to do a gross examination, no microscopic work or chemical analysis." Microscopic work would be conducted at the army's main headquarters in Rawalpindi; chemical analysis generally was carried out at a laboratory in Lahore. Some skin samples were prepared for microscopic examination. Some samples were extracted for gross examination. But at the same time, orders were dispatched from the base commander to the hospital commandant to prepare coffins immediately. A special coffin-building unit arrived at the hospital in the night, commanded by a colonel, and began construction. The major said he went home in the early hours of the morning, and when he returned early the next day, what little preparatory work for autopsies had occurred was now finished, "and the bodies were being prepared for shipment in coffins." He said he never learned why these decisions were made, whether the initial specimens were preserved at all, and if so, what became of them. "Everything was top secret," he said.

That night we got back to the hotel and I flipped on the BBC. A military coup attempt was underway in Kabul, the Afghan capital. News flash! Awwoooooogah! Awwoooooogah! We had to check out and drive through the night to Multan so I could file a story by telex. The next morning, I had to fly off for the Afghan border. Kamran agreed to keep working his Pakistani sources and to start looking for some of the other army doctors who had been on duty at the Bahawalpur hospital that night.

But as the weeks drifted by, we kept hitting dead ends. We couldn't find the doctors. The Pakistan army wasn't saying anything. The Americans were saying less. Saddam Hussein invaded Kuwait and suddenly I was in the Persian Gulf. I called Kamran every now and then to see what

else we could do. We worked a few other stories together in the meantime. And then Kamran got a break.

A well-placed source of his in the Pakistan government told him that on October 19, 1988, two months after the C-130 crash, a man holding an American passport had been arrested in Quetta, the mud-rock provincial capital of tribal Baluchistan province. The American was a black man and he had visas in his passport indicating recent visits to Iran. Kamran's source said the American had been detained at the airport for possession of a small amount of hashish. Later, the police discovered in his luggage and at his hotel what they described—in writing, at the time—as the manual of a C-130 aircraft, a hand-drawn sketch of a military airfield, a map of the airports at Islamabad and Istanbul, Turkey, photographs of the Ayatollah Khomeini, and the names and telephone numbers of pro-Iranian Shia activists in Pakistan. In addition, the American possessed unidentified radio equipment, possibly transmitters. The police were so alarmed by these materials that the chief martial-law bureaucrat in Baluchistan—this was prior to the restoration of democracy—flew to army headquarters in Rawalpindi and demanded a meeting with the chief of the Pakistan intelligence service, ISI. The intelligence chief at the time was a general named Hamid Gul, an Islamic hard-liner who between 1987 and 1989 was the principal liaison between the CIA and the Afghan mujaheddin rebels in the United States–funded secret Afghan war. Gul, informed of the case, dispatched a plane to Quetta to pick up the arrested American. Five days after his arrest, the American was turned over to the army and flown to Rawalpindi. The officials in Quetta never heard what happened to the American. They were ticked off now and willing to talk to Kamran because they had thought they were going to get medals and reward money for detecting and arresting Zia's assassin, but instead the army now refused to answer their queries about the case.

Kamran flew to Quetta to check out the story. Three sources in the civilian government told the same tale independently of one another. One produced a contemporaneous memo recording the materials found in the American's possession.

As soon as the Gulf War was over I flew to Karachi to meet again with Kamran. We went over the details. It wasn't clear what we had, but it sure was interesting. There were radical black American Muslims scattered all around the Islamic world, fighting in holy wars such as the one in Afghanistan. Some were U.S. Army veterans. It seemed plausible enough

that one might be recruited by Iran or otherwise volunteer to carry out an assassination. Tehran and its allied Shias in Pakistan had plenty of reason to be angry at Zia at the time of the crash. They also had a proven track record of assassinations, although none involving anything nearly as sophisticated as pressurized mildly exploding poisonous gas bombs, if such things even existed. Anyway, even if this particular American had nothing to do with the crash, his case sounded intriguing.

We didn't know if the American was alive or dead. Kamran had taken the Quetta sources about as far as he could. We agreed that the American government must have known about this case and decided, for whatever reasons, to keep it quiet. I had working relationships with the senior American officials in Pakistan. After thinking about it and talking at length with Kamran, I decided the best way to pull the trigger on this was to go see the Americans and ask for answers, trying not to let on how little I knew. If there was something to it, the Americans might react defensively and give us some sense of direction.

I flew to Islamabad, checked into the Holiday Inn, and called for an appointment with senior diplomats at the American embassy. I had had some problems with a particular diplomat, exceptionally knowledgeable, who had lied to me on a story in the past. After that incident, we made up and agreed there would be no more lies. Particularly, we agreed that if there was something that he didn't want to talk about, he would just decline to discuss it, rather than spin some disinformation tale. This time I invoked that agreement in advance. I said I had something highly sensitive related to the Zia crash. I didn't want to be lied to about it, so if the diplomat found he couldn't discuss it for whatever reason, I wanted him to just say so, and not make something up. I was told by the chief embassy public relations officer that this proposal had been transmitted and agreed upon. A naïve deal, you might say, but it was the best I could come up with.

While I was waiting for the appointment, Kamran called. He had talked again to Quetta and clarified the name of the American. He was Mark Alphonzo Artis, of 733 Watson Street, Aurora, Illinois. (Originally, we had merely been given the name Alphonzo, no address.) I called the *Post*'s Chicago bureau. A researcher checked out the address. It was in a middle-class, mostly black neighborhood. When the researcher went there, the man who came to the door laughed and said he knew of no such person, but the researcher had doubts about the encounter, so she went back. This

time a woman told her that she was the mother of Mark Alphonzo Artis's wife. From the Islamabad Holiday Inn I made calls all over Illinois and found a few people who knew Artis well. They described him variously as "mentally sick" and suffering from "manic depression." He lied a lot and traveled in strange circles. He went abroad frequently and called home from places such as Turkey, Iran, and Sudan. After his arrest in Quetta in October 1988 he had disappeared for nearly six months.

During this time, relatives who were worried about him had contacted the U.S. State Department. Months passed. Finally, in March or April 1989, the State Department reported that they had found Artis. He had been held in a Pakistani prison for six months without notification to the U.S. government, Artis's relatives were told. The Pakistanis were now letting him go and he was being put on a plane back to the United States, the State Department said. Artis himself did not say much to his friends in the United States about what happened to him in Pakistan, these people said.

"We have no idea about what went on over there," said one person who knew Artis well. "When he came back he was in the worst condition, physically and mentally. They said it was drug charges. Later, I heard about the rest of it, the plane crash. . . . Only Mark and whoever he was involved with can tell you what happened. And nobody knows if he's telling the truth."

The next morning I went to the embassy. Surely the Americans knew about this, one of their own citizens held incommunicado by the Pakistani intelligence service on suspicion of blowing up Zia's plane, with the U.S. ambassador aboard.

"I was not aware of it," said the senior diplomat. He had brought along a man he described as a "security officer" to take notes about our conversation. My inquiry was "the first time we had heard about being involved," the diplomat said. "They're supposed to notify you if they arrest one of your citizens. Sometimes they do, sometimes they don't. . . . We wouldn't have any reason to believe they would withhold information from us on something like this." He seemed to be shocked, shocked to hear about it.

I asked about the crash investigation. He said the American government side was "very strongly inclined" to think it was all an accident caused by hydraulic problems on the C-130. I asked about General Gul, the Pakistani spy chief who had held Artis in jail on suspicion of killing

Zia, apparently without telling the U.S. embassy that he held the prisoner, all the while meeting with the CIA daily to run the secret Afghan war. The diplomat said Gul "was pretty cooperative, as a matter of fact, fairly frank about things."

The diplomat and the security officer made a big show of concern about this new information I was bringing to their attention. The diplomat stood up, went to his desk, and said, in effect, Doggone it, I'm going to call over to General Gul right away and ask what this is all about. I asked for a check of the embassy files on Artis. They agreed to look immediately.

I went back to the hotel and waited. The public relations officer called and said they had checked the files and had come up with a "total blank." There was no record of the name, nothing. I said this couldn't be possible. I was absolutely certain that relatives of Artis had put through a request to the State Department and that the embassy had eventually gotten Artis out of jail and sent him home on a plane. There had to be something. Check again. He did. I called back and he said he had found a single file card. The card made reference to "illegal activities" and "mental instability." There were no other details, no indications of contact between Artis and the embassy.

I called my boss in Washington, who was by now getting nearly as sucked into this whole thing as I was. I said there were two possibilities. One was that the embassy did not know about Artis's arrest and detention by ISI, and that therefore I had just told them about the case for the first time. The second possibility was that the American embassy had just staged an elaborate drama to deceive me. I was not yet prepared to succumb to all the conspiratorial implications that would arise if I accepted the second hypothesis. So if the information about Artis was brand-new to them, that meant the government might now go looking for Artis to sort the case out. I wanted to find Artis before the government did. My boss agreed. Within eight hours I was in the air, flying Islamabad–Lahore–Delhi–Frankfurt–Chicago, to hit the streets and find our man.

Dazed and jet-lagged, I checked into a Marriott Hotel beside a freeway south of O'Hare airport the next afternoon, took a nap, and then drove to Aurora to drop in on some of the people I had been talking to on the phone from Islamabad. I got more details on Artis's erratic travels and apparently schizoid personality. Evidently Artis professed to be a Mus-

lim, an enthusiast of the Iranian revolution. But nobody had a lead on where he might be now. On the telephone, I reached one person who had previously been especially helpful. This person mentioned a new name, that of a white woman, Josephine Viecelli, who allegedly did a lot of deals with Artis and funded his travels abroad. Viecelli was Italian, my informant thought. Had a son. I asked where she lived.

"I don't want to tell you any more. Let's see how good a reporter you are."

Great. I asked whether I was at least in the right part of the country to look for her. I was.

Got a spelling of Viecelli?

Not really. My source tried out of a few phonetic possibilities. I tried for more, but this was as much as I was going to get.

The next morning, a Saturday, I drove in to the Loop and parked myself beside a pile of Chicago-area phone books in the *Post*'s downtown bureau. I listed every possible spelling of Viecelli I could think of and then went through the phone books, copying down all the numbers I could find. There were about 150 Viecellis of various spellings. No Josephine, but a couple of initial Js. I started calling. I had the usual weird and semihostile conversations you have with strangers when you bother them at home looking for somebody they don't know. By sunset I had scratched off about 135 of the listings and was looking at a dead end. Only one of the initial Js was not a confirmed washout. That phone number had been disconnected. The street address was listed in Des Plaines, Illinois, near the airport. I got out my Chicago-area street atlas, traced a route to the address, and drove out. I was starting to feel a little ragged.

The place was a lower-middle-class garden-apartment complex with trash blowing through the parking lots and at least fifty units in identical two-story buildings. I had no apartment number, so I started knocking on doors, asking if anybody knew a Josephine Viecelli. The residents appeared to be mainly elderly immigrants from Eastern Europe. I spotted the building manager in one of the parking lots, a huge man in a T-shirt with his belly hanging over his belt of keys. I approached and asked if he had a tenant named Josephine Viecelli. He asked who I was. I told him.

"Vuck you! Vuck you!"

The screaming drew about half the residents to their screen doors.

Some came outside and pretended to sweep their walkways to get a better look at what was happening. I was pissed off at this guy for yelling at me just because I was a reporter, so I yelled back a little, but then I shrugged and walked away. I approached the sweepers, elderly women. They were sympathetic. The building manager yelled at everybody, they said. One of them mentioned that they had been afraid to tell me when I knocked, but, yes, there was a Josephine who had lived in the building.

Josephine Viecelli? Not so sure. But Josephine, definitely.

"What happened to her?"

"Government came and took her away. Immigration police. Happened about a month ago."

"Where did they take her?"

"Back to Albania, I think. She was an Albanian."

"Did she have any children? What did she look like?"

"She was young, attractive, dark. She had one son. His name was Castro." A pause. "You see, she was probably a Communist."

Christ. Now what? I drove off into the darkness, trying to connect up all the pieces. All I can tell you is, that night, back at the Marriott by the freeway, too jet-lagged to sleep, I sat on the edge of my bed, smoking, and figured it all out. The Soviets wanted Zia dead. So they sent an Albanian case officer to Chicago to recruit a black American Muslim manic-depressive. Then they sent him to Iran, loaded him up with sabotage equipment, and sent him to Pakistan to kill Zia. The American government had covered the whole thing up because they were afraid that nobody would believe they didn't do it themselves, since Artis was an American. Sure, sure, it was all plausible.

Coffee and Sunday morning sunlight rescued me briefly. Before driving back to Des Plaines to check with the police about the Albanian, I called back my source on the original Viecelli tip. I bluffed and said that while I had had a very successful day and had found Viecelli's apartment in Des Plaines, I had discovered that she had moved, and I just wanted to double-check a couple of details.

The person asked what street I'd been looking on. I read out the name. No, no, came the reply, Viecelli lived in Des Plaines, the town I had been in, but on a different street, which the source named casually, before remembering that this was something I wasn't supposed to be helped on. I wrote the new street name down. I said that the Josephine I'd found the

day before had a young son named Castro. Ring a bell? No, the real Josephine had an older son, Paul. Josephine was not young, dark, or attractive. She was in her fifties at least.

All right, forget Castro. Find Viecelli.

I retrieved my atlas and drove back to Des Plaines, to the new street. It was about a mile long in a quiet residential neighborhood of middle-class brick homes on quarter-acre lots. There were lots of yellow ribbons on the trees and doorways to welcome home the troops from the Persian Gulf. I had no address for the Viecellis, so I drove down to one end of the street, parked, and started walking up, knocking on doors. Sunday morning is a good time for that. People are too groggy to be angry.

Two blocks along I got a "yes." It was from a mild couple in late middle age, he a retired employee of the phone company, she a housewife, baking muffins in the kitchen. The Viecellis, Josephine and Paul, had lived next door for several years, they said. The Viecellis were weird. People in the neighborhood called them the Addams family. They had a shooting range in their basement, a rope with pulleys for targets, shells all over the place. They were famous in the area because they had ripped off nearly all their neighbors, for tens of thousands of dollars. Josephine was always looking for investments in various schemes that she had going. Some of them involved Artis. Artis was supposed to go to Iran to sell blue jeans and video recorders to the people over there—you know, in Iran, they don't have blue jeans and video recorders, the couple told me.

Josephine Viecelli said that if the neighbors put up ten thousand dollars each to finance the trip, they would get double their money when Artis returned. Everybody had decided to go in on it—double your money sounded pretty good in Des Plaines, Illinois, the couple said. But then in the fall of 1988 Artis disappeared mysteriously. No money, no blue jeans. Josephine Viecelli said she was expecting riches "any day, any day, any day," the neighbor said. "It just got to the point where it became a real joke. The stories would always change so much." Eventually, the Viecellis went broke. They sold their house and moved away. Many of the neighbors were angry. They never got their money back. Then, after the Viecellis were gone, investigators started showing up.

"One man told me he was from the CIA, an investigator who came by," said the wife. "We were going through our own craziness. There was a woman who was here. She did have a badge. Then there was a man.

I'm sure it was CIA. The IRS was here, too. State police, private investigators. The only thing I heard from Josephine [about Artis] was that he had gone to Utah, the Cayman Islands, Denver, someplace. The only thing she told me was that what he was doing was investments. Well, we're writing it off on our taxes."

They were very nice. They gave me the Viecellis' new address, said it was not far off. And they gave me a muffin.

I talked to a few more neighbors. It just kept getting more and more weird. The Viecellis were con artists, it seemed. They raised money from their neighbors and gave some of it to Artis, who then traveled overseas on unspecified business in Iran and other Islamic countries.

I asked one neighbor to describe Artis and the Viecelli household. He answered with a string of impressionistic non sequiturs: "There were moving vans, insurance policies, a lot of old cars that would pull up and people, migrants would come out. There was some kind of deal going." I was wandering now through a Don DeLillo novel.

The Viecellis lived in a basement apartment underneath the freeway—two rooms, crammed with boxes. She was an enormous woman with white hair who never got out of her chair. Her son, Paul, was big, too, with long stringy hair and tattoos on his arms. I told them I had come to talk about Mark Alphonzo Artis. They invited me in.

I sat on a box and asked what had happened to Artis when he was arrested in Pakistan on suspicion of killing Zia. "He said he had business and he asked me if I could basically help him with the funding," Josephine said. "Nothing came out of it. I lost every cent I had. I don't know anything about any arrest by the Pakistanis for any plane crash. Afterward, he just said he couldn't get to a phone." They told me Artis was currently on the run. He had just pulled a scam in California, swindled a woman in Seattle out of fifty-three thousand dollars, and disappeared.

Paul took me outside. We stood next to his motorcycle. Paul said that when Artis came back from Pakistan, after he was released by Pakistan's intelligence service, he acted very strange. "He said stuff about these beads," Paul said. "He said stuff about the jeeee-had [jihad, or Islamic holy war]. He was always talking about the jeeee-had and stuff. He said nobody would fuck with him because he had these beads on him. They called him Syed Ismail. . . . When he got back from Pakistan, he was in the nuthouse for a while. He was really into this thing, this religious thing.

He used to scare the shit out of me, the way he talked. . . . He said he was going on Oprah Winfrey and blow the whole thing up [the mystery of Zia's death], to tell everybody what it was all about."

That night I flew to Washington. I felt my intuitive connection to Middle America unraveling, and my intuitive connection to Pakistan deepening. Who *were* these people, with their yellow ribbons and Iranian blue jean schemes?

On the way out of Chicago, I called a local FBI agent. He said the Viecellis and Artis were targets of a federal fraud investigation, but he didn't know if or when arrests would be made.

At the *Post* I sat down with Jim McGee, one of the paper's best investigative reporters. I told him what I had. He arched his eyebrows. McGee is so unflappable that if you introduced him to a nine-armed space alien with antennae sticking from its eyes, his first question would be, "So, what's this we hear about your *supposedly* being a space alien?" I welcomed his sobriety.

McGee set up a meeting with a senior Bush administration official. The official told us that the CIA didn't know anything about Artis's being held by the Pakistanis on suspicion of killing Zia. The official said the CIA would be upset to hear about this because even if Artis was a flake, the agency should have known about him. The official ran computer checks on Artis. Nothing, he said.

Then McGee set up an appointment with Oliver Revelle, then the chief of counterterrorism at the FBI. We walked over together to FBI headquarters. We noticed on the sign-in sheet in the lobby that a couple of men from the CIA had signed in just ahead of us. In Revelle's outer office there were two guys in suits standing around against the walls, trying to look as if they belonged but not doing a very good job of it.

We sat down with Revelle and I told him what I knew about Artis. "If someone like this had been developed as a suspect, I would have known about it," he said. "To my knowledge, we know nothing of this case."

At his request, I read out Artis's full name and passport number. He wrote it down on a slip of paper and buzzed for a secretary. She picked up the paper and left the room. We talked about the crash investigation in general terms. On the question of the bodies, he said, the forensic and pathological investigations "were all done by the Pakistanis." The FBI had found "no indication of a criminal cause." Going back over the forensic

evidence in detail now would be "really impossible. Some forensic evidence is perishable. Some can be disturbed. Our responsibilities, while significant, are secondary to the Pakistani responsibilities." So the FBI's forensic investigation, now that it was on the case, "would not be the same as one that would be conducted here."

Revelle's secretary came back with a note. He read it and hit a button on his phone. He talked briefly, out of earshot. No more than five minutes later an FBI agent named Al Finch walked into the room with a thick file in his hand. He sat down. Revelle explained that Finch had traveled to Pakistan twice to work on the FBI's investigation.

And *he* knew about Artis.

"He is known to us," Finch said. "He is a mentally unstable individual." Finch confirmed the details of Artis's arrest and his detention by Pakistani intelligence. Finch said Artis had probably been tortured while in Pakistani custody. He said he had heard about the case in the same way Kamran did, from a source in the Pakistan government.

Finch's investigation of the matter, he continued, consisted of a single act: He went to see Hamid Gul, the Pakistan intelligence chief who had held Artis incommunicado and interrogated him for six months. At this meeting, Gul told Finch that there was nothing to be concerned about. For one thing, the materials in Artis's possession at the time of his arrest were not so incriminating. The C-130 manual was not actually a manual but "a book on airplanes," Finch said, quoting Gul. The supposed airport maps were "tourist maps of Iran and Afghanistan." The electronic gear was a transistor radio. Finch never saw the materials. Nor was he troubled that Artis's arresting officers in Quetta had described them otherwise at the time of the arrest.

The FBI "accepted the findings of ISI," Finch said. Artis was not a suspect because "his mental capacity was definitely in question"—as if mental imbalance disqualified somebody from being an assassin. "There were all types of conspiracy theories going about in 1990," Finch said. "The Pakistanis suspected a lot of things. There were theories concerning Shias from Iran. Hamid Gul, being the ISI director at that time, was dead serious about all the conspiracy theories. They were exploring everything. If there had been any indication that this guy Artis had been involved in the crash, he would have been tried."

All right, that sounded reasonable. But, I wondered, if Finch had

investigated the Artis case in Pakistan, what about this senior American diplomat in Islamabad, the one who told me so elaborately that he had never heard of it before?

"Sure, [he] knew about it. He knew about it after it happened," Finch answered.

I thought to myself: So why had he lied to me about it just a week before?

The problem with all of this, Finch went on, is that the Pakistanis "do not need a reason. They just need an idea. Someone's imagination. They will go on and on ad nauseam. Until we could be shown a real motive, it would not be in our interest to go into these." He sounded pretty disgusted.

I asked about the possibility that Artis worked for the Iranians, that the Iranian government had wanted Zia dead. The Iranians had a track record of assassination, didn't they?

In fact, Kamran had by now been told by a member of the joint Pakistani intelligence board that had interrogated and apparently tortured Artis for six months that the reason Pakistan finally let him go was that they were convinced he was a CIA plant sent to make them think Tehran killed Zia. The evidence on Artis, this Pakistani intelligence official told Kamran, was too convincing to be real. Mirrors on top of mirrors.

Finch said Gul had indeed believed Artis was a CIA plant sent to make the Pakistanis believe, falsely, that the Iranians killed Zia. "Apparently Artis did have the names of several Iranians" at the time of the arrest, Finch said. But Finch didn't take any of this seriously because of "the reputation and ability of Hamid Gul. He does not play around. He does not fool around. This particular concoction was not part of our investigation."

Walking back to the office, I talked with McGee about two possibilities. One was that Finch and Revelle had told the truth, that they had responded spontaneously to my detailed questions. The other possibility was that the FBI, like the American embassy in Islamabad, had just staged an elaborate drama for our benefit. I was relieved to find that McGee also noticed how quickly and conveniently Finch came into the office with a thick file full of materials on Artis, after Revelle said he had never heard of the case. But this meant nothing, really. And I was exhausted, dizzy.

I felt certain about a few things. One was that it was foolish for the FBI to take Hamid Gul, the former Pakistani spy chief, at his word. Perhaps

Finch had read the U.S. Defense Intelligence Agency's biographical sketch of Gul. In January 1989, while Artis was being held incommunicado by Gul's ISI on suspicion of being involved in an American plot, DIA produced a classified sketch of the Pakistani intelligence chief that described him as "a strong supporter of Pakistan's ties to the U.S., generally friendly towards the U.S. and the West and very comfortable around foreigners. . . . His religious practice does not appear to affect his political views. . . . Gul is a cheerful, ambitious officer, who has a very professional outlook . . . a sincere and caring individual." The trouble with this bit of "intelligence" was that even apart from the issue of mutual U.S.-Pakistani suspicion, nearly everybody in Pakistan saw Gul as a master manipulator, a professional liar. American diplomats I talked to about him used words like "devious" and "untrustworthy." I asked one who had been in Pakistan during the Zia crash and the period of Gul's reign as spy chief to assess the general. "In retrospect we cannot say that relationship was a good one," the diplomat said. "We put an awful lot onto that effort and he certainly profited from it. He was profiting from the relationship both personally and in terms of his ideological bent. I think we misunderstood the depth of his anti-Americanism." That the FBI had settled the Artis matter on Gul's word seemed preposterous. But Finch said that's just what he had done.

Another thing I felt certain about was that I had been lied to. I just didn't know by whom or about what.

The only way to move forward was to find Artis, a man who reportedly lied about most things to everyone he met. But Artis was on the run and I couldn't trace him.

I wrote a story about the Artis case for the *Post*. The editors couldn't quite figure what it was about. It was hard to blame them. They put the story in the paper anyway, mainly to humor me. Afterward I had a meal with my boss, the spy novelist David Ignatius. He listened to my narrative and urged me to see *The Grifters*, the movie about con artists based on a Jim Thompson novel.

In the parking lot, Ignatius joked, "We killed Zia, didn't we?" He meant the American government.

"We killed Zia," I said, also joking. More or less.

Some people explain the inexplicable with conspiracy theories. This is certainly the tendency in South Asia. I regard this point of view with some sympathy—for one thing, it lies close to religion, to the postulated

existence of God and the Devil, which is the grandest and most attractive conspiracy theory of all. The opposing assumption is that political events are shaped more often by pedestrian human incompetence than by cunning. This is my view and I cling to it, provisionally. There is plenty of historical evidence on each side. In the case of the Zia crash, I could have spent the next few years wandering around in the hall of mirrors, searching for the Devil. It was tempting. The other choice was to go back to South Asia, back to work. I decided to go back to work.

I laid a few trawling lines, telling friends and relatives of Artis that I still wanted to talk with him. That summer, when I was on vacation in Connecticut, Artis telephoned *The Washington Post* and asked to speak with me. Ignatius took the call. Artis had a whispery voice, wouldn't say where he was calling from. He wanted to meet me in August. In Nigeria. Ignatius said he wasn't sure I would be in Nigeria in August, but he urged Artis to call me directly and work something out. He set up an appointment for Artis to telephone me in the New York bureau the next morning.

I got up before dawn to drive to Manhattan and wait for his call. It never came. It's been a year now. Artis has never called back. I haven't been able to find him. So what if I did?

"Pak One, stand by," said Mashoud. And then he was gone.

7

Rulers

A river without water, a forest without grass, a herd of cattle without a herdsman, is the land without a king.

—*The Ramayana*

One night back in New Delhi about a month after Artis made his phantom telephonic appearance, I wandered downstairs late to check the news wire that ran incessantly in my office, producing a rhythmic screech. I was about to flip the machine off when a small Associated Press item out of Karachi passed across it. Kamran Khan, my friend and partner in the Pakistani wonderland, had been attacked and stabbed outside his newspaper office.

By the time I touched down at Karachi's smoky, sprawling airport the next night, it was clear that Kamran would survive his wounds, but it was not so clear whether or not a fresh attack would be mounted against him. On scratchy phone lines to India, Kamran's friends and colleagues had described what passed for the facts of the case. Since the tentative termination of our plane crash enterprise, Kamran had published a running series of brave if arguably foolhardy investigative reports on political and police corruption in Karachi and surrounding Sind province, a region writer Ian Buruma once described aptly as "a kind of sandy Sicily." The province is controlled by sometimes interlocking, sometimes competing mafias—political, ethnic, and purely criminal. Heroin trafficking, ransom kidnapping, and abuse of political patronage are the mafias' main endeavors. They wage their competitions through young toughs armed with

some of the tens of thousands of AK-47 assault rifles pumped into Pakistan by the CIA in its effort to aid the Afghan mujaheddin. Kamran had written about the Karachi mafias in local newspapers for years and had endured many threats. But what seemed to have finally provoked an attack was a series on Pakistan's CIA—not the Central Intelligence Agency but the Criminal Investigative Agency, a police unit in charge of looking into serious crimes. He wrote that the CIA had itself become a criminal enterprise manipulated by the corrupt administration of Sind province's chief minister, Jam Sadiq Ali. Immediately Kamran received death threats at home. Goons showed up at his doorstep in the night, shouting abuse and daring him to come outside. Friends called to warn privately that Jam Sadiq Ali was furious and ready to strike back. Kamran wrote desperately to the prime minister of Pakistan, Nawaz Sharif, putting on record his demand for political protection. It didn't work. Two days later, as he stepped from his Suzuki car outside his newspaper office, he was attacked. Two young goons who had followed him on a motorcycle got down and asked his name. After confirming that he was Kamran, they asked why he had written nonsense in the papers. One thrust a knife at Kamran's chest and throat. Kamran lifted his arm and blocked the blows, which severed his forearm to the bone. He then dashed inside his office, bleeding badly. Colleagues took him to the hospital.

There was little doubt but also little direct evidence that Jam, as the Sind chief minister was universally known, had ordered the hit on Kamran. Jam—who died of cancer in early 1992 after denying brazenly for months that there was anything wrong with him—was the sort of charming, effective thug who provoked chuckles of admiration in the parlors of the cynical Pakistani elite. He had been a longtime ally of Benazir Bhutto's father, Zulfikar Ali Bhutto, and had gone into exile in London when Zia hanged Bhutto and imposed martial law. People who saw Jam during the London years described him as a little lonely, a fish out of water in the hip, cosmopolitan exile scene surrounding Benazir. Obviously Jam felt snubbed by her. Returning to Pakistan, he waited for his opportunity and then turned on her, agreeing to serve Benazir's enemies by becoming Sind chief minister when the establishment tossed Benazir out of office in August 1990. Jam seized his chance by cracking down ruthlessly on Benazir's political machine in Sind. Beginning in late 1990, he arrested thousands of Benazir's allies and tossed them into jail without charges. He handed out twenty thousand AK-47 licenses to the best-organized politi-

cal and ethnic opponents of Benazir in Sind, the Mohajir Quami Movement, or MQM, an ethnic mafia that had been formed originally to
represent the legitimate political interests of refugees but had become, by
1990, a well-oiled criminal machine. After arming the MQM, Jam took
control of sections of the police force, using it to assert his will over
Karachi and some rural areas in Sind.

Watching all this and then digging into the details, Kamran began to
write about the boss. Jam took notice. Zafar Abbas, the BBC's stringer in
Karachi, told me that shortly after Kamran's reporting began to appear,
Jam took Abbas aside at a dinner to ask him, "Who is this Kamran Khan?"
When Abbas explained, Jam said that Kamran had better learn that he,
Jam, was a different sort of chief minister. Abbas told Jam that he ought
not to threaten journalists. "Many people in Karachi are kidnapped," Jam
replied. "Kamran could find that he, too, is kidnapped." Nobody I talked
to—police, army officers, journalists, politicians—doubted that Jam had
been behind the knife attack. Of course, nobody was prepared to testify
to that in court, either.

After I learned that Kamran would survive his wounds, my main
objective was to get him out of the country before Jam or somebody else
tried again to kill him. By the time I landed in Karachi, Jam was already
well into the old feudal game of "First I kill you, then I love you, then
I kill you again." The chief minister had personally ordered that Kamran
receive the very best medical care available in Karachi, expense be
damned. He had ensured that Kamran was transferred to the Aga Khan
hospital, funded by the multimillionaire leader of the Ismaili sect—a
hospital that looked cleaner and better managed than most of the ones
you see in the United States. Kamran's room was filled with bouquets of
roses sent by the chief minister and his various allies. Kamran and I joked
that the bouquets had no doubt been ordered in advance, appropriate for
either funeral condolences or get-well wishes, depending on how the
attack turned out. Police under the chief minister's control had been
posted outside Kamran's hospital room. This did not strike either of us as
reassuring. Kamran was already on the phone to friends in the army,
asking them to please send someone around to replace the provincial
police guards.

It seemed to us an open question whether the knife attack had been a
warning to Kamran successfully executed, and thus the episode was for
the moment finished, or a botched murder attempt, in which case we

would want to move quickly to avoid a second attack. Obviously, in Karachi, if you really want to kill somebody, you open up on them with an assault rifle. A knife attack is a little antiquated and suggested less-than-lethal intent. Since the only man who could really answer this question about intent was Jam himself, I made an appointment to see him.

He invited me to a dinner at his official Karachi residence for a visiting delegation of Chinese Communist officials from Beijing. Multicolored cloth tents had been erected over his front lawn and tables were set atop Persian and Afghan carpets. The Chinese hunched together in their ill-fitting suits and white socks. Jam's retainers lingered around the buffet table, stuffing themselves with slabs of boned lamb. I mingled with a few Pakistani friends, waiting for the boss to summon me. He did, finally, after slapping the Chinese delegates on their backs and ushering them through the tall, spiked metal gate that guarded his driveway.

One of Jam's retainers took me inside a carpeted reception room filled with tacky ornate furniture and buffeted by subarctic winds from air conditioners on full blast. A few businessmen and ministers in Jam's government drifted in, either to watch my audience or to wait for one of their own when mine was through. At last Jam entered grandly through sliding glass doors, dressed in a flowing white salwar kameez. He had white hair and a trimmed white beard. When he smiled, a gold tooth sparkled.

Before we began, he pushed a button by his chair and summoned in the publisher of Kamran's newspaper, Mir ul-Rehman. Jam stood and embraced him, then made the introductions.

"I am his servant," Rehman said.

"No, I am *his* servant," Jam replied. Then he ushered Rehman out.

Our conversation was cordial, occasionally intense. Jam criticized Kamran repeatedly, calling him an agent of intelligence services. Kamran's reporting was never correct; it was "yellow journalism" against Jam's government. Yet he said that he liked Kamran personally and did not want any harm to come to him.

I suggested that there were legal means available to control the press if Jam felt it was irresponsible, and he said, yes, there were, but he went on to talk animatedly about how ineffective the legal means were because the government could never win lawsuits and reporters never felt the pinch of having to pay legal bills. Somehow, the reporters had to learn their lesson. At this point, I ventured that attempted murder was a hard

lesson to swallow. Jam said dismissively that the attack on Kamran was not murderous. Twice he accused Kamran of inventing the story that he had raised his arm to block a blow aimed at his chest or throat, saying that, in fact, the assailant had deliberately—politely, even—cut Kamran across the arm.

I asked what evidence he had for this contention, as Kamran was the only witness to the attack to have come forward.

"No one meant to kill Kamran," Jam answered confidently.

I said that one of my biggest concerns was that I could not tell whether this attack was a warning satisfactorily executed or a hit not yet completed. Jam answered that he thought the matter would go no further.

"That's what I'm very concerned about, that it go no further," I said with as much force as I could muster.

"It will stop here," Jam replied firmly, staring at me intently. Then he lifted the large glass of imported beer he was drinking. "Cheers," he said.

Jam talked about the unusual nature of the crime problem he inherited. He said he could not defend his police force, but could I defend the New York or Washington police?

I asked what he meant when he said earlier that Kamran was an intelligence agent.

"I am not an agent, I do not know how these things work," he said. "Kamran does not only work for you, he works for agencies, and those agencies are all trained in Washington." I pressed him for evidence of this charge. He took my hand and said, "Let's discuss this sometime in a better mood."

At the end of our conversation, Jam invited me to be his guest during an upcoming three-day tour that the prime minister of Pakistan intended to make in rural Sind province. Jam said that all my needs would be taken care of if I accepted his invitation—except wine, which he said was difficult to find in the countryside, and women, which he did not think he could arrange very easily.

At his spiked metal gate Jam said farewell and presented me with a gift—a package of white silk fabric trimmed with lace.

"Good night," he said, extending his arms in warm, prolonged embrace.

———

For much of history, South Asia has been ruled by men—and occasionally by women—like Jam. Some controlled fiefdoms no larger than a Wiscon-

sin family farm. Others led vast empires, waged long wars, and erected prodigious monuments to themselves. Many embodied the attitudes of successful patriarchs, simultaneously asserting their will by force and seeking popularity through patronage. The British slipped comfortably into this system, rewarding indigenous rulers who were willing to cooperate with the empire and quashing those who were not. At independence, despite the exposure of many in the South Asian elites to Western ideas such as democracy, capitalism, socialism, and bolshevism, the subcontinent had precious little experience with systems of governance other than those dominated by rulers who derived their legitimacy from land, power, force, wealth, charisma, patronage, and divine sanction.

In theory at least, one of the advantages of democracy is that it permits peaceful arbitration, even co-optation, of these old, narrow, often bloody political arrangements. Hold an election for the first time in a tribal area and the traditional autocratic tribal chief will duly collect all the votes. That may not seem Jeffersonian. But if the chief does a lousy job in office and the democratic system holds fair and firm, then in the next election his colleagues have a way to shunt him aside without shooting him in the head and sparking regressive, chaotic mayhem. A dozen successful popular elections later and suddenly the younger generation is running its campaign on a platform of abolishing the tribal codes altogether. Thus, a peaceful revolution. In theory.

In this respect, South Asia's experience with democracy since independence is one of those glasses half full or half empty, depending on your inclination toward gloominess. Many of the autocratic political structures present on the subcontinent when the British withdrew have withered away through democratic arbitration. Obviously, this is most true in India, which has held to its parliamentary democracy, with one brief interruption, for more than four decades, and which possesses a vigorous independent press and a judiciary that occasionally asserts an independent voice. It is true to a significant extent even in Pakistan, Sri Lanka, Bangladesh, and Nepal, whose democratic experiments have been more fitful and less evolutionary.

But while South Asian democracy can boast of many achievements, it has also generally failed to produce institutions strong enough to withstand the perfidies of politicians. It has failed to produce political economies prosperous enough to unify decisively tentative nation-states. And

it has failed, to various degrees in various countries, to undermine the potential of autocrats, that is, to banish the kings.

Why it has failed to do this is an enormously complicated question best addressed in volumes that trace in detail the political histories of independent India, Pakistan, Sri Lanka, Nepal, and Bangladesh. But there are a few general points worth making here. One is that successful democracies depend on the strength of independent state institutions, and on this score the Nehruvian state has had a decidedly mixed record. Another is that democracies depend on free and fair elections. Here again, South Asia's record is mixed, although hardly dispiriting. Most important, even if the democratic experiments in South Asia had not been interrupted by the many cataclysms of the past four decades, it would be too soon for us to predict their ultimate success or failure—you cannot mediate away two thousand years of feudal and imperial history in four decades, no matter how hard you try, no matter how many free and fair elections you manage to hold.

Even healthy democratic systems produce bad leaders, so it is perhaps not surprising that South Asia's imperfect systems have thrown up a remarkable list of truly awful ones since independence. What is interesting about these leaders is not the particular chronicles of their incompetence, foibles, and quirks, but rather their common failures of temperament and outlook. Time and again South Asian democracies have been betrayed by elected leaders who chose to govern as if they were kings or queens. In this they have been tempted by the strains of subcontinental history, the weakness of their countries' democratic institutions, and the universal inability of human beings to disbelieve the adulation of crowds.

Most interesting of all in this regard are those who should have known better. There are, of course, many who don't know better. You meet a lot of people in South Asia like Jam, minor thug-rulers who appear to be unencumbered by political conscience. Such men feed on the weakness of the state, exploiting opportunities for profit and glory with the tenacious ruthlessness of your average Wall Street bond trader. The system expects little of them and they give back even less. But there are others who have properly seen themselves at the center of South Asia's modern struggles, leaders of destiny empowered to tilt the national course and to discipline the minor thug-rulers who hold the nation back. When such leaders take center stage—an Indira Gandhi, a Rajiv Gandhi, a Benazir Bhutto—they

promise ideas, progress, a further break with the past, and at the same time continuity, unity. And they promise modern democracy. Yet they quickly find themselves at the epicenter of a political culture infused with the most undemocratic temptations. The Jams beneath them rush to offer their fealty, opening their arms in friendly embrace. The suffering crowds throng to the roadsides, begging pitifully for salvation. The permanent political bureaucracy—the courtiers and the generals—conspire and dissemble and maneuver for position. All this can trigger a psychological struggle bordering on the Shakespearean, made no less so by the culture's tendency to melodrama.

Often, one of the first symptoms of this interior struggle is Nixonian paranoia. Consider Indira Gandhi, for example.

She grew up at the political knee of Jawaharlal Nehru, her father, one leader in recent South Asian history who proved decisively able to resist the temptations of traditional, personalized autocracy. But Nehru's successor died suddenly of a heart attack and by then Indira Gandhi was in a position to make her bid. The Congress bosses backed her because they thought she could be manipulated. This proved a miscalculation. But as Indira asserted herself, rushing from crisis to crisis and from one corner of the subcontinent to another to project herself as Mother India, she began at first to overwhelm and then in time to undermine the democratic institutions her father had built. By the mid-1970s she had managed to organize the Congress Party and the sprawling state apparatus on principles of strict personal loyalty to her and to her court. She was isolated by sycophants and supplicants, including her son Sanjay. At the same time she was confirmed in her high self-regard by the enduring enthusiasm of the great crowds that flocked to greet her public appearances. The South Asian crowd is vast and impressive but its importance is easy to overestimate. A colleague mentioned before I left for India that he could attract a crowd of twenty thousand in South Asia just by changing a tire on the roadside. That is not much of an exaggeration. Why a woman like Indira Gandhi begins to believe in this crowd at the expense of everything else she may once have thought about democracy is hard to say. But at the end of the process, in 1975, you have her throwing out the cabinet, jailing her opponents, suspending freedom of speech, and declaring a National Emergency in response to a perceived conspiracy to dethrone her from her rightful rule.

Failure must be rationalized and the easiest way to do that in South

Asia is to blame your enemies. Couple this with the isolating traditions of the royal court and you do not exactly have a prescription for stable democratic checks and balances. A personally insecure ruler, such as Indira Gandhi, begins to see the democracy she once championed through the prism of her court. Conspirators dart in the palace shadows. Political manipulations course through the popular press. The idea of democracy becomes intertwined with the person of Indira Gandhi and thus both must be defended with vigor against the conspirators.

When Indira topped arrogance with stupidity and called an election in the midst of her Emergency to ratify what she believed was her overwhelming popularity, Indian democracy found a way to reassert itself and tossed her out of office. In an interview with David Frost immediately afterward, Indira was shameless, unrepentant. She believed the whole fiasco of the Emergency and the election defeat was a conspiracy against her. Frost asked if she had been ill served by the people around her, the courtiers.

"That some people kept the facts [from me] is evident from what happened subsequently," she answered.

"Which people?"

"Intelligence people and so on."

"You say intelligence people kept facts from you?"

"Well, I don't—I mean, I think—I mean, I imagine that they did."

Substitute for Indira Gandhi in India Zulfikar Ali Bhutto in Pakistan or Sheikh Mujib in Bangladesh, and you have a partial glimpse of what went wrong, psychologically and materially, with South Asian democracy during the 1970s.

Rajiv Gandhi was less cunning than his mother, milder in temperament, but he inherited her sense of entitlement to rule. Or, at least, he did not reject very firmly his courtiers' advice that in him lay the salvation of the Congress Party and the unity of India.

There was nonetheless something likably befuddled about Rajiv, a contentedness that beamed across his face when he went wandering among the crowds in his khadi and jogging shoes. But this charming aspect of the boy-king—and all his ennobling talk about science, technology, and modernity—masked political programs that sanctioned, whether by neglect or calculation, the continuation of his mother's authoritarian abuse of the party and the Indian state. On Rajiv's watch elections in Kashmir were violently rigged in 1987, stirring an armed

rebellion that remains the most politically dangerous of the many under way on the subcontinent today. In revenge for his mother's murder, and because he did not wish to control his most thuggish henchmen, he perpetuated a reign of police violence against Sikhs in Punjab that turned a tricky political situation into an impossible one. He manipulated religious feeling. He eschewed internal Congress Party elections, thereby further entrenching the network of regional thug-rulers installed by his mother. He did nothing to discipline or clean out the convicted murderers and kidnappers in northern India who sat in legislative assemblies under the banner of his party and the glow of his charisma. He talked about radical capitalist reforms when he first came to power late in 1984, but he backed away from the plans quickly when the old Congress bosses— the Jams of Bombay and Lucknow, Agra and Bhopal—resisted economic liberalization, presumably because it might empty the state patronage trough at which the party and its leaders fed. Later, after his death, friends and partisans of Rajiv attributed these failings to his being overwhelmed initially by the challenges of dynasty and office, and they argued that had he lived, he would have changed his ways. Perhaps. Only Rajiv's most hardened enemies accused him of innate malevolence. As the Ruler of Oz once said of himself, Rajiv was not a bad man, he was just not a very good wizard. For a little while at least, he did much to inspire the Indian middle class's emerging, progressive demands for modernity. He sustained his family's symbolic but arguably useful role as the embodiment of a post-independence unified Indian nation-state. But in a political culture heavily influenced by sycophancy, autocracy, and the psychology of the ruling court, good intentions will not win out. On the contrary, they are easily subsumed.

All this seemed frequently to confuse the outside world, particularly the West. The West wanted to believe in Rajiv the airline pilot, the track-shoed scientific modernist, elected leader of the world's most populous democracy, etc., etc. It did not want to believe in, or sometimes could not apprehend, Rajiv the boy-king, whose tantrums and manipulations flowed through the autocratic machinery he sat atop, occasionally expressing themselves at the far end as sticks wielded on skulls or large sums of hard currency transferred by wire to front companies banking in Switzerland.

During much of my time in South Asia, Rajiv was mainly a shadow. An Indian electorate fed up with his manipulations and the steady deterio-

ration of the state machinery threw him out of office late in 1989, only to find his successors worse than many imagined possible. Because of this and in spite of himself, Rajiv seemed on the verge of a modest comeback when Dhanu blew him up in the late spring of 1991. The West would miss him, but not much. It was distracted as always, busy with Saddam and the end of communism. Besides, by the turn of the decade, the West was once burned, twice wary in South Asia. It had fallen in love with another democratic modernist, gone right off the deep end. But that affair had turned out badly.

————

I first saw Benazir Bhutto in New York's Grand Hyatt Hotel in 1989, on a June night of driving rain. She had been elected seven months earlier as Pakistan's first democratic prime minister since the overthrow of her father in 1977. She stood that night in the hotel's third-floor ballroom, a striking figure with her flowing robes and cascading black hair, preaching to the converted, as she so frequently did in the West. In this case the assembly was a tuxedoed convocation of the Asia Society, big spenders and big thinkers in the stylish foreign policy set. Benazir wowed them with a prepared text about her plans for privatization and capitalism in Pakistan, plans she spoke about convincingly to Western faithful but did little to implement at home.

Toward the end of her speech, warming to the theme of democracy's recent and triumphant return to Pakistan, she departed from her text to tell a story about a recent political tour she made in Sind, Jam's country, where she was raised. Benazir described it as a long, blistering hot day of political rallies before "the masses," as she so frequently called them. In an unnamed dusty provincial backwater, she paused for rest. As she sat in the shade, panting, a small boy brought her a Coca-Cola. She drank gratefully and then asked him how much it had cost. The boy said two rupees. She asked what the boy did for a living. He said he put air in bicycle tires. She asked what he earned. He said thirty rupees in a month, the equivalent of about $1.25. At this point, Benazir turned to her New York audience in white ties and gowns and said with utter seriousness, "This boy, he gave so much of his salary to buy me a Coca-Cola because he believed in an idea—an idea of freedom and democracy." And then Benazir concluded to an ovation.

I stood listening in the back of the ballroom. I was leaving for South

Asia in a couple of weeks and I had come to hear Benazir mainly out of curiosity. This Coca-Cola story made me very curious indeed. Fealty equals democracy and freedom.

But the story makes perfect sense when you set eyes on the feudal world where Benazir was raised on a sprawling estate as a landlord-politician's daughter, whose birth signaled to all around her that she was entitled to rule should she choose to try. The acute misunderstanding of Benazir in the West—where throughout her long exile during the 1980s she courted opinion makers and the public with her smart looks, her credentials from Harvard and Oxford, her poise, and her undeniable courage—arose from the West's inability or unwillingness to see this other Benazir, the princess-from-birth.

Ian Buruma proposes two Benazir Bhuttos, one whom he calls the "Radcliffe Benazir," the other the "Larkana Benazir," after the feudal Sind town of her birth. "So much about the Larkana Benazir smacks of kitsch; so much of the Radcliffe Benazir strikes one as half-baked," Buruma wrote. That's an apt formulation. Her autobiography brims with Larkana kitsch. Detained during martial law on a family estate, she writes with earnest outrage that the martial law regime is causing flowers in her family gardens to die because the regime has cut the number of gardeners from ten to three. "I join in the struggle to keep the gardens alive," she writes. "I will them to survive, seeing in their struggle to live denied adequate water and nourishment my own struggle to survive denied freedom." Ultimately, for all her courage and accomplishment, the most important prisons in Benazir Bhutto's life have turned out to be not the physical jails in which she and her family were held at various points during the 1980s by the Zia martial law regime but the prisons of perception erected by her feudal origins.

Buruma and others wrote early on about the schizophrenia in Benazir's outlook, contrasting among other things the privileged liberalism imparted by her Western university professors with the mythical romanticism taught by her father, who studied the life of Napoleon and modeled himself upon the French emperor. But few in the West paid attention. Benazir helped to promote this myopia not only with her dazzling charm but with her plausible insistence that there was no middle ground in Pakistan, that either you believed in Benazir and thus in democracy, or you believed in Zia and in the regressive, U.S. government–backed authoritarian rule of the Pakistan army's martial law. People in and out of

Pakistan who should have known better initially accepted her personalization of democratic politics, partly because, for as long as Zia refused to yield and hold elections, Benazir was a symbol of change and hope rather than a vessel of Sind's traditional autocracies. But when Benazir was elected prime minister in 1989, after Zia's death, the balance of her identity began to tilt.

As a young woman at Harvard and Oxford during the 1960s and 1970s, Benazir moved with ease through the Western liberal upper-middle classes, rewarded by that world's admiration for individual achievement, even if it is propelled by privileged birth. She adapted like a chameleon to the West's emerging emphases on appearance, style, wit, strength, feminist independence. She often said what those around her wanted to hear. But beginning in 1989, she adapted less well to the complexities of governing Pakistan after twelve years of martial law. She still told those around her what they wanted to hear, but this did not promote effective administration of a large, diverse, and impoverished country. More important, the longer she was in Pakistan, the more she seemed drawn psychologically and in very practical ways to Larkana, to the culture of the old estates. She embraced many of the Jams around her, doling out political franchises to the minor thug-rulers, including convicted murderers. She sanctioned corruption by refusing to act against, or even investigate, senior ministers and allies accused of stealing from the state. She did nothing to discipline a "student wing" in her party that waged an open, sustained war with automatic weapons against a rival ethnic group in Karachi. She rationalized these failures by trying to draw a distinction between corruption and patronage, saying the former was unacceptable but the latter was just part of business as usual in South Asia. But some of the deals she considered mere patronage certainly would have landed her in prison had she attempted to put them together in the West, whose democratic values she so conspicuously promoted in Pakistan. In any event, before this question could be fully resolved, Benazir succumbed, as Indira Gandhi did, to the paranoia of the court, seeing her enemies at work in every administrative frustration. She felt from the beginning of her reign as prime minister that she was being "destabilized from within," as she put it in one conversation.

In response to this perceived destabilization campaign, Benazir and her allies in the Pakistan People's Party undertook during the nineteen months they held office an elaborate game of "Spy versus Spy" in the

capital of Islamabad with their enemies in the army and with the former political allies of Benazir's arch-enemy, Zia. They spent their time and energy setting up videotaped "sting" operations to capture army officers attempting to bribe politicians into defecting from Benazir's coalition. In fairness, having been persecuted by the army and having seen her father hanged and one brother murdered in exile, Benazir had far more reason than Indira ever did to believe in conspiracies. But like Rajiv, with whom she said she felt a kinship, Benazir wished to believe in the future, yet she could not shake off her past.

Each time I sat down with Benazir to talk in detail about her predicament in office, the conversation drifted toward the conspiracies she saw around her in her court. I would press her to elaborate, looking for facts that might yield an interesting story. She would begin cautiously, worried about being lured into foolishness or dangerous disclosure. Then she would plunge in, talking enthusiastically but often vaguely about the combinations at work against her. Over time, this tendency grew worse and worse. On August 6, 1990, the night she was finally thrown out of office by her opponents on corruption charges relating to the business activities of her husband and her senior ministers, she sat stunned on a couch in her brightly lit official home on a wooded hill in Islamabad. By now there was a single conspiracy and the leaders of this grand plot were merely "they." "They killed my father because they knew that he would win any election he stood for," she told us, the reporters gathered at her feet. "They know that I will win any election that I stand for." Moreover, "they" made certain that she could not govern and now were determined to ruin her once and for all. "I repeatedly received reports about the attempts being made by certain quarters to destabilize my government," she announced.

Would "they" ever give her another chance? "I doubt it. I doubt it," she answered. "I don't believe that they can face me politically. They couldn't face me politically yesterday and they can't face me politically today."

By the fall of 1990, campaigning to regain office in a national election and fighting off a series of kangeroo-court corruption hearings, she reached the point where she apparently believed that her opponents were releasing secret gasses to cause her to faint in public. This particular allegation surfaced in October, when Benazir was crushed by one of the usual maddening crowds at a court hearing in Lahore. All of us inside the

courtroom fought for our lives to get out of that crowd; it was killing, suffocating. But it did not seem terribly mysterious. Benazir fainted. So did others. But at a friend's house the next day, she told us that she thought "it might have been some gas. I've been in much larger crowds. But I started blacking out. I would have fallen and been totally trampled. Not only myself but my former adviser felt he was getting heart failure. We feel that something was planned by the authorities."

By that time it was hard not to feel sorry for Benazir, after all she had been through, after all she had once symbolized. Many of her former friends around the world were writing her off as a self-deluding despot, telling her to get help before it was too late. Her husband was in jail. Her father was dead. Her party was falling apart, breaking under the pressure of its opponents. All Benazir had left was her disintegrating court and her courage. But her courtiers were incompetent and her courage only gave her the strength to believe in fantasies. So you thought of her, blacking out in the midst of the crowd that for so many years had sustained her courage and ambition, feeling that she was having a heart attack, suffocating, and believing that it was all the work of her enemies.

Pakistanis tend to be far less tolerant of Benazir, remembering, as they do, her father's opportunistic demogoguery twenty years ago while he ran his populist campaign for office. They remember, too, Zulfikar's decidedly authoritarian streak as prime minister—his persecution of opponents, his assertion of personal power at the expense of democratic institutions, his princely self-image. These characteristics contributed to the bloody breakup of Pakistan in 1971, when Bangladesh gained independence. Pakistanis are also aware intuitively of what the Bhutto family's attitudes, rooted in their status as feudal landlords and imperial servants, represent: the enduring power of land, and the susceptibility of the weak Pakistani polity to manipulation.

Around the time of Benazir's dismissal from office, I went to see Tahira Abdullah, a women's rights activist in Islamabad who felt thoroughly betrayed by Benazir's reign. Tahira sneered articulately about the princess. "Have you seen her on American TV? She's young, she's charming, she's Harvard and Oxford. She's what the media dreamed of. Charm just oozes out of her. On *60 Minutes*, with Ed Bradley, there she was in her diamonds and pearls, talking about the poor women of Pakistan. It stinks. It's hypocrisy of the highest order."

I told her that she sounded disappointed.

She laughed. "We are totally disillusioned, if any of us had any illusions."

What Benazir could never accept is that many who disagreed with her, or even despised her, nonetheless wanted her to succeed, not for herself but for the country. If she had accepted this, if she had been able to detach the idea of democracy from herself, she might at least have lasted longer in office.

On the day before she was thrown out as prime minister, I went to see another formidable Pakistani woman in Islamabad, Maleeha Lodhi, a contemporary of Benazir's and a newspaper editor who is one of the country's brightest political writers. Neither of us knew what was to happen the next afternoon, but you could sense that the end was near.

"Her father deliberately set out to undermine and destroy independent institutions—the party, trade unions, any other sort of independent power," she said. "Benazir has behaved in the same way but for different reasons. He came in through the institutions and struck back against them. She came from the outside. It's the great-leader syndrome. Everything has to be me. . . . 'Compromise' is a dirty word in her vocabulary. During the martial law period, yes, that can be a very successful strategy, but not now. Half these people around her she saw as her father's murderers. It couldn't have been easy. She's an emotional person anyway. I just feel so sorry for her, personally. She had such an opportunity and she's come very close to blowing it for herself. I guess you need a different kind of leader to handle that."

Shortly afterward, in Lahore, I met Mubashir Hassan, who served as finance minister in the government of Benazir's father and has known the family for several decades. I asked him why he thought Benazir had failed.

"The phenomenon of Benazir cannot be properly understood unless we note that for the last ten years, the state structure in Pakistan has been rapidly collapsing," he answered. "It's not just a problem of a leader going this way or that. The police are no longer the police. The magistracy is no longer the magistracy and the tax collector can no longer collect taxes. The collapse of the state has given rise to kidnappers, murderers, bank robbers, drug dealers. At least the old-time feudal lord was a stabilizing power. But now these emerging money powers need new political backing. They poured enormous amounts of money into the coffers of Benazir and Nawaz Sharif. The whole scene has become a bazaar. Previously the

top leadership was never so corrupt. But now, you name it—the top ministers, public corporations, heads of banks. They're all corrupt.

"I think what makes Benazir go is her conviction that she is the People's Party and she finds justification in the crowds she attracts. And anyone who tries to tell her that this is not politics, that it won't last, she simply doesn't believe them."

I asked why he thought, as all of this unraveled around her, Benazir seemed to find a kind of refuge in paranoia. Like so many in the South Asian elites, Hassan referred to his countrymen as "they," as if he were some sort of nineteenth-century colonial officer.

"Indo-Pakistan society is paranoiac by nature," he answered. "They are extremely insecure. They have always been ruled by force and power. They have yet to learn to rule over themselves. The more they learn, the more they become afraid of what will happen to them. They keep looking for protectors at every level. . . . Salvaging the Pakistani state might require a combination of a Caesar and a Plato. But Benazir is not even in the running."

In the national Pakistani elections of October 1990, after she was thrown out of office, Benazir and her party were defeated in a landslide vote. She announced immediately that the tally had been secretly and systematically rigged to ensure her defeat. Outside election monitors looked carefully at this charge, and while they found irregularities, they could find little evidence to support the broader charge of a big fix. These days, Benazir crosses Pakistan with a diminished train of courtiers, still seeking solace in the crowds. She may yet make a comeback; she relishes the public role of victim, and her enemies oblige her with persecution. Her husband has been charged with serious crimes and cannot possibly count on an impartial trial. Her beloved party—the embodiment of herself—is splintered. To compensate, she has been meeting recently with Islamic fundamentalists to talk about a new alliance. Sometimes, perhaps for rejuvenation, she flies off to America or Britain for a lecture tour. She appears dressed in pearls on talk shows like *Good Morning America*.

If you are inclined to optimism about South Asia, then you might say that in time, if Pakistan finds a way to sustain parliamentary democracy as an antidote to its spasms of military rule, the repetition of elections will slowly file the edges off this story and gradually mute all the high drama and despair. Anything is possible, and of course there is much greater strength and resiliency at the base of Pakistani society than those on top

can see or credit. But for now, watching Benazir and her rival claimants for the right to rule wandering among their crowds, it is difficult to imagine that the promise of modernity she made with such charming conviction will be realized anytime soon.

8

Crossed Lines

On one side the whole world is after us and [on] another side the
internal enemies are going to finish us. But at least we have one
satisfaction, that from one end to the other end we have made
other people sleepless.

—*A. Q. Khan, father of the Pakistani*
nuclear program, to a colleague

The West misunderstood Benazir, but Benazir also misunderstood the
West. She seemed so often to believe that a key to the successful
governance of Pakistan was to seduce the foreign policy crowds in
Boston, New York, Washington, and London. Given the magnitude of the
U.S. economic and military aid program in Pakistan, her impulse to foster
cordial relations was understandable. But Benazir's relationship with the
West, like that of so many others in the South Asian elites, moved beyond
calculation into pathos. The Pakistani journalist Ahmed Rashid reported
the story of how, near the end of her reign as prime minister, in the midst
of a dispute with her enemies in the Pakistan army, Benazir turned up one
night at the door of the U.S. ambassador in Islamabad, asking him to
please intervene and tell the generals to behave. Manipulated by Benazir's
opponents, the image eventually angered many Pakistanis and helped to
feed a surge in angry nationalist politics beginning late in 1990 that
contributed to a near-total break in the U.S.-Pakistani alliance.

The misunderstanding between South Asia and the West plays itself
out as overwrought tragedy or exaggerated comedy, but it is rarely
inconsequential, at least for South Asians. For two hundred years the
political economy of the Indian subcontinent has been shaped in decisive
ways by the ambitious power of Western armies and Western ideas. If the

South Asian political classes today seem entangled in obsessions and misperceptions about the West, that is at least partly because they have been forced continually to reckon with Western political interests at crucial moments of a volatile and rapidly evolving history. But the converse is not true at all; the relationship is terribly unequal. The West today ignores, misunderstands, or tramples over South Asia at no great expense to itself. The occasional exceptions are relished with pride by South Asians, even when they turn out badly. The construction of nuclear weapons, perhaps the most popular government-sponsored endeavor on the subcontinent after cricket, is one example. The Bank of Commerce and Credit International was another.

The BCCI story erupted in the summer of 1991 when the Bank of England led a raid against BCCI's London headquarters and many of its branches, accusing the bank's officers of massive criminal fraud. A $20 billion financial empire with branches in seventy-two countries, BCCI was now broke, and with the Bank of England's raid its millions of ordinary depositors became overnight victims of what New York district attorney Robert Morgenthau called "the largest bank fraud in world financial history." Suddenly all the world wanted to know about BCCI and its founder, Agha Hasan Abedi, a Muslim financier of Indian origin who built his reputation and his bank in Pakistan. Congress convened hearings to explore the bank's links to organized crime and to its financial allies in the United States, particularly Clark Clifford, the Washington political fixer and elder statesman who was an adviser to several presidents before finding wealth in partnership with a South Asian entrepreneur. The Western media went berserk over the story. It was an otherwise slow summer, and the BCCI tale was one of those amorphous, sinister scandals that seem to link up, to those of a conspiratorial bent, many disparate phenomena—drug trafficking, gun running, political corruption, intelligence gathering, and financial fraud. BCCI was said to have run a "black network" out of its Karachi branch that performed dirty tricks, even murder, in service of such evil entities as the Saudi Arabian monarchy, the Colombian cocaine cartel, the CIA, the Pakistani nuclear establishment, the Iranian revolutionaries, the Nicaraguan contras, and so on. If you looked at it from a certain angle, you could believe that BCCI was the link that bound all the scandals of the 1980s into one. Or so it seemed in the humidity of a slow-news summer. And at the center of it all was a man who fit neatly Western preconceptions and prejudices about South Asia,

a swarthy Pakistani with a name few knew how to pronounce. (AH-beh-dee is correct.)

Abedi was depicted in the West as one of the great criminals of the twentieth century. In truth, he probably was. Prosecutors indicted him on fraud charges and the Federal Reserve Board named him in an action seeking his permanent exclusion from U.S. banking. In these documents, Abedi was described as a swindler who stole billions from his depositors, gave away money recklessly to friends and cronies, laundered illegal drug profits, lied repeatedly to regulators, and covered up his crimes by currying favor with prominent political figures around the world. That Abedi did all this, and more, is indisputable. But fraud itself is prosaic; Abedi is not. What was most interesting about him, as a criminal and a contemporary South Asian, was his struggle to reconcile South Asia's past with its future. Like Benazir, Abedi was suspended between two incompatible worlds. He fell because he found it profitable for a time not to reconcile the contradictions.

Abedi was born and raised in Mahmudabad, an isolated Muslim kingdom in what is now north-central India that was alive fifty years ago with intrigue, wealth, and idealistic politics. His ancestors served for generations as courtiers to the once-powerful Mahmudabad rajas. Besides Abedi, dozens of other senior and mid-level BCCI managers were raised in or trace their roots to Mahmudabad. As Benazir learned about politics in Larkana, so Abedi first learned about finance, wealth, power, and law in Mahmudabad's centuries-old feudal world. In Mahmudabad a series of bejeweled Muslim rajas administered great tracts of land from a gold and silver throne. They financed idealistic politicians such as the Mahatma Gandhi and Pakistan founder Mohammed Ali Jinnah. They doled out gifts to their subjects, paid stipends to renowned poets and intellectuals, plotted against the British Empire, and finally witnessed the birth of independent India and Pakistan in a bloody spasm of post-Partition riots. Abedi and nearly all of BCCI's senior executives migrated as young adults from what is now India to newly independent Islamic Pakistan in 1947 and 1948, when the kingdoms that the British had employed to rule South Asia fell. In Pakistan, Abedi and other refugees confronted the challenge of building twentieth-century institutions from scratch in a culture still rooted in seventeenth-century feudalism. Among other things, Pakistan at its birth had no large banks and very few bankers.

Abedi set out to change that. Driven by high ambitions and relying on

the loyalty of young men from his Mahmudabad clan—a clan knit by family, religion, ethnicity, and a shared, convulsive history—he erected an international banking empire that sought to carry into the realm of modern finance the romantic idealism of a lost feudal kingdom. Along the way, Abedi and his clan achieved a degree of wealth and fame befitting the decadent Mahmudabad rajas he and his ancestors had served for generations. To the West, Abedi was merely a criminal. To some Pakistanis, he was a man born into a family of minor royal servants who became obsessed with transforming himself into a king.

In 1922, when Abedi was born, Mahmudabad was the second or third largest princely state in northern India, encompassing 530 villages and thousands of hamlets and generating half a million pounds sterling in annual income. Its line of Shia Muslim rajas dated to the seventeenth century and commanded respect from the British colonial officers they served, as well as from Indians struggling for liberation from the British Empire. The Mahmudabad rajas lived in exorbitant luxury and owned several palaces in the countryside and the city of Lucknow. But they were also deeply involved in anticolonial politics and Shiite religious movements. As far back as the mid-nineteenth century, Abedi's family served the rajas as revenue officers, administrators, and private secretaries. Their position as courtiers provided them comfort, stability, and middle-class status. Abedi's father and grandfather were confidants of the rajas, although not among the most senior advisers. Abedi himself grew up hearing stories of royal splendor and fierce anticolonial struggle against the British. Mahmudabad lore has it that his great-great-grandfather participated in the legendary Mutiny of 1857, when Muslim soldiers in northern India revolted against the British, only to be slaughtered when the rebellion was quashed in short order. Abedi's ancestor was subsequently hung in a cage by the British on the streets of Lucknow to serve as an example to the population, the story goes. Whatever the truth of that, it secured the Abedi family's stalwart reputation among the Muslims of Mahmudabad. The kingdom was at once extravagant and impoverished. Landless peasants tilled the fields for subsistence and paid tithes to revenue officers, who filled the rajas' coffers with treasure. Neighboring minor princes also paid stipends to the Mahmudabad rulers. The rajas, in turn, prided themselves on their philanthropy and devotion to high culture. They toured the countryside in times of trouble to hand out donations to the poor, provided shelter and finance to independence-

movement leaders, and paid stipends to Muslim poets, intellectuals, and religious scholars.

"They were impractical people, I suppose," explained Ahmed Abdul Bari, the son of a neighboring Lucknow raja whom I met in Karachi after BCCI had failed. The rulers for whom Abedi's family had worked were "impulsive, emotional, romantic," he said. "There were lots of people with power to be looked after," added a friend of Abedi's, Humayan Gouhar. "That did affect [his] thinking."

Abedi's career in banking began amid the trauma of Partition, when as many as one million people died in religious riots and millions more were forced to abandon their lives and belongings to seek refuge in a new country. The Mahmudabad raja left his throne, emigrating first to Karachi and then to London, where he helped to build the Regent's Park mosque, ate simple meals from a hot plate in his apartment, and finally died in exile. Abedi and thousands of other Shia Muslims fled with the raja to Pakistan. But they could not afford to go on to London. There was hardship but also opportunity in their new country, and Abedi pushed ahead. He rose to a senior position at Habib Bank but felt stymied by the Habib family clan's tight control. In 1959 he struck out to start the United Bank Limited with money provided by the Saigols, a family of industrialists in Lahore who were also refugees from India. When UBL was nationalized by Zulfikar Ali Bhutto's government in 1972, Abedi started again by founding BCCI.

In the Pakistani world of clan, family, ethnicity, and religion, Abedi was at a double disadvantage as a Muslim Shia refugee from India, suceptible to discrimination by Pakistan's dominant group, native ethnic Punjabis from the Sunni Muslim sect. Like so many others in Pakistan and India, Abedi protected himself from such discrimination by surrounding himself with people from his own clan—Shia refugees, particularly Shia refugees from Mahmudabad. If you were a Shia with family roots in Mahmudabad or its environs, you had merely to walk into BCCI's headquarters to be offered a job. As the bank grew, so did the clan's rewards. Salaries skyrocketed. The bank expanded internationally. The clan struck it rich. Many of Abedi's trusted aides at BCCI were not only from his clan, they were from lower-middle-class or landless families with few resources and no reputation. They often treated Abedi sycophantically, a practice he did little to discourage. He was, after all, their raja.

Abedi also sought status in emerging Pakistan by surrounding himself

with relatives of the country's most important people. "He wanted the sons of somebodies," explained politician Abida Hussain, at present Pakistan's ambassador to the United States. "If you were a civil servant, you got your son hired at BCCI. If you were a general, you got your son hired. They were paid more than they were worth and they swanked all over the world. It was inevitable that it would go broke." In the 1980s, Abedi hired a descendant of one of the greatest "somebodies" he had ever known—the raja of Mahmudabad. Imran Imam, a grandson of the Mahmudabad ruler whom Abedi's father had served, became a senior employee of BCCI's headquarters office in London. His position: Abedi's personal assistant.

In some ways, Abedi saw BCCI less as a twentieth-century multinational bank than as a seventeenth-century feudal kingdom with international horizons. From BCCI's beginning, Abedi declared publicly and repeatedly that his would be a different kind of bank, one devoted among other things to philanthropy and the uplifting of Third World poor. In Pakistan, he poured about $60 million of bank profits into a foundation ostensibly devoted to funding antipoverty projects. He doled out stipends to Pakistani politicians, journalists, and poets. He gave low-cost or free housing loans to all his employees and many of his friends, some of them important Pakistani politicians. If an employee or a relative fell ill, Abedi sometimes paid for expensive operations or treatment abroad. He routinely paid for scholarships for the children of employees to attend universities in the West. Many of the beneficiaries of this largesse, of course, were members of his Mahmudabad clan. But as BCCI expanded, Abedi took the feudalism he knew and went international. He gave $10 million to former U.S. president Jimmy Carter's Global 2000 organization and millions more to philanthropic foundations he established in England and other countries.

But the money did not belong to Abedi personally. It came from BCCI's revenues and from the bank's depositors. His impulsive generosity extended to the bank's basic lending business. He apparently lent hundreds of millions of dollars to people who had no intention of paying it back. When Price Waterhouse, BCCI's auditors, uncovered these giant black holes in the bank's lending portfolio in 1991, they were stunned to find that Abedi had apparently doled out unsecured, nonperforming loans totaling as much as $5 billion to friends and business associates. Pakistanis found this pattern of lending huge sums of money without collateral or

tight repayment agreements perfectly comprehensible. "If they had done something for him, he would make sure that he did favors for them," said Bari, the son of the Lucknow raja. "That is something the West finds very difficult to understand. But he [Abedi] had seen how princely things are done."

One of Abedi's patrons was a genuine prince—Sheikh Zayed of Abu Dhabi. After flying to the sheikh's then-underdeveloped desert kingdom in the early 1970s to persuade the ruler to fund BCCI, Abedi and his bank devoted the ensuing fifteen years to catering to Zayed's every need. This was something an old courtier like Abedi know how to do well. He set up a "protocol department" in BCCI's Karachi branch and spent as much as $5,000 a day to maintain the sheikh's Pakistan palaces and to serve the Abu Dhabi ruler's visiting relatives. Abedi took this idea international as well. As BCCI expanded internationally, he sought out businessmen with close family or social connections to the new country's government, rewarded those intermediaries generously, then sought to expand his bank's deposit base. In Washington, he turned to former U.S. defense secretary Clark Clifford, whose reputation as an accomplished courtier was well established long before he met Abedi.

Ultimately, this pattern of growth became untenable—the total amount of the unrecoverable loans, gifts, stipends, and charity donations outstripped the amount of deposits and other obligations BCCI owed to its customers. New York district attorney Morgenthau called this type of fraud a "giant Ponzi scheme," meaning that Abedi kept racing to raise new deposits from customers in order to cover his fraudulent dealings with friends, employees, and cronies. In South Asia, the pattern was seen differently. There it seemed obvious that Abedi had tried foolishly to extend to the West a style of business commonplace in his own world but unacceptable abroad.

To many South Asians, the fall of BCCI was further confirmation of continuing Western plots to keep South Asia in its place. To them, when the Bank of England raided and closed BCCI to save what depositors' money was left, another Abedi was being hung out in a cage by colonials, as an example to the population.

That the West might not view South Asia as a rising threat to be contained by the continual enactment of secret conspiracies against its leaders sounds implausible to many Indians, Pakistanis, Bangladeshis, and Sri Lankans. After two hundred years of imperial history and forty years

of the cold war, the existence of such conspiracies has become an article of faith. After Rajiv Gandhi was assasinated, the Indian press brimmed with articles offering the theory that the CIA had killed Gandhi because as a strong subcontinental leader, Gandhi posed a threat to George Bush's "new world order." When I published a story describing these theories and ridiculing them lightly, one Indian media critic took up two pages of a leading national magazine to excoriate me for naïveté and arrogance. It was obvious, he wrote, that I did not understand how the CIA really worked, what it really wanted.

In the case of BCCI, it was the Western media who saw the CIA's faint hand connecting prosaic fragments into an artful pattern. But this time, for once, I was headed in the other direction. After hearing lengthy stories about Mahmudabad's lost feudal splendor from friends and associates of Abedi in Karachi, I was desperate to see the kingdom and talk to the reigning raja of Mahmudabad, the son of the ruler Abedi's father had served. His name was Mohammed Amir Mohammed Khan, but his friends referred to him as Suleiman. He was born and raised in London during his father's exile and trained as an astrophysicist at Cambridge University. During the 1970s, he gave up on the West, married a Hindu, the daughter of a distinguished Indian couple, former foreign secretary Jagat Mehta and author Rama Mehta, and then returned to his family's old, decaying palaces to take up residence. His friends described him as one of the great characters of the cultural divide between South Asia and the West; V. S. Naipaul had met and written about him, they said, as if this were the ultimate endorsement. But when Rama, my New Delhi researcher, telephoned and asked for an appointment to talk about Abedi and BCCI, Suleiman declined. So, figuring that South Asian imperatives of hospitality would overwhelm his reluctance, we decided to fly down to Lucknow and knock on his palace door.

We drove first to what the locals call the "city palace," a crumbling, sprawling estate in the heart of teeming Lucknow. We entered through a faded gateway, waving the guards aside with regal gestures. At the end of the stone drive we found that most of the palace was shut; Suleiman occupied only a handful of rooms to one side. Servants and barefoot boys milled about. Of all the wonders in South Asia, the most glorious is this: that history just lies around in heaps, crumbling slowly, open for anyone to wander through and examine. No velvet ropes, no guided tours, no souvenir shops with overpriced postcards, just a few *chowkidars* with not

much to guard against. We presented our cards and sat in a hallway. A servant returned to say that Suleiman was in the bath, but if we waited, he would grant us an audience. For an hour we milled through the hallways, staring at the sepia photographs of Mahmudabad's history— the raja and his court, the raja's father and his British sponsors, the imperial ladies in wide-brimmed bonnets and white dresses wilting in the summer sun.

Finally Suleiman invited us into a sparsely furnished study filled with musty physics books. He was a short, balding man with tufts of graying hair and tortoiseshell glasses. He mentioned nothing about our rudeness in showing up uninvited. I explained that I wanted to learn more about the history of Mahmudabad. It was the last complete sentence I uttered for three hours. Suleiman was off—he talked and talked and talked, leading us on a journey through ten centuries of history, religion, and Eastern thought, digressing here to the fourteenth-century Caliphate of Baghdad, turning there to the rulers of the Gilgit Shias, looping back around to resume the history of Mahmudabad. Eventually his narrative found its way forward to the twentieth century. He talked of Abedi's family.

"Abedi's father and paternal grandfather are Syeds, which means descended from the Prophet. They were all with us since the nineteenth century. They were loyal, people of integrity, moral probity. Maybe they had their weaknesses—rumor has it, with women, but very discreetly. They were generally not known for any controversial behavior. As far as financial matters, revenue matters, their service to the state, their record was unimpeachable. There were no inappropriate embezzlements." (Left unaddressed was the complicated question of what, in feudal economic arrangements, constitutes an appropriate embezzlement.) Abedi himself was "very moved" by the feudalism of Mahmudabad. "As he grows ill and old he is emotional. I saw him in London last year and he wept. He looks upon me almost as he would my father and my grandfather. I went to shake his hand and he took it and pressed it to his chest and began crying. I pulled it away and said he should not be emotional. When my father died, he [Abedi] looked at me and tears flowed from his eyes."

I asked Suleiman what it was like being king. He talked at length about growing up with his father, the last semi-independent raja of Mahmudabad. His father had been caught in palace intrigues at the age of fourteen, accused of conspiring against his decadent father. Later he

became influenced by Gandhi and others in the independence movement. His father was an ascetic. He shunned the splendor of the palace but could not escape it, either. He quarreled with the founders of Pakistan and then abandoned the subcontinent altogether, living out his life in spartan middle-class exile in London, struggling with such mundane challenges as how to hail a taxi and pay the driver. "My father by degrees became extremely religious," Suleiman said. "All alcohol was destroyed. He slept on the floor. He was a cross between a Tolstoy and a Gandhian— romantic, idealistic, very passionate. He was greatly conscious of the fact that wealth cannot be acquired without some injustice. He was not a revolutionary. He did not have any place for Stalin. Yet he was fascinated by Lenin. Gandhi was around a lot and greatly admired him. He constantly emphasized the need to live side by side with the masses—no Savile Row suits. He was very keen to earn his own living. . . . But he felt somehow that money was not quite right."

Suleiman described his own recent homecoming to Mahmudabad's abandoned palaces in the patchwork era of modern, democratic India. The people flocked to see him at the old Mahmudabad fort outside of Lucknow. Suleiman decided to run for political office, for a seat in the state legislature, and he won. At a rally in the fort after his victory, tens of thousands of former Mahmudabad subjects packed themselves inside, chanting and swaying with emotion.

"It was not just the elections—it was some kind of unspoken feeling, a return, a replacement," Suleiman said. "A bond had been reestablished. It showed what my father meant to them. I'm sure there were instances of tyranny and repression during our family's reign, clashes between the cultivators and the peasants. We were not revolutionaries." Mahmudabad's meanings, Suleiman said, are "not irreversible, but it's a part of history."

We said we wanted to see the main palace out in Mahmudabad proper, fifty miles from Lucknow, and he gave us directions. He mentioned the somewhat confusing fact that his wife, a Hindu Brahmin, was at present staying in the Mahmudabad palace in purdah, the Islamic system of strict segregation of women. Thus she could not receive me, but she would probably be glad to talk to Rama. In New Delhi and London, Suleiman's wife enjoyed a modern, liberated life. But when in the kingdom, she did as the kingdom does, covering herself from head to toe and living in

isolation with women from the palace grounds and the surrounding village.

We rattled out to Mahmudabad in our hired Ambassador, antique pride of the centralized Indian automobile industry, a chugging bubble replicating Britain's 1953 Morris Oxford. We passed through the green fields of Uttar Pradesh farm country—paddies, cane, groves of fruit trees. At the palace a corniced yellow archway rose before a shaded lawn. An old man with a white beard and a Nehru cap guarded the entrance with a stick. He ushered us through the decaying grounds and into the musty palace. The drawing rooms and ballrooms and dining room were virtually empty, the furniture having been carted off and sold for cash years before. Lizards darted across the throne-room floor. Goats brayed in the yard. Ten-foot oil portraits of Queen Victoria and the bejeweled rajas loomed from the walls. There was no electricity. We wandered into the rear grounds to take some pictures, past an empty ritual pool. A shower rolled up and doused us with rain. Crows and vultures fluttered to the palace eaves.

When we started back to Lucknow, the Ambassador broke down, so we hiked back to the palace to wait for help in the form of Suleiman, who had said he was coming to Mahmudabad in the evening. We sat with the guards among the yapping stray dogs. Rama went in to visit with the raja's wife, who sat on a carpet in a mildewed, darkened room, instructing local women about their marriages and their problems. When Rama returned, we talked through the sunset about Mahmudabad, and the way history fades and the future rises on the same decayed ground, and everybody—Suleiman, his London-bred wife, Abedi, the Mahmudabad villagers—is understandably confused. As we talked, monsoon clouds raced across the sky. The bell tower struck five times at six o'clock. A bearded mullah sang the call to evening prayer. "Allah O Akbar . . ."

When Suleiman showed up, he agreed to send us back to Lucknow in his own Ambassador, but he said there was a problem. His wife's cousin, a public relations executive from Dubai, was visiting, and he had promised her, too, a ride to Lucknow. In Dubai, she went to work in a skirt and heels, but here she was in purdah and thus could not sit in the backseat with me without offending the sensibilities of Mahmudabad's former subjects and present citizens. Suleiman's scientific mind devised a solution. A black curtain would be erected between the front seat and the back seat of the Ambassador. The car would then back up to the section of the

palace reserved for purdah. Servants would draw enormous black drapes around the car. In this privacy, the cousin and Rama would enter the backseat and secure the curtains. Then the drapes would be withdrawn and I could enter the front seat. I watched this solution unfold in a state of disbelief. Finally climbing into the car, I thanked Suleiman for his hospitality and apologized for the problem caused by our failed Ambassador. He replied that it was no bother. "Uttar Pradesh is a mess," he said. "Nothing works."

In this way we made the two-hour drive to Lucknow, segregated in seventeenth-century Islamic tradition, but chattering all the while in English about shopping and business in Dubai.

––––––

South Asia cannot escape the West, however much some sections of its leadership may wish to do so. The most important commerce in ideas is carried on by people like Suleiman, the millions of South Asians who move freely between the two worlds. The large subcontinental cities mark the intersection. There great tribes of native professionals and business-men and minor royalty, whose families have partially emigrated over the last few decades to countries such as Britain, the United States, and Australia, return to "find" themselves and to cook up a few political and business deals along the way. These émigrés, half in and half out, exude a heightened energy, uncertain about which world to conquer and which set of values to build upon. Often they seem determined to do everything at once. Benazir and Abedi and Suleiman are hardly the only ones. Their stories are replicated hundreds of thousands of times these days in more obscure but no less vivid dramas involving college-age students search-ing for identity, trading families searching for opportunity, writers search-ing for language. Strike up a conversation in the jumbled economy-class cabins of the overbooked 747s jetting between South Asia and the West and you will hear yet another tale: the young Indian engineer coming back from America to an arranged marriage about which he feels ambiva-lent; the expatriate Keralite Muslim construction worker shuttling be-tween his jungle village and Dubai, ferrying bags of electronics and fistfuls of gold; the carpetbagging businessman with a different visiting card for each of his two dozen offshore companies; the daughter of disenfranchised South Asian royalty who observes that for all the privi-leges of living in the West, what she finds most liberating is that every-

body has to clean their own toilet. South Asia and the West talk to each other in a babel of jumbled, misunderstood conversations. The cultural collision resembles the South Asian telephone network, with its "crossed lines" on which you hold a conversation simultaneously with three or four other parties. You can try to talk through the chatter, or you can sit there and yell "Crossed line hai!" until everybody else gets off. Either way, the conversation is fragmentary.

Although South Asia's history raises obstacles to its future, the future's call remains insistent. For one thing, the truth of the cliché about a rapidly shrinking world is nowhere more visible than on the subcontinent. Satellites now beam American and British twenty-four-hour news and sex-pop videos into vast blocks of cable-wired middle-class apartments in New Delhi, Bombay, Madras, Karachi, Lahore, and Islamabad. So large is the appetite for this programming that even the present governing Islamic conservatives in Pakistan have decided to permit domestic CNN broadcasts, though they employ a censor to turn the picture fuzzy whenever a woman appears in a short skirt.

In my New Delhi neighborhood rival underground cable operators literally battled to win the profitable right to sell Western programming. The founder of our particular local franchise spent six years in American prisons on heroin-trafficking charges; presumably he knew the value of a captive audience. He strung his cables on trees and through bushes, and when the system failed, as it did frequently, he sent around circulars blaming his troubles on his enemies and promising victory. One that turned up on our doorstep went like this, the English as found:

THIS IS AN EMERGENCY. Don't Panic. After Receipt of this Circular, immediately DIS-CONNECT our CABLE input Socket from your T.V. Set. Our system has been Sabotaged once again. As promised in our earlier circular, regarding the Re-Vamping of the Cabling, we had somehow accomplished the task to a certain extent, and taken the cables from Rooftop to RoftTop. The same culprits who had earlier indulged in massive sabotage of the cables, after finding that they could no longer reach our cables physically, have in a maddenning Frenzy, adopted the worst method possible. They have run a 220 Volts of Electrical current in our cables; This ugly trick surpasses all moral and Ethical behaviour. It is no more Business!! This Criminal Act has been committed with the slightest regard for human life. . . . Two of our Technicians were badly wounded. We shall have no objection in case you prefer not to wait, by making Alternate Arrangements, from the same people, who have thus far, shown no Mercy, for our members. They could'nt careless whether human

lives are lost, in a Tragic Manner, so long as their coffens are being filled in. . . . We genuinely feel SAD, for this disruption caused by anti-social Elements trying to do hegitimate business, but again in an Illegitimate manner. WITH PROFOUND SORROW . . .

Even totalitarian governments have trouble managing the Information Age; in wide-open South Asia, controlling the spread of new technologies and ideas is a lost cause. In obscure Indian market-town bazaars, entrepreneurs in dilapidated stalls hawk videotapes of Swedish erotica and maudlin American made-for-TV dramas about surrogate motherhood and euthanasia. In all but the very poorest villages television antennae protrude from mud-brick homes that lack piped water. Once, covering an election in Punjab, I drove for hours from timeless village to timeless village with Dinesh Kumar, a young reporter at the *Times* of India. There were few paved roads in the villages but plenty of antennae. In Ludhiana, we weaved through hordes of bicycle rickshaws and stray cows and found a hotel, where we planned to eat lunch. Sikh separatist guerrillas had forced the hotel to close its restuarant, so in order to eat we had to check in and order room service. Our room overlooked a rancid mud garbage dump, but it did have a TV, and we turned it on while waiting for our *samosas*. Up came talk-show host Phil Donahue, speaking earnestly to a New York audience about mother-daughter prostitute teams. Dinesh stared in silence for a while, then turned to ask, "Do people in America really watch this?"

The degree of confusion that arises at the cultural intersection is difficult to overstate. South Asians tend to see their roles as tragic, as was the case with Benazir and Abedi, and it is hard to blame them. But the clash of cultures is also sometimes comic. N. T. Rama Rao, a wildly popular, self-aggrandizing movie-star-turned-politician in south-central India, a man who routinely cast himself as God on the big screen, had a fondness for grandiose symbols. He was especially enamored of statues, and when he got elected as chief minister of Andhra Pradesh state he began erecting them all over Hyderabad, the state capital. A significant percentage of the bankrupt state budget was allocated to commission statues of mythical and historical figures from the region's past. Then Rao fell ill, and like nearly everybody in South Asia who can afford it, he flew off to the West for diagnosis and surgery. In New York, he saw the Statue of Liberty and was awestruck. He pledged to outdo the statue on

behalf of the huddled masses of Andhra Pradesh. On his return to Hyderabad, Rao earmarked more than $5 million in public funds to commission an enormous statue of the Buddha, which he planned to install on a platform in the middle of Hyderabad's central city lake. It would be the largest monolith ever erected. For several years, hundreds of shirtless stone masons chipped away at a granite hillside outside Hyderabad, painstakingly carving the Buddha's figure. But when it was finished, state engineers pointed out to Rao that he had misunderstood something about the Statue of Liberty—it was hollow, and thus not so heavy, whereas the Hyderabad Buddha was solid rock and extremely difficult to move. Unfazed, Rao allocated more money to construct a widened road between the granite mountain and the city center, and he hired transport engineers from Calcutta to build special trucks and barges to move his statue. It took days to roll the Buddha into town, but it was done. At an auspicious dawn selected by astrologers, Rao gathered with city fathers at the shore of the Hyderabad lake to watch the statue be loaded onto a barge and ferried to the platform at the lake's center. But as the barge pulled away from shore, it began to list under the weight of the huge Buddha. The boat tipped this way and that. The statue plunged toward the water, broke free from its straps, and splashed into the depths.

"I worked so hard, found the rock, brought it from such a long way," Rao told me afterward at his house in Hyderabad, where he summoned up what I took to be stage tears during our conversation. "I am sorry. The great saint is lost in the waters of the Hussain Sagar. . . . You [Americans] have the appreciation of the liberty of the nation. I wanted something like that. . . . That would have been my contribution to society."

After several years resting at the bottom of the lake, the statue finally was hauled out of the depths by an engineering company and set on its pedestal. Rao, not coincidentally, did not fare so well. He is at present out of office, trying to decide whether to cast himself as God again in the movies.

You figure that a politician like Rao gets what he deserves. But then there are the ones like Amir Shroff, the Hyderabad junk dealer who once spent an afternoon with me talking about how the West had ruined his life. Shroff caught my attention with one of those unsolicited letters Western correspondents in South Asia frequently receive, the ones describing massive conspiracies afoot to ruin innocent citizens. I read all of these carefully, out of my growing fondness for expressions of political

paranoia. One persistent correspondent in Kanpur wrote every few months to express his outrage that the world was not paying attention to his astrological earthquake forecasts. As for Amir Shroff, it was difficult to tell from the documents he sent—astrological sketches of concentric circles and lotus flowers describing his spiritual and financial predicament—what, exactly, had gone wrong. At first I thought that he might have gotten fleeced by American businesses, and that it might be a good thing to help him. But when Rama and I arranged to see him at his splotched, fetid apartment in Bombay, the problem turned out to be nothing quite so straightforward as that. Shroff had fallen into the great sea of American junk mail and had been unable to climb out. His was a tale of confusion and crossed signals in the postmodern global village.

For twenty years Shroff made a living buying and selling junk in Hyderabad, Rao's city of statues. A brother had moved to Illinois and wrote that America was a land of splendor and opportunity, a place swirling with business deals and millionaires. He invited Shroff to visit. During two stays at his brother's apartment between 1989 and 1991, Shroff found himself dazzled by the ethos of American capitalism. What amazed him most was the mail: the business offers, magazine offers, lottery games, astrological forecasts, and franchise advice brought to his door each day by the letter carrier. Eager to become a millionaire, Shroff dutifully wrote back to the solicitors. By his count, he sent out and received three thousand letters while in the United States. "I just got the idea of how your people live in your country and grab the business," he explained. "I wanted to be a millionaire. I wanted to associate with the big people, no doubt."

And the replies poured in. "Will Amir Shroff win a share of $250 million?" a letter from a magazine clearinghouse began. "Very likely!"

"Now you can add $50 million to your personal Nest Egg," said another.

"Great news!" reported a self-described property researcher in Florida. "My investigative report indicates that there could be many—MANY SHROFFS—that are currently owed unclaimed money from government offices nationwide and YOU, AMIR SHROFF, could be one of them." Shroff could not figure out how his ancestors might have left unclaimed property in the United States, but he assumed it must be true. "To be frank with you, I don't know," he told me. "My forefathers must have some interest in your country. A person living in your country for nine

months has been given so much opportunity." Indeed, letters seemed to come from every corner of the continent and beyond: the Winners Club, the American Constitution Coalition Foundation, American Family Publishers, Global Lottery Agency, Lucky Lottery Service, the Jupiter Pioneer stamp club, the Trade Leaders' Club, and on and on. "I have joined so many clubs over there," Shroff said. "These all came to my residence—I never went anywhere. This was the miracle, I'm telling you."

Moreover, the letters were personal. They called Shroff "my dear." He explained: "All the mail contained the appreciation of Mr. Shroff. Why, I don't know—maybe the destiny and confidence behind me." Inspired, Shroff even wrote to President George Bush at the White House, telling him what a great job he was doing. And the president—or one of his franking machines—wrote back. "Thank you for your warm and thoughtful message," said the signed letter on White House stationery. "I appreciate your comments and am encouraged and strengthened by your kind words as I face the many challenges and opportunities before our country. I am grateful for your support." Shroff, recognizing regal patronage when he saw it, now figured that he had hit the big time. "The postman said to me, 'Mr. Shroff, are you a politician? Why do you get a letter from George Bush?'"

Shroff stumbled into another corner of America's get-rich-quick subculture, the lotteries. He played—and won. "To be frank with you, Lady Luck is with me," he said. "I played twenty dollars and won five hundred dollars instantly. Even sitting in India, I am still playing with the Canadian people. This pays me money the easy way."

Finally it came time for Shroff to return to India. He brought with him all of the correspondence and information about business opportunities he had received through the mail, carefully encased in plastic sheaths and folders. He brought the club membership cards he had been sent—his Discover America at a 50 Percent Discount card, his *Faith Magazine* Life Study Membership Card, his Hertz United States Golf Association card, his Authorized Mason Shoe Dealer Card—and the letters promising he would win millions of dollars soon. Back in Bombay, he gathered up all of his family members and his voluminous files of correspondence and went to the U.S. Consulate to apply for a visa to go back to America. But the consulate turned him down. Its visa department felt, in the circumstances, that Shroff did not intend to return to India, which meant he was ineligible to receive a nonimmigrant visa. The only way he could ever get

an immigrant visa would be to win in the lottery held annually by the U.S. Immigration and Naturalization Service. Devastated, Shroff began calling, writing, faxing, and sending telegrams to Washington daily, looking for help. He said he was disappointed that his friend Bush would not return his calls, but he rings the White House four times daily just in case. He said he was wasting away in his Bombay apartment, waiting for results.

"I want to disclose something very, very important," he said, leaning forward in his stark living room as if about to divulge a secret. "Something is wrong with the government machinery in the United States."

––––––

Since the end of the British Empire, the West has occasionally perceived that it has interests in South Asia, as the United States did during its proxy war against the Soviet Union in Afghanistan. But even the most serious of these interests can hardly be described as vital. Any Western newspaper correspondent filing stories from New Delhi and then looking for them on the front page comes to understand the point quickly. Some South Asians chalk this relative dearth of attention up to racism. But that does not explain very much. The West produces mountains of academic writing, think-tank reports, and journalism about the Middle East and Japan. The point of much of this material is to promote mutual understanding. This is not because of any ebbing of racist attitudes toward Arabs and Japanese. It is because the West perceives material interests in the Middle East and Japan. It sees no comparable interests in South Asia.

The West's indifference matters in South Asia for several reasons. It reinforces the self-interested arguments of the local elites, which use the specter of Western malevolence to resist full integration in the international economy and to protect their own positions of domestic privilege and control. It feeds, too, the subcontinent's traditional fear of things foreign, a state of mind developed during centuries of coping with foreign invaders. Most important, it means that South Asia must struggle—against very great odds—to implement resurgent Western ideas such as democracy and capitalism at a time when the West itself does not seem to care very much about how it all turns out.

The West is indifferent to South Asia but it is not absent. Imperial and cold war history cannot be erased, so they are there to be manipulated by those who benefited most from the postimperial and cold war arrangements. Fragments of ascendant Western culture and material prosperity

flow through on the satellites and crossed lines, but without explanatory footnotes or warning labels. This again leaves those in power, or in pursuit of it, free to supply their own explanations while seeking some version of national liberation or self-aggrandizement. South Asian nationalism and religious revival are two of the obvious, if complex, responses. Blend this landscape of modern, even futuristic, confusion with the rubble of history—the enduring inequities of the old orders, the decomposition of the Nehruvian state, the surging numbers in self-conscious search of opportunity—and there is fertile ground for conflict. The future and the past are simultaneously up for grabs, and there are accounts to be settled before either is won.

STATES

OF

CONFLICT

9

Among the Death Squads

If you have a government that promotes people because they are mass murderers, you have a problem.

—*Mangala Samarweera*

O f all the bonehead mistakes I ever made, arguably the most bone-
headed was the decision to drive away at sunset from the Madhu
bishop's compound. War was on again in Sri Lanka and we had been
driving around in it all day. For reasons I no longer retain it seemed
important to record what we had seen in a brief news story. The difficulty
was that we were stuck in the jungle and the light was going. The bishop
of Madhu had offered to put us up for the night at his cool, whitewashed
compound, a sanctuary in the battlefield where thousands of civilian
refugees were arriving daily to take shelter from the soldiers, guerrillas,
and paramilitary hit squads roaming around their villages. To get back to
the land of international telephone lines from the bishop's place, we
would have to drive along narrow dirt roads through checkpoints
manned by Sri Lanka's Sinhalese security forces. Of course, I was not
planning to do any actual driving; I would leave that to Ron, the cherubic
Sri Lankan madman who had developed a highly lucrative, monopoly-by-
default business of driving journalists around his island's several wars.
Ron's advantage, aside from nerve, was his divided ethnic lineage—half
Sinhalese, half Tamil—which conveniently allowed him to claim that he
was a partisan of whatever side of the ethnic conflict he happened to be
on at any given moment. This kept him alive and kept his passengers

moving through the checkpoints. Ron once drove for the Colombo Hilton but was discharged after returning his polished Toyota with fifty-caliber machine gun bullet holes in the roof and sides. One of these bullets, fired from a helicopter tracking him from overhead, had passed between his parted legs and through the driver's seat. The car company seemed indifferent about the near-miss but was terribly upset about the Swiss-cheese ventilation. So now Ron worked out of his home near the airport and drove scavenged cars on which he erected great white banners proclaiming neutrality in several languages. He was unfailingly cheerful and game for anything, even bonehead ideas like the drive from Madhu.

For thirty minutes we raced along abandoned narrow tracks through elephant grass and groves of palm. We had the windows down and the tape deck on and we mouthed falsetto accompaniment to Michael Jackson. We passed a couple of checkpoints with ease and thought we were nearing the edge of the fighting zone. Darkness fell quickly and the passing palms faded to black.

Suddenly Ron slammed on the brakes. He killed the headlights and the tape deck and the motor.

Somebody was shouting at us in Sinhalese from a distance. Ron interpreted under his breath. Put your hands up. Open the car doors slowly. Step with your hands in the air to the front of the car. Get down on your knees. Move forward down the road on your knees with your hands still up.

Flashlights glanced across us as we followed these instructions. Gun bolts clicked. We couldn't see a thing. Ron began a dialogue in Sinhalese with somebody in the shadows. I could not understand a word but it did not sound as if it was going very well. We moved twenty yards down the road, shuffling humbly in the dirt. Ron, still talking like a Gatling gun, finally rose to his feet and walked forward, telling me under his breath to stay where I was. I knelt like this, reaching to the sky, physically and emotionally frozen, until I heard Ron begin to chuckle. Then he began to laugh. Now three or four people were laughing.

"It's all right," Ron said. "Come ahead." An army captain in fatigues and a T-shirt stood near a barbed-wire bunker. He had a pistol in his hand. Soldiers with assault rifles and shoulder-fired grenade launchers joined the group. They were chattering in rapid Sinhalese and still laughing. Ron,

now in full salesman's mode, had his arm on the captain's shoulder to express collegial intimacy. I asked Ron what the hell was so funny.

"The captain says this is our lucky day—really our lucky day," Ron answered jovially. "He thought we were the enemy. He was this close"— Ron squeezed his thumb and forefinger together—"to ordering his men to open fire. Then I heard him shouting and stopped the car. They had machine guns and grenades trained on our headlights. He was about to yell 'fire' when we stopped. He says this is really our lucky day."

Ron was gritting his teeth but he was laughing nonetheless, so I laughed as well. The captain now felt a need to explain six or seven times what a lucky day this was for us, since he had not killed us. He even digressed into the field of astrology to describe the scale of our good fortune. Yucks all around.

By now I was getting annoyed. I said to Ron, "Tell him that this is certainly our lucky day, but it is also his lucky day, because killing an American reporter, even by innocent mistake, would not be a good thing for a fine officer like himself."

Ron passed this thought along and the captain seemed puzzled by it. He answered in Sinhalese. "He says," Ron explained, "that this is Sri Lanka. If they had killed us, they would have just burned the bodies. Nobody would have ever known."

Right. I had forgotten about that.

We asked for permission to pass through. The captain said there were a few more checkpoints and that he would radio ahead that we were coming. We did not believe him. For two hours we rolled at a crawl, in silence, through the darkness. Whenever we saw a light, we stopped the car, turned off the headlights, got out, raised our hands, and surrendered. We surrendered to two old ladies sitting on their front porch. I believe we surrendered to an old man walking down the road with a flashlight. I definitely recall surrendering to a couple of dogs in somebody's floodlit front yard. Nobody seemed to mind our errors. Sri Lankans understand fear.

The Sri Lankan death squads normally worked at night. They were led by people like our checkpoint captain, mid-level Sinhalese army and police officers at the front lines of the island's counterinsurgency campaigns. From their barbed-wire military and police compounds in the jungle the officers and small squads of soldiers in civilian dress drove out

in Japanese-made jeeps after sunset, yanking young men of certain castes from the streets or from cars or from their homes. Often the young men, suspected revolutionaries, were beaten and interrogated for a few hours. Then they were shot in the head at close range and burned with kerosene. Sometimes their bodies were dumped just before dawn into the muddy rivers that snake through the Sri Lankan jungles. At the Jae-la bridge just north of Colombo, morning commuter traffic into the capital would congeal each morning as drivers and bicyclists stopped to lean over the rails and count the corpses floating down the Jae-la River to the ocean. In the island's south, where the death squads were most active during 1989 and 1990, a popular tactic was to cut off the heads of victims. Soldiers then placed the heads at dawn outside the home of the victim's relatives as a kind of calling card. Estimates of the total number who died or disappeared in this way between 1988 and 1990 are in the tens of thousands. The death squad violence in the south peaked late in 1989 and petered out by the end of 1990. It continues at a reduced level in the north today, amid the war between the Sinhalese army and the Liberation Tigers of Tamil Eelam. But the vast majority of victims of the Sri Lankan death squads have not been northern Tamils allied with the suicide-charging Liberation Tigers. Rather, most of the victims have been southern Sinhalese supposedly allied with the Maoist People's Liberation Front, known as the JVP because of its Sinhalese initials. Those who died in the south shared ethnicity and religion—but not political ideology—with their murderers.

Western polities are organized partially around the assumption that to pluck people from their homes in the night, shoot them, behead them, and burn their corpses at dawn is morally and otherwise intolerable. But what made the Sri Lankan death squads in the island's south so politically peculiar was that few Sri Lankans, even those in parliamentary opposition to the national government, found it possible to draw such firm conclusions. For example, consider that Ranasinghe Premadasa, the Sri Lankan president who presided over the bloody reign of the death squads, was more popular after the terror than before. When a popular democracy in a country with a 90 percent literacy rate is prepared to endorse death squads at the polls, does it tell you that democracy is fatally flawed or that the work of the death squads represented some sort of utilitarian achievement? You could hear both answers on the island.

Sri Lanka is a country that has carried to the most vivid extremes the

same conflicts—over ethnicity, nationalism, religion, political ideology, social equity, economic opportunity, the nature of the state—that bedevil and occasionally threaten the stability of its larger neighbors to the north. The island is a gruesome political laboratory where the rest of South Asia observes and analyzes a possible future that it wishes at all costs to avoid. The difficulty is that the island is so rich with terrible anecdotes, intractable conflicts, and competing theories that it is possible to draw reasonable but diametrically opposed conclusions from the same evidence. By the late 1980s Sri Lankan society had become so polarized by violence and so beset by organized evil that the country, as a Colombo friend put it, quoting Czechoslovakia's Václav Havel, had "lost its ability to distinguish between right and wrong."

Why this happened is a question that arises in part from language of political morality generally muted today in the industrialized West—language used to explain, justify, or defeat revolution.

The People's Liberation Front is—or more properly, was—a self-proclaimed Marxist revolutionary movement that capitalized on the grievances of impoverished but generally well-educated Sinhalese Sri Lankans who felt they had gotten a raw deal from the Nehruvian model erected on their island by the postcolonial English-speaking Sri Lankan elites. Rohan Wijeweera, the son of a small-time Sinhalese Communist politician, was the Liberation Front's leader. He spent years studying Marxism and history in the Soviet Union. While developing the ideology of his revolutionary movement, he traveled extensively around the world and met or corresponded with representatives of China, Cuba, the Southwest Africa People's Liberation Organization in Namibia, the Palestine Liberation Organization, and various Basque separatist guerrillas. He read Che Guevara's and Fidel Castro's speeches and books, titles such as *Those Who Are Not Militant Revolutionaries Are Not Communists* and the tellingly phrased *History Will Absolve Me*. Wijeweera was a charismatic man of modest birth and great ambition who understood intuitively how to push the hot buttons of Sinhalese racial, ethnic, and religious culture. But as for politics, the vocation to which he devoted and ultimately gave his life, he spoke of the crucial questions only in the most wooden language of Marxist theory.

Justifying the mass killing he unleashed first in an aborted revolutionary strike in 1971 and then with greater effect during the late 1980s, Wijeweera said, "Counterrevolutionaries resort to violence. Therefore to

ensure the safe delivery of the new social system it becomes necessary to resort to revolutionary violence against the violence employed by the capitalist class. . . . I am a Marxist-Leninist. I am a modern Bolshevik. I am a proletarian revolutionary. Marxism-Leninism is a clear doctrine. In no way is a Marxist-Leninist a conspirator. I, a Bolshevik, am in no way a terrorist. As a proletarian revolutionary, however, I must emphatically state that I am committed to the overthrow of the prevailing capitalist system and its replacement by a socialist system." This sort of thing sounded as if it were copied from a borrowed revolutionary phrase book. But in all the years of his revolutionary fervor, it was the most Wijeweera ever offered his adherents as theoretical justification for following him into death. There were other emotional buttons that Wijeweera pushed at crucial moments of his revolution—buttons that aroused Sinhalese nationalism and xenophobia. But the leader's politics were unapologetically modern and Bolshevik. He was deeply absorbed by the absurd doctrinal debates and splits within the international Communist movement. At one point, for example, he decided that isolated, tropical Sri Lanka's future depended to a large extent on which side it backed in the Moscow-Beijing split. Wijeweera chose China, devoted many jungle speeches and propaganda pamphlets to explaining his choice, and declared himself a Maoist.

Why such a significant number of Sri Lankan Sinhalese were willing to follow Wijeweera into battle in the late 1980s is a difficult question. Sri Lanka had been for years a center of Trotskyite politics. Yet Wijeweera never commanded anything like a majority, even among the Sinhalese. The baseline of his support is perhaps best measured by the 273,428 votes he won in a 1982 presidential election, the only one he ever participated in. This placed Wijeweera third in the balloting, way behind the two major parties but strong enough to surprise Sri Lanka. Rohan Gunaratna, the Sinhalese historian who has published the only thorough, balanced history of the Liberation Front, writes that aside from his personal charisma, ruthlessness, and ambition, Wijeweera built a meaningful movement because he "successfully blended Marxism and racialism and created a doctrine which attracted the Sri Lankan rural educated unemployed youth," of which there were many, as there are in all of South Asia. Wijeweera preached of paradise—free education, jobs for all—but also of revenge, the rightful taking back of the state's resources from the post-colonial elites. Wijeweera "became the first Sri Lankan politician to come

from a village background, from a family with less wealth, less influence and less education—and to challenge and to threaten the average Sri Lankan politician who came from a wealthy, influential and elitist background," Gunaratna wrote.

Wijeweera's "success" remains disturbing to many members of neighboring South Asian elites, in part because he operated in social and economic conditions that were not fundamentally different from those in, say, India or Pakistan or even Bangladesh. If you ask Sinhalese Sri Lankans to short-list the inequities and failings of the Nehruvian state that fed the rise of Wijeweera and his brutal Liberation Front, you will hear a list of problems found to one degree or another across all of the subcontinent. You will hear about the divisive language problem on the island, and the greedy mendacity of the Colombo elites, and the historical cycles of ethnic and religious conflict, and the lingering problems of caste and landed feudalism, and the high unemployment rates, and the inequitable economic consequences of the island's government-dominated mixed socialist and capitalist system. All this combined in southern Sri Lanka to give birth to a generation of idle, intelligent, ambitious young people susceptible to rebellious ideology and to manipulation by a man like Wijeweera. Most of the serious writing in Sri Lanka about the reasons for the Liberation Front's rise concentrates on specific, avoidable mistakes the Colombo government made—the decision to segregate Sinhalese and Tamil language education in 1956, the ambivalence about democracy during the early 1980s, the decision to ban the Liberation Front in 1984 on the pretext that Wijeweera led the horrible anti-Tamil riots in Colombo in 1983, when in fact it was the government's own thugs who led these attacks. These errors were indeed serious and they strengthened the Liberation Front. But once the revolutionary movement began, the dynamics of insurgency and counterinsurgency also influenced its development. The Sri Lankan security forces cracked back with brutal violence, creating martyrs, which further inspired the revolutionary movement. At the same time, the movement's adherents discovered that in impoverished, insecure societies such as those in South Asia there is unusual profit in revolution—with a gun and a bandana and a threatening pamphlet, you can walk into any shop in town and extort decent amounts of money, even if you don't know Marx from Engels.

Every South Asian insurgency is unique. But the several dozen under way in the region today do have in common a backdrop of postcolonial

state failures. And many share a pattern of violence—an internal dynamic of insurgency and counterinsurgency—that dates to the colonial period and before. Modern South Asian governments are quick and thorough when deploying force to defeat prospective revolutions, as were the British, who taught their successors what they know. Arguably Sri Lanka's counterinsurgency campaign against Wijeweera and his People's Liberation Front is distinguished not so much by the fundamental conditions in which it occurred as by its extreme brutality. At a moment of exceptional weakness in the history of the independent Sri Lankan state, Wijeweera and his followers nearly brought the whole house down. They were defeated in a bloodbath the likes of which South Asia has not seen since the partition of Pakistan. This is the aspect of Wijeweera that does, and should, interest the rest of South Asia most today. Whether it is the Indian government in Punjab and Kashmir, or the Pakistan government in Baluchistan and Sind, or the Bangladesh government in the Chittagong Hill Tracts, the present, often structurally weak subcontinental regimes wrestle continually with how they should calibrate counterinsurgency in order to prevail and survive. Particularly, they wrestle with the question of force versus negotiation. And when they look to Sri Lanka, they find ambiguous lessons about the uses of death squads.

In the summer of 1989 Wijeweera and the People's Liberation Front had the Sri Lankan state on its knees. The entire capital of Colombo seemed to feel the way I did kneeling on the dirt road that night near Madhu: frozen, waiting for the sound of the end. When you drove in from the airport, the only people on the streets were soldiers. On that thirty-mile stretch there were perhaps fifty checkpoints and roadblocks manned by jittery teenagers. Wind came in off the ocean and blew trash all about the roads, much of it dire propaganda posters pasted up by the invisible cadres of the Liberation Front and then torn down by the security forces to tumble in the abandoned streets. There were no cars or buses—the Liberation Front had banned them as part of a general strike it called in anticipation of the state's imminent overthrow, and its cadres had shot dead enough drivers to put the point across. In the previous year Wijeweera, after two decades of planning, had taken his revolution to the edge of the envelope. His followers threw hand grenades into buses and shops to kill those who refused to pay extortion money. They carried out random assassinations of civil servants, policemen, and soldiers. They infiltrated the ranks of national police and the army, distributed pam-

phlets, and delivered secret lectures about the coming revolution. To demoralize those in the security forces who would not go along, Wijeweera ordered his men to enter the homes of policemen while they were off at work, slaughter their wives and children with knives and guns, and then leave the bodies to be discovered when the policemen came home. As these gruesome attacks multiplied, the demoralization of civil society worsened. By late July, the end seemed near. Sri Lanka would fall to the Liberation Front—this was no longer Wijeweera's pipe dream, it was a serious possibility. The Front issued propaganda declaring that they were soon going to do to the families of army officers what they had already done to the families of the police—that is, murder them in cold blood—if the officers did not resign. The army was the ticket to national power and it seemed in danger of crumbling from within.

There were few illusions in Sri Lanka about what the Liberation Front would do if it seized national power. These were not cuddly Sandinistas with a Hollywood auxiliary. Wijeweera spoke of ethnic, religious, and class conflict in the most violent terms. He endorsed and practiced political murder on a wide scale. If he took Colombo, there would be slaughter—widespread "ethnic cleansing," as it is called today in the former Yugoslavia, as well as large-scale political retribution. Everybody in the capital knew it. It was already happening, incrementally.

At this point Premadasa's government, in a spasm, abandoned its attempts at negotiation with Wijeweera and unleashed the death squads in full fury. According to Sri Lankan politicians, security force officers, and international human rights groups, the Colombo government deliberately recruited policemen who had lost their wives and children in bloody Liberation Front attacks, sent them into the areas of the south where the Front had made the most progress, and told them to do whatever was necessary to defeat the enemy. This method of counterinsurgency, acknowledged only in elliptical terms by its architects, such as state defense minister Ranjan Wijeratne, had begun in 1988. In July of 1989, with the state apparatus teetering, the government let it be known that it had adopted a new, modified policy: for every relative of a policeman or soldier killed by the Liberation Front, ten allies of Wijeweera would be rounded up and summarily executed.

After this announcement, to travel in Sri Lanka's death squad country was to tour a strange landscape of slaughter and silence. This was the time of the Mitsubishi Pajero jeeps with no license plates and the midnight

knocks and the burning bodies rolled up on the pristine white beaches. In the Liberation Front strongholds, young men began to disappear at a rate of four hundred to five hundred per week. Diplomats at one Western embassy in Colombo counted six thousand actual corpses. But thousands of other young Sinhalese just disappeared. Some of them undoubtedly fed the smoldering piles of ash and bone fragments that I would come across from time to time on southern roadsides, usually a few hundred yards from a security force checkpoint. When a severed head or a full corpse with a burning tire around it turned up, crowds of villagers gathered and stared, mute. The message delivered by the besieged government got around quickly.

One of the strange things about Sri Lanka was that the tourists kept coming—Italians, Germans, and East Europeans drawn by the fine sands and budget prices. They went jogging when the sun came up, literally hopping over the bodies of the dead. Both the Liberation Front and the government declared foreigners off-limits in their war, to encourage the uninterrupted flow of vital foreign exchange.

I drove with Ron one afternoon through the jungle to Kotagoda, the seaside fishing village that was Wijeweera's birthplace. Since nearly any organization in South Asia begins with family and clan, to defeat the Liberation Front the death squads had decided to slaughter every young man they could find who traced his roots to the place where Wijeweera belonged. As a consequence, there were only old men and a few women left in Wijeweera's village. They wandered into Kotagoda by day to do a little farming and fishing. Nobody would sleep there at night, they said. Too many severed heads. One woman had been beheaded ten days before, the villagers said. It was unusual for a woman to be murdered by the death squads but not unheard-of, they added. The villagers stood talking like this in a spectacular setting—coral sea sparkling in tropical sun, lush palms and wildflowers all around. They pointed around the horizon as if directing a tourist to a hotel. Over there, see, is where they burn most of the bodies in the night. Here is where the tide brings the corpses ashore. Down there is where most of the severed heads show up.

As we spoke, a jeep raced into the village. It stopped thirty yards down the road. It had no license plates. Armed men in civilian dress climbed out, charged up a hillside, then returned a few minutes later yanking a teenager by the collar. They threw the young man into the back of their jeep

and sped off. Brazen—it wasn't even dark yet. For all practical purposes, we had just witnessed a murder. What were we supposed to do now, call the police?

In the nearby town of Matara we drove to the headquarters of the local commander of the security forces, appropriately housed inside an old Dutch colonial fort. At the razor-wire gates were hundreds of women standing in clumps under the hot sun, some holding umbrellas. They wore colorful saris and blouses. They were the mothers of the disappeared, lined up in search of answers. Every morning they showed up at the fort at dawn, hoping for an audience with the colonel inside. It had reached the point where the colonel handed out numbered tickets to control the flow. Only the first hundred mothers got numbers, so they had to leave their homes in the jungle at two or three in the morning each day to reach Matara in time to get a ticket. Even then, the mothers said, they rarely got any answers. Occasionally a son turned out to be alive and in a detention camp on suspicion of being a member of the Liberation Front. Mostly, though, there was no news. The colonel usually said that the boy in question must have been killed by Wijeweera's men, the mothers reported. They clustered around Ron and me, wailing and crying, thrusting forward photographs and identity cards of their missing sons.

I pushed inside the overheated, concrete building. There were more mothers inside, seated in silence on wooden chairs beneath spinning ceiling fans. After a time, the colonel invited me in. Death squads, shmeath squads—he didn't want to talk about any death squads. But he would be glad to talk about the Liberation Front and how he was on the verge of ending their revolution.

"The Liberation Front were virtually in control when we came in," the colonel began. "People were living in fear. They were collecting funds. They were saying, 'Stop work. Stop buses.' Once, when I first arrived, the presidential mobile secretariat came down here and the Liberation Front tried to disrupt it with bombs and grenades. But they have not succeeded. When we established control the fear went out from the public. You see, for an insurrection to succeed, it must have public support. But the public resented it. They did not have the public sympathy. It was forced on the public. Anybody would fear for his life. It went on and on and people started becoming disenchanted."

I mentioned that a previous Sri Lankan government had felt once

before, in 1971, that it had beaten the people's Liberation Front with violence. They had been wrong. What made him think it wouldn't happen all over again, this time worse than before?

"We've taken on youth training to try to prevent future insurrections," the colonel answered. "We're training hundreds of young people in the army youth-training program. There's no pay but there are one or two courses under way. We have about thirty-five hundred applicants in Matara alone. We're teaching them secretarial skills, masonry, carpentry, and how to make garments."

In fact, Premadasa was smarter than that. As a southern Sinhalese of low-caste birth, the first leading mainstream politician of that background in Sri Lankan history, he was well positioned to steal Wijeweera's revolutionary thunder by challenging some of the power of the English-speaking high-caste elites whom Wijeweera held up as the implacable enemy. By his birth alone, Premadasa assured many ordinary Sri Lankans that he had their welfare at heart. He mixed free market reforms with visible welfare schemes, modernism with obscurantist, apoplectic Sinhalese nationalism. By these means Premadasa tried after 1989 to overtake Wijeweera's original appeal and substitute a political vision grounded in a functional, if brutal and flawed, parliamentary democracy.

But Premadasa surely knew as well as anyone that it was the death squads, and not his calculated political chauvinism, that defeated the People's Liberation Front. This was accomplished by mid-1990 and brought Sri Lanka back from the brink of revolution. The decisive event occurred on November 12, 1989, when roving security force units in plainclothes found Wijeweera in hiding in a southern village called Ulapane and arrested him. He died of multiple gunshot wounds in the early hours of the next day. His body was burned. After that, the Liberation Front began to dissolve and then to collapse. The Sri Lankan government claims Wijeweera was shot trying to escape and that he was cremated according to tradition, "under conditions of maximum security," as the official release put it, as if a corpse might be prone to rash acts. Nobody in Sri Lanka believes this claim, there are witnesses who contradict it, and it does seem an unnecessary fiction. If it is possible to suggest that death squads have moral authority, the authority of the Sri Lankan death squads arose from the belief—held not only by Premadasa and his henchmen but by what seems in retrospect to have been a solid majority of Sri Lankans—that the mass state-sponsored murder of 1989 and 1990 was

justified in the circumstances by the greater evil contained in the imminent triumph of the People's Liberation Front. The climactic act of this essentially popular campaign of national murder now appears to have been the summary execution of Wijeweera himself, an event most Sri Lankans actually celebrated.

Premadasa did not speak in these terms because it remains the official position of Sri Lanka's parliamentary democracy that state-sponsored paramilitary death squads operating beyond the reach of law represent a political crime. Premadasa and the Western governments that poured hundreds of millions of dollars in public and private capital into the Colombo government throughout the death squad campaign must operate instead by the tacit understanding that while the death squads were acceptable this one time because of the extremity of the Liberation Front threat, they are not acceptable in principle. This allowed Premadasa to posture as a man of peace and it allows squeamish Western governments to posture about their commitment to the protection of human rights. Premadasa suppressed the full truth about how the death squads won the war in the south because he controlled the government and found his approach politically expedient; the Western governments generally sidestep the full truth about the death squads because Sri Lanka is too obscure to make it necessary to do otherwise, and because now that the war in the south is won, they wish to get on with the business of rescuing Sri Lanka from itself and profiting from Premadasa's commitment to international capitalism. In the jungles are the ghosts of at least twenty thousand murder victims. The Colombo government and its outside sponsors are not morally capable of exorcising them.

To neighboring South Asian governments the lesson is clear enough. If you are prepared to cope with some public-relations irritations, you can get away with state-sponsored murder on the subcontinent in the late twentieth century if you succeed in arguing that national survival is at stake, if you succeed in painting your opponents as a greater evil than your own government, and if you are otherwise prepared to cooperate with the larger international priorities of the West. And another lesson has been reaffirmed: Death squads, properly calibrated with the will of a beleaguered majority, can be a decisive means to tactical victory.

After the death squads had finished their work in southern Sri Lanka, I sat down for a few hours one afternoon in Colombo with Neelan Tiruchelvam, a lawyer and research analyst whose ability to articulate

questions of political morality in a country that seems to have so little of it is truly astounding. I asked about the legacy of state murder.

"There are very deep scars, I think. In the southern areas there are so many people who are victims of violence or people who have been tortured and who are still struggling to reconstruct their lives. There is very little support for them in terms of emotional support, legal support. But what is very, very strange about Premadasa's government and its relationship to those areas where there was the greatest oppression is that in the most recent local government elections, the government did better in those areas than in previous years. This shocked people. Part of the explanation is, I think, the way the Liberation Front itself behaved. They were so ruthless that the restoration of some degree of normalcy was welcomed."

What about the argument, the lesson of the war for many Sri Lankans, especially those in power, that the death squads were a necessary and even justifiable evil?

"Well, as far as the government is concerned, they won't apologize for what happened. There are lots of people, I think, in the middle class also who would say that. That is, we had no other choice. But I find it difficult to accept the inevitability of repression in any situation, even one as bad as what happened here with the Liberation Front. But they say, Well, you are only able to talk like this because we went in and cleared the ground for you to survive. So it's an extraordinary instance. I don't see a parallel in history. . . . It's extremely dangerous as an example. People are genuinely convinced this is the right thing to do."

I was in a hotel room in Istanbul, Turkey, on May 1, 1993, the day an unidentified young Sri Lankan man with high explosives strapped to his body approached Premadasa at a political rally in downtown Colombo and pushed a detonator. The suicide bomber, Premadasa, and about a dozen others died instantly in a massive explosion. The news came through on CNN, whose announcer mourned the loss of a great Sri Lankan statesman who had dedicated his life to the unity of his fractious island. The death squads were not mentioned. The story passed from American television screens within a day—another ethereal, violent mystery of the East.

———

Organized, state-sponsored political murder is practiced regularly and on a significant scale in South Asia today not only in Sri Lanka but in the disputed Indian states of Punjab and Kashmir. Government counterinsurgency campaigns also persist in the Indian northeast, in Pakistan's Sind Province, in the hills of Bangladesh, and in other areas. At the moment, most of these other counterinsurgency programs are in various states of remission.

In Punjab and Kashmir several thousand people die annually in low-intensity wars of insurgency fought between Indian security forces—police, paramilitary troops, and regular army soldiers—and a fractured array of dozens of separatist, religious, and revolutionary guerrilla groups. In Punjab, guerrillas claiming to represent the state's ethnic and religious Sikh majority are attempting achieve total independence from New Delhi. In Kashmir, guerrillas claiming to represent the state's Muslim majority also seek total independence from New Delhi. The Indian government, arguing that neither guerrilla movement represents the popular will and that in any case secession of any part of the Indian union is unacceptable, has suspended most of its civil and criminal legal code and deployed hundreds of thousands of troops to defeat the guerrillas with force.

In Punjab, this years-long counterinsurgency campaign has been accompanied by sporadic but unsuccessful attempts at political negotiation with the separatists. In Kashmir, the government does not yet feel that the "situation on the ground," as Indian officials refer to it, has "ripened" sufficiently to warrant meaningful political initiative. This process of ripening involves an attempt to weaken the guerrilla groups—which are not as unified or as committed as Wijeweera's Liberation Front was in Sri Lanka—with unbridled force. A substantial number of the annual victims of violence, perhaps several hundred in Kashmir and as many as one thousand or more in Punjab, are young men suspected of being insurgents, who are arrested and murdered in custody by Indian security forces.

After an extensive investigation in Punjab during 1989 and 1990, the human rights group Asia Watch concluded that these killings "are not aberrations but rather the product of a deliberate policy known to high-ranking security personnel and members of the civil administrations in Punjab and New Delhi. Moreover, there is credible evidence to indicate

that, in some cases, the police have actually recruited and trained extra-judicial forces to carry out many of these killings." In other words, death squads. Everything I saw and heard during half a dozen visits to besieged Kashmir suggested the same was true there as well. In both places, however, death squads operate on a considerably lesser scale than they did in 1989 and 1990 in southern Sri Lanka.

The political heirs to Jawaharlal Nehru and Mohandas Gandhi have a much tougher time coping with the political morality of their death squads than Premadasa had in Sri Lanka. India's international credibility depends on its self-image as a humane, even spiritual, democracy. Confronted with evidence about state-sponsored murder in the half-empty chambers of the United Nations Human Rights Commission in Geneva or the General Assembly in New York, Indian diplomats respond by chanting the mantra of democracy—the basic syllogism is, we have elections, therefore we are not killers. They fall back, too, on the old xenophobic defenses, accusing human rights investigators of undermining India's sovereignty on behalf of neo-imperial interests. At the same time, the Indian diplomats do all they can to assure the world that their opponents in the insurgency wars represent a greater evil than themselves—the Sikh guerrillas are international terrorists implicated in plane hijackings and bombings and massacres of unarmed civilians, the diplomats remind us, and the Kashmir guerrillas are Islamic fundamentalists armed by outlaw states. This tack, despite the counterpropaganda efforts of Sikhs and Kashmiris living in the West, works reasonably well. The Indian government has every reason to believe that it can get away with its present level of state-sponsored murder in Punjab and Kashmir indefinitely, particularly now that New Delhi's embrace of free market reform has enlivened the interests of Western governments.

Consider, for example, G. N. Saxena, the Indian governor of Kashmir at the time of my visits. Saxena, a senior civil servant with a pencil mustache, sat in a sprawling, well-tended colonial mansion on a hill above Srinagar's picturesque Dal Lake. He rarely left his mansion except by helicopter because if he had driven through the valley below, the rebellious Kashmiris would almost certainly have killed him. From his aerie he supervised the Kashmir counterinsurgency—the long curfews, the daily house-to-house searches, the retaliatory arson attacks against entire villages, the mass arrests, torture, and murder. Each time I went to Kashmir, I stopped in to hear the governor explain in his isolated mansion how,

while it might not be entirely evident to a foreigner like me, the situation on the ground was actually getting better and better. During one recent visit, we were discussing some incremental evolution in Kashmiri guerrilla tactics when the governor suddenly intervened in a tone of great annoyance, not with me but with the pesky revolutionaries who filled his life with such stress.

"This kind of tinkering with the war is a nuisance," the governor said, referring to the new guerrilla tactics. "What are they achieving? This kind of thing—we can live with it for centuries."

It was a rare outburst of honesty, but hardly anyone in or out of India doubts it, except the faithful among the Kashmiris and the Sikhs. Of course, as was true in Sri Lanka, the prediction depends on the stability and durability of the Nehruvian state. Those in the senior ranks of the Indian counterinsurgency programs—governors, army officers, police officers, intelligence officers—do not often question the state's strength or righteousness because they are its living embodiment. They see the challenge before them in terms of centuries not so much because of some abiding faith in the future but because of the historical continuity in their own roles. In effect, they did this work for the moguls, they did this work for the British, they did it earlier for the independent Indian government in places like Bengal and the tribal northeast, and they will carry on doing it in the name of Nehruvian democracy. As members of a permanent and prosperous class, they can afford the long view.

K. P. S. Gill, the Sikh chief of police in Punjab and the director of that state's counterinsurgency programs—a man widely held responsible for the extrajudicial killings of hundreds, if not thousands, of Sikh youth—insisted that I understand this point one evening at his official residence in Chandigarh, the Punjab capital. The occasion for my visit was one of those sporadic attempts by New Delhi to quell the Sikh rebellion through some sort of democratic negotiation, rather than purely by force. This time the initiative was an election. I wanted to hear what such a champion of force as Gill thought of the idea, and he invited me over. His house, on one of Chandigarh's broad, suburban, semiprosperous streets, was surrounded by barbed wire, sandbags, and bunkers. Floodlights shone over the lawns and the driveway. When I arrived, Gill was not there, so turbaned soldiers ushered me into his drawing room to wait. A few aides passed through, some hobbling on canes necessitated by wounds inflicted in past terrorist attacks. Gill turned up long after dark in a convoy of

Ambassadors weaving this way and that through the streets, red lights flashing, curtains drawn across the windows, decoy cars turning back and forth to confuse potential assassins.

The chief strode in, greeted me perfunctorily, sat down in an armchair, propped up his feet, and ordered a full bottle of Royal Velvet Scotch Deluxe Malt Whisky, brewed in Bombay. He seemed the personification of the colonial Sikh—a tall, bony man with a waxed mustache, a trimmed gray beard, and clipped Oxbridge diction. He wore that night a maroon turban, a smoking jacket, and a tie. He poured himself a tall glass of whisky, downed it, and continued drinking one after another. Within an hour he had imbibed at least seven. Our conversation turned to the problem of revolution and terrorism. Democracy, Gill made clear, was no solution.

"The situation is evolving too fast for the human rights activists to keep pace with it," he said. "Ultimately terrorism will die a natural death. It may take a little time. It may take a longer time. But there is no ideology behind it. The problem with the Sikhs today is that it is a progressive community saddled with a backward-looking political leadership. . . . Their killings are so pointless. They don't even send a message. The creation of terror by itself, I don't think that was advocated by any of the ideologues. The classical theory is much different from what is being worked out here."

Well, then, I asked, what should be done?

"Has any democracy answered that question in the face of a problem like this?" he replied. "Against state power, you can't use violence. It just doesn't work. What a political solution boils down to today is elections. But elections are no solution. . . . Look, in Punjab there has always been this grudging admiration of the outlaw. Even when I was a child, if a *dacoit* [bandit] was killed by the police, a thousand people would come to see the body of the dacoit, which would be displayed. And we would hear exaggerated details of the dacoit's physical prowess. Today it is that same thing. The militant is fighting. He is battling the police. It's a grudging admiration. The police have never been popular in Punjab. I remember as children the idea was, when we traveled to a village, we had to reach it before sunset. It's the same thing today. And the so-called 'fake encounters' [death squad killings] were a part of the Punjab administration in those days, too. Some district commissioners were remembered popularly for wiping out dacoitaries through fake encounters. . . . The general who

fought Napoleon in Russia, his motto was 'Time and patience.' All you need is time and patience."

His speech was milky now, cloudy and fluid, and he began to talk about religion, what stands between a man and the Creator. I came back to democracy. If you organize yourself around that idea, then don't you have to have faith in it in a situation like the one in the Punjab? Won't the violence Gill advocates—indeed, practices unapologetically—finally undermine democratic society?

"Elections are a very minor episode," Gill said. "They don't matter at all. Only you people are sold on elections. The problem is human nature. Terrorism is an inevitable product of human expression. I don't know how much time I've spent reading Walt Whitman—a lot of time. Now, with all this, there's so little time to read and recollect. I sometimes think I could turn and live with the animals. Not one of them is dissatisfied. Walt Whitman, he was not a poet. He was a saint. 'I Hear America Singing.'"

Now Gill began to recite stanzas of Whitman. He began to recite Ezra Pound.

I asked again about terrorism and counterterrorism in Punjab, the uses of state power that he endorsed. Gill stood dramatically and walked to his bookshelf. He returned with a copy of *Any Old Iron*, a 1989 novel by Anthony Burgess that concerns the recovery of King Arthur's sword, Excalibur, and how there no longer seem to be any human causes worthy of the sword's might. Gill thumbed through the pages and then handed me the open book, his finger on a particular paragraph.

"Read this," he pronounced in a deep voice.

The passage concerned the narrator's recollected impressions of the Wailing Wall in Jerusalem. It read:

I saw fists and howling mouths and then Weizmann's own acetone at work, and I was visited by a philosophical speculation rather mature for a boy of nine: that religious and political causes were only pretexts for smashing things and people; it was the smashing that mattered. Human beings were balls of energy, masses of fleshly acetone, and the energy could best be fired to a destructive end, creation being so difficult and requiring brains and imagination. But since man is a creature of mind as well as nerve and muscle, some spurious cause has to justify destruction. Destruction, best expressed in this age in which I write as terrorism, is truly there for its own sake, but the pretence of religious or secular patriotism converts the destructive into the speciously creative.

I wondered afterward whether it becomes easier or more difficult to do what Gill does—round up the angry young men, supervise the interrogations and torture and killings, take the war to the enemy—if you think like this. Gill seemed to find some solace in it, or else in his whisky. To me, this sort of nihilism was more chilling even than the purposeful, visible state murder in the Sri Lankan jungles. There the death squads operated in a twisted, brutal climate of political morality. Gill's vision was darker. It existed outside of conventional political morality because it rejected politics—rejected, even, human nature.

Soon Gill wanted to go to sleep. He poured a last whisky and recited more poetry. Then he shook my hand and said good night. Tomorrow, he reminded me politely, was another day of counterrevolution.

10

The Boys

We don't call this mass action. We are playing and kidding with
our weapons.

—Amir, Twenty-two-year-old
Kashmiri guerrilla

The publicists over at the Party of God agreed one afternoon to take
me out to see some of their kidnap victims in the Kashmiri countryside. They wanted to talk about their revolution and make me understand
just how strong, righteous, and humane they really were.

We arranged to meet in the hallway of a public building in Srinagar,
Kashmir's once-idyllic summer capital. The separatist insurgency in Kashmir is such that it is possible to meet and commune with armed young
Muslim guerrillas just about anywhere in the valleys that meander
through the region's snow-capped Himalayan peaks. The Indian government's several hundred thousand heavily equipped counterinsurgency
troops, non-Kashmiri and non-Muslim, are certainly a visible presence,
but they generally have little clue as to what exactly is going on in the
slum warrens and villages around their sandbag bunkers and barbed-wire
encampments. Or, if they know, they prefer not to intervene casually out
of fear of the consequences. So the guerrillas move freely through the
civilian population with AK-47 assault rifles cradled beneath traditional
draping Kashmiri *phirans*. They go shopping like this, hang out at ga-
rages, repair their motorbikes, and attend the extraordinary number of
secret strategy sessions necessitated by the existence in Kashmir of at
least one hundred fifty distinct separatist guerrilla organizations and

factions. In this environment, meeting a conspicuously white man in a public building and taking him out to see a couple of kidnapped Hindus is no problem at all.

My escort was a clean-shaven seventeen-year-old who smiled and chattered a lot. I felt a little sorry for him because as much as the guerrillas are confident about their control of the Kashmir Valley, the foot soldiers they send to escort foreigners through enemy lines must be low indeed on the guerrilla organization chart. But my friend didn't seem to mind. He was having fun. He climbed into the front seat of my hired Ambassador. I scrambled into the back with Ghulam Nabi Khayal, the Kashmiri journalist with whom I traveled regularly. Khayal's credibility with both sides in the war made working in Kashmir a relative breeze. As we rolled out of Srinagar, he struck up a rapport with the young man from the Party of God, or Hizbollah, an affiliate of the notorious Iranian-backed Lebanese Shiite outfit responsible for Western hostage-taking and other acts of political terrorism in the Middle East. The leader of Kashmir's Hizbollah told me he met with and received training and support from brethren in the Lebanese Hizbollah, but despite all the talk of pan-Islamic holy war on both sides, it was hard to see that the two parties had much in common. For one thing, the Kashmiri version of the Party of God was not Shiite, it was Sunni. For another, it was not especially anti-Western—there had been no American troop presence in South Asia to stir its wrath. Moreover, the Kashmiri members had so many cousins in America that they seemed more interested in obtaining visas than in vanquishing the Great Satan. I had the impression that the Kashmir Hizbollah chose its affiliation primarily for the terrorist cachet, hoping the Lebanese party's tough reputation might rub off on them. Besides, in South Asia people may find reason to treat each other brutally but they are almost uniformly hospitable to outsiders. In traditional South Asian culture, hospitality is a code of honor and any lapse can be a cause for shame. In tricky situations, I put my faith in the old codes, although there were times when I worried, in self-interest, about the degree to which modern ideology, particularly militant Islam, might be overtaking traditional attitudes. In any event, that afternoon in Srinagar, my young escort to the holy war offered no cause for alarm. We had talked for only ten minutes and were not yet out of Srinagar when he turned around from the front seat and announced, "My colleagues said I should blindfold you but I have not—because I trust you."

For an hour we wound on narrow asphalt roads through ripe paddy fields. The air was cool and dry. It was a fine day for the harvest. Village women wrapped in scarves bent in the fields with sickles. Above them rose mountains cast violet and blue in undulating light and shadow. Occasionally we passed a dozen or more Indian soldiers on patrol, clad in full camouflage combat gear. They walked in rank along the roads with their weapons pointed forward. In search of an invisible enemy, they looked exceedingly anxious and unhappy. I thought inevitably of Vietnam and the predicaments of armies of occupation, for that is what the Indian counterinsurgency forces in Kashmir resemble these days. For the most part, the villagers paid them no mind and the soldiers kept to themselves. As in Sri Lanka, Kashmiris say the soldiers turn brutal most often in the night, when the darkness cloaks their faces and provides them a kind of moral and military parity with the invisible guerrillas.

We stopped the car in a grove of trees beside an icy, olive, swift-running river and began what became a two-mile single-file walk, with our escort at the lead. A weapon appeared in the boy's hands and he moved confidently through bucolic scenes—children diving into river water from rickety footbridges and trees, duck families nesting beneath houseboats, bulls and cows wandering languidly along village footpaths. Villagers waved to our guerrilla, whether in affection or prudence it was impossible to tell. Our escort commandeered a river boat and stood at its bow as we were poled across. "Where we have taken them, even the angel of death cannot reach them," he said dramatically over his shoulder.

In the rice fields beyond, bearded mujaheddin, or holy warriors, emerged from picket posts in the surrounding trees and approached with assault rifles. They patted us down and pointed us on to an isolated three-story brick house encased in trees beside a narrow, cold stream.

Inside we met Hizbollah's military leadership. The oldest of them was twenty-six. They wore Western urban fashions—blue jeans, jacked-up athletic shoes, mirrored sunglasses—but also long Islamic beards. There was some discussion about my Nike Air Jordan basketball shoes and where these might be obtained. Laughs and emphatic soul handshakes were offered. We asked in ritual fashion to see their weaponry and they obliged with pride. There were the usual Chinese-made imitation Russian assault rifles, the kind originally supplied by the CIA to the Afghan resistance. Normally the Kashmiri guerrillas will trot out a few heavier weapons, such as mounted machine guns, land mines, or long-range

sniper rifles, to impress visitors. But this time our hosts were concerned about their ability to break down quickly and move out with their hostages as soon as our interview was complete, so they did not have much of the top-drawer stuff with them. Shaheed-ul-Islam—a nom de guerre—Hizbollah's acting chief commander (the real chief being in prison), did, however, have an impressive hunting knife, which he unsheathed conspicuously and fingered as we talked. I asked him about it and he said he acquired it in Afghanistan, where some of the Kashmiri guerrillas have sought training from their brethren in holy war.

"It is the same kind that Rambo uses," Islam said with a smile. Rambo, you may recall, in one of his Roman-numeraled fantasy adventures, singlehandedly slaughtered dozens upon dozens of evil Afghan and Soviet Communists while attempting the rescue of a captured American military adviser. For this reason and perhaps others, among South Asian guerrillas, Rambo is hip.

The hapless captives, Mr. and Mrs. Wakhloo of Srinagar, sat on the carpeted floor of a damp, empty room downstairs. As Hindus, they were members of a religious minority in Kashmir, but they were also heirs to their community's traditional role of privilege in the Kashmir Valley. This inheritance had now been taken from them by force by a gang of teenagers. The Wakhloos seemed understandably ambivalent about this meeting, anxious on the one hand to convey greetings and messages to relatives, but worried on the other about saying something that might annoy the boys with the guns. I had no intention of writing about the Wakhloos' case at any length, and certainly no intention of giving public credit to Hizbollah for their civilized conduct of kidnappings. Many of the hundreds of Hindus who have been kidnapped at gunpoint from their homes by Kashmiri Muslim guerrillas eventually find their way home safely. Some, however, are murdered, shot and dumped by the roadside. Hizbollah had been attempting to negotiate an exchange of the Wakhloos for their imprisoned chief, and frustrated in this, they had apparently decided that a little publicity about what good souls they were might move the bargaining along. For my part, I had made the trip mainly to see how the guerrillas moved in the countryside, although if there was anything I could do privately to help the Wakhloos, I intended to try. For now, that meant walking through the generic script of an interview with kidnap victims as carefully and

quickly as possible, with an eye less to the acquisition of information than to the preservation of good vibes all around. The Wakhloos, sitting cross-legged in purple and powder-blue salwar kameezes, did their part, saying how much they had come to understand the cause of their enemies and what nice boys the guerrillas were once you got to know them.

Mrs. Wakhloo had passed the time playing games with her captors—mostly puzzles and tic-tac-toe, she said. "They have been very good, very kind, no doubt," she said. "I have been debating the Islamization of Kashmir with some of them. The situation of Kashmir is really grave this time. My heart bleeds, really it bleeds. But one should be able to talk freely, politically and otherwise. We may differ here in this room but I must say, the people of Kashmir, they are one. There are no conflicts. If there are some misunderstandings, they can be solved by dialogue."

In this spirit, Hizbollah's military commanders served us biscuits and tea on a plastic tray. But as the weight of the dialogue shifted to the knife-wielding acting guerrilla chief, Islam, the tone became more martial. I asked how he justified kidnapping civilians as a tactic of a supposed war of liberation.

"This is the first type of situation for us like this," he answered uneasily. "They compelled us to do this. This is all for the exchange of prisoners. The Indians understand the language of guns. They don't understand anything else. So now we will go to any length. We won't stop now. India says it is ready to have talks around the table now. The Indian media are saying that they are ready to give us the 1953 position [full autonomy from New Delhi, except for defense, foreign policy, and communications]. But we are not interested. We have achieved something else—Kashmir is an international issue now—and to gain this we have had to sacrifice a lot. The army wanted to put the people under pressure but they failed in their efforts. Now they're going in for a political solution. It will not work. Many politicians have come in and tried to activate the political situation, but they can't come out in public or they will be shot. . . . We have sophisticated weapons now, the kind you will come to know about in the phase of guerrilla war. We are more organized now. We think a hundred times before we go into an action. Before, we were just playing."

He added: "The people have to decide about their future, but we have to keep a check that our course is not a suicidal one."

Translation: no compromise, no mediation by the traditional leaders, only war, dictated by the new generation. Among the Kashmiri guerrillas, this is generally what passes for revolutionary thought.

———

Whether they are from Hizbollah or Hizbul Mujaheddin or the Jammu and Kashmir Liberation Front or the People's League or Al-Ummar or the Zia Tigers or any of the countless other factions and subfactions, the Kashmiri separatist guerrillas frequently refer to their warfare to date as "just playing." By this they mean to boast that great feats of military prowess lie over the horizon, as opposed to the present state of grim, bloody military and political stalemate. But I always understood the references to "playing" in another sense as well. Not only in Kashmir but in much of South Asia, the present business of armed social and political revolution seems to be confused at times with adolescent coming-of-age fantasy. There is a *Lord of the Flies* feel to all of it. Teenagers in places like Punjab and Kashmir see themselves in the vanguard of change. The difference between them and teenagers elsewhere is that they can act on this perception with weaponry—and without much discipline. Unemployed, frustrated, politically aware, surrounded by an unmistakable landscape of recent injustice, they throw themselves into the fight, only half comprehending what those in the older generation—their parents and teachers and doctors—say about the goals of the ethnic, separatist political and religious struggle that is their inheritance. On the ground, weapons in hand, these young guerrillas may believe that they are serving the historical cause of their people, exacting revenge or finally replacing useless talk with meaningful direct action. But they do not convince you that they understand the difference between growing up and waging a revolution. And when you ask to be taken to their leaders, you find neither young people wise beyond their years nor adults immediately at hand to compensate. Other, that is, than kidnap victims.

What is generally referred to as the "overground" leadership of the separatist rebellions in Punjab and Kashmir does consist of lawyers, doctors, university professors, religious philosophers, professional politicians, and the like. But these venerated if currently radicalized community leaders tend to form exile governing bodies or local human rights committees and leave the actual fighting to the kids, affectionately known to all as "the boys." One consequence is that the older generation has

watched helplessly during the last several years as the center of gravity of the rebellion has shifted from traditional institutions to scattered, quarreling makeshift boys' clubs supported by foreign governments or religious obscurantists. And as the boys make more and more sacrifices in blood, they become more and more confident of their own righteousness and strength, and less and less amenable to adult supervision or mediation.

Of course, that is partly because many of the guerrillas think it was their parents' generation that helped to ruin Punjab and Kashmir in the first place. The historical roots of separatist politics in Punjab and Kashmir are deep. At present, the government of India is the enemy in these wars; the nominal, oft-stated goal of the separatist guerrillas is full independence, or in some cases confederation with Pakistan. The cycle of political abuse and mendacity that led ultimately to the eruption of violence in the 1980s can be—and is—blamed by young and old alike primarily on New Delhi's relatively recent political errors, such as vote rigging and state-sponsored killing. But the younger guerrillas know, too, that much of their older community leadership—the interlocutors between Punjabi Sikhs or Kashmiri Muslims and the Nehruvian state—contributed to and profited from the disastrous politics that led finally to armed rebellion. Now the boys are going to do things their way. And they are sufficiently well armed to dissuade their elders from telling them otherwise.

Islam, the acting Hizbollah chief, is one among many. He was in law school and had just begun a practice in the Srinagar high court when the latest separatist, anti-Indian rebellion began to swell in Kashmir in the late 1980s. He dropped out of formal law and politics and took up the occupation of guerrilla war. As with many young Kashmiri guerrillas, the crystalizing event in his political education was the rigged state election of 1987, when Prime Minister Rajiv Gandhi's corrupt local ally, the golf-playing Farooq Abdullah, a nominal Kashmir nationalist, used the Kashmir state machinery to deprive his local political opposition, the rising Muslim United Front, of seats in the state legislature. Young organizers and poll workers for the Muslim United Front were summarily rounded up, jailed, and beaten on suspicion of subversion. In their absence, it is widely agreed, the vote was stolen, which seemed excessive even for a thug-ruler like Abdullah, since the Islamic politicians were not going to win a legislative majority no matter what. In any event, when the jailed poll workers were let free after the deed was done, they drifted toward the radicalized guerrilla

clubs, of which there were by now several dozen. The separatist guerrilla organizations drew their strength from Kashmir's disputed and ambiguous past, its inequitable present, and from India's enemies abroad, notably Pakistan, conveniently situated across a mountain border.

Since the popular Kashmir rebellion erupted in full fury late in 1989, much attention has been paid abroad to Kashmir's unresolved historical grievances. These are significant. But this attention has been largely drummed up by Pakistan and by Kashmiri émigrés because the more important causes of the rebellion—the political, social, and economic failures of the Indian state in Kashmir—do not provide Pakistan with any diplomatic right to meddle.

Kashmir is the only state in India with a Muslim majority. By Lord Mountbatten's ill-considered rules of the Partition in 1947, it did not go to Pakistan, as it almost certainly should have. But the state was ruled by Hindus and it remained with India. This deal later contributed to two of the three wars between India and Pakistan. But it is worth keeping in mind that before the late 1980s, Kashmir's historical wounds had been bound up rather satisfactorily. The governments of India and Pakistan had dropped the subject. The Vale of Kashmir was one of the most popular tourist destinations in South Asia. The local agricultural economy was booming. The culture was secular, pluralist, tolerant, and ardently commercial. Ethnically and culturally distinct, ordinary Kashmiris were self-conscious and proud. They possessed no shortage of politicians willing to exploit the past for present gain, but armed rebellion, and particularly Islamic holy war, was hardly inevitable.

By now, more than two years into low-intensity guerrilla warfare, the internal dynamics of revolution and response have taken over in Kashmir, so if you ask the boys what they really care about, they will not talk about history or even very much about Islam. What they will talk about instead—shout about, more likely—is the blood that has been spilled, the torture meted out by Indian counterinsurgency forces, the deaths in prison, the rape cases, the martyrs. This widely shared popular anger fuels the fighting and protects the Kashmiri guerrillas for now from the sort of public disenchantment with undisciplined violence that has stalled the parallel rebellion in Punjab. But it does not do very much to explain the origins of the decision to take up arms.

If you listen to the autobiographies of the boys, attentive to that moment in the narrative when they describe dropping out of school and

picking up weapons, the most repetitious theme concerns the ways Kashmir's version of the Nehruvian state failed a generation of youth whose expectations were raised with the valley's growing prosperity. A complementary theme concerns how Islamic schoolteachers, some supported from abroad, exploited this frustration.

The ethos of Nehruvian socialism teaches directly and indirectly that opportunity is centered in the state apparatus through school placements, government job placements, and the distribution of infrastructure. In Kashmir as in some other places on the subcontinent this channel of upward mobility was clogged by corruption and inequitable patronage controlled by the local elites, Hindu and secularist Muslim. For a student to pass college entrance exams or win a place at the oversubscribed colleges, it was necessary for his family to pay large bribes. To win a government placement required either a bribe or clan connections, with the latter dominated by local Hindu pandit clans. This sort of systemic corruption has become common in South Asia. In Kashmir it was perhaps worse than in most areas, but more important, the perception of injustice was aggravated by the grievances of history.

On top of this, a significant minority of young men were educated to the high school level in Kashmir in a system outside the state's control, in schools run by what is known across the subcontinent as Jamaat-Islami, or the Islamic Society. In these schools small-time mullahs, some of them politicized by the regional rise of militant Islam after the Iranian revolution, taught their Kashmiri students that the obvious failures of the Indian state could be explained by the failure of Kashmiris to be true to their Muslim religion. The Islamic Society has long been present in Kashmir and for many years represented a religious fringe alien to the secular Kashmiri mainstream, which tolerated much imbibing of liquor and smoking of cigarettes and the wanton enjoyment of Indian *masala* cinema. Islamic Society teachers did not preach armed revolution but they did forecast inevitable conflict between true Islam and the secularism advocated by Nehruvian socialists. When these Islamic teachers ran for the state assembly in large numbers in 1987, with their eager students out doing the polling work, they showed themselves ready to play by the state's rules—the mullahs would become big men, free to enjoy the privileges and patronage of state office. Instead, the vote was rigged and the students were beaten and jailed. Ideology acquired a grievance.

Finally—and the Indian government prefers to see this as decisive—

neighboring Pakistan's pan-Islamic military, and the Afghan mujaheddin it armed, worked their way during the 1980s into the Islamic Society network in Kashmir, encouraging young boys from the Islamic schools to come across for arms and training. When these boys returned, they were revered as local heros by their classmates. And as their numbers swelled, they began in important ways to leave their teachers behind.

For now, the older generation views this history with sympathy and offers its support. "They are youth and they have taken an extreme position," former Kashmir chief minister G. M. Shah explained one cold morning early on in the rebellion. "There was such widespread rigging of the 1987 elections, and after that the youth were highly hurt. Everybody can be brought to the table if you are honest about what you want—but you cannot do anything with this Indian government that has failed on every front. From drinking water to food to industry to terrorism. Show me one place where they have succeeded. Incompetence breeds corruption. And corruption has bred rebellion."

A gray-bearded mullah named Abbas Ansari, one of the Islamic teachers and candidates whose youthful supporters now form a spur of the armed rebellion, put it this way: "This generation of youth does not belong to the issues of [Partition] in 1947. They do not even belong to 1953. They belong to the age group between fifteen and thirty. They were certainly born after 1957 [when Kashmir received a form of autonomy from New Delhi] and they came to the conclusion that it is not India who are our well-wishers."

India, he continued, "created a generation of mistrust. The government of India never looked into the basic economic structure to remove poverty and unemployment. . . . It seems that so many people around the world have gotten freedom by fighting. We [in the older generation] have not resorted to arms. But we feel suffocated. These youths who have come out with these arms, they have provided a sort of relief to this suffocation."

Within the guerrilla movement, there is a division between the boys who grew up in the Islamic Society nexus and those who are the children of the traditional, secularist Kashmiri elite and commercial middle class. The nominally religious guerrillas have the closest ties to Pakistan, the best weapons, and in militant Islam an ideology that transcends local politics. The secularist guerrillas, represented by the Jammu and Kashmir Liberation Front and its splintered affiliates, speak for the urban classes

and almost certainly for a majority of ordinary Kashmiris when they call for full independence, not confederation with Islamic Pakistan. The Indian government hopes to exploit this division through covert counterintelligence operations and to set the militants against each other, as they have done to a degree with Sikh guerrillas in Punjab. But the Kashmiri guerrillas are aware of this strategy and have tried mightily to resist it. For now, among the boys, the disagreement between Islamic guerrillas and secularist guerrillas suggests a high school football rivalry, not internecine war. Many of the key guerrilla faction leaders knew each other earlier at school and they remain able to communicate and occasionally cooperate. Hatred of a common enemy, the government of India, and homogeneity of culture and language sustains the movement's broad popularity.

The degree of this popularity is impossible to miss on the streets of Srinagar. During my time, as a foreigner, you could wander into any slum quarter, step over to a fruit stall or a car repair shop, declare yourself a journalist, and ask to see some of "the boys." Much mumbling in Kashmiri would follow, neighboring shopkeepers would be summoned over, and soon you were off walking in a small group through the narrow warrens of three- and four-story tenements. You stopped in one place, then another, then a third, took a seat, drank some tea, and suddenly here were the boys, lifting up their draping phirans like flashers to show their weapons beneath. If you sat for as long as an hour while the word circulated through the neighborhood, an entire regiment would show up, utterly unconcerned about the bunker of Indian counterinsurgency troops just beneath the window.

On one recent visit I was anxious to meet with some of the leaders of the Hizbul Mujaheddin, a Pakistan-backed guerrilla group that grew out of the Islamic Society and is arguably the most influential in Kashmir today. But for the first few days in Srinagar, I had trouble making contact. The night before I was scheduled to leave, the guerrillas finally telephoned. I said I very much wanted to meet them, but I had a ten o'clock meeting with the governor in the mansion on the hill and a two o'clock plane to catch. No problem, came the reply. When you're finished with the governor, just drive out. We'll meet you outside the mansion gate and take you to our headquarters. Then you can go on to the airport. This seemed a little bold. The governor's mansion is surrounded by Black Cat commandos, squads of army troops, and scores of paramilitaries.

Wouldn't they prefer to meet somewhere else? Not at all—nothing to worry about, they said.

The next morning, after our talk, the governor said he had to drive out of his mansion grounds to a nearby defense compound. So I waited for his heavily armed convoy of vehicles to head down the hill, joined the rear of the line, and drove through the gate. I looked for possible guerrillas but saw none. Rumbling in the Ambassador, no more than thirty yards from the governor's car, I heard a thump on my door. Rolling alongside was a bearded young man on a motorbike. He cocked his head and we followed him. I waved to the governor as we passed. Best of luck with the counterinsurgency, sir.

At Hizbul Mujaheddin downtown headquarters, a guerrilla named Khalid, of the Zia II regiment, fondling a telescopic sniper rifle with an estimated range of 1.5 kilometers, laughed when I expressed my astonishment. "Kashmir is completely under our control," he boasted. "The mujaheddin are showing their mettle. Every young man in Kashmir is a militant." And then, the standard invocation of teenage rebellion: "It is now or never."

———

The odds are it will be never.

A perennial question about South Asia is whether its recently created nation-states will break up under separatist pressure. The catastrophic split of West and East Pakistan in 1971 makes this more than an abstract speculation. At present, the most serious rebellions in the region—in northeast Sri Lanka, Kashmir, Punjab, Sind—are being run on the ground by teenagers who, while often courageous and certainly well-armed, seem much too unfocused or too prone to criminal indiscipline to defeat the mustered power, however decayed, of the Nehruvian state. In Kashmir and Punjab particularly, to the degree the guerrillas have any coherent long-term vision, they are counting on the state's gradual weakening over a period of years, even decades. If it does not reform itself successfully, the Nehruvian state's long-term staying power is indeed questionable. Among other things, counterinsurgency at the scale India now practices it is highly expensive, and the state is short on funds. Moreover, New Delhi's historical blindness and mendacity in Kashmir and Punjab are difficult to overestimate.

But given India's emotional attachment to the land in Kashmir—a

sentiment not confined to the governing classes—it is hard to imagine the territory ever being permitted to secede unless Pakistan defeats India in a war, and that is a prospect that would draw long odds at Harrah's. The same is doubly true in Punjab, where secessionist history is more shallow, the rebellion is less popular, and the political disorganization of the boys is more obvious.

So what you have instead of imminent revolution on the borders of South Asia today are these bubbling, brutalizing half-wars, where generations of teenagers are drawn into the radicalizing vocation of extortion, terror, and seemingly unwinnable revolt, motivated and even ennobled by the death-squad nihilists on the other side such as Punjab's K. P. S. Gill, whose attitudes make it even more difficult for the state to recover its reputation or its authority. The long-term consequences of this sort of youth education, during a time of accelerating, irreversible social and economic change on the subcontinent, are potentially disturbing but not so easy to predict.

Just after the Soviet Union fell in on itself, Shekhar Gupta, one of India's most energetic and independent journalists, published a long essay that asked in part whether what happened to India's great patron to the north could also happen to India. Gupta has covered separatist insurgencies in South Asia for fourteen years and probably knows the dynamics better than anyone. Yet in his essay he dodged the question he raised. I went to see him in his office at *India Today* in New Delhi to ask what he really thought.

"I don't think anyone who has been exposed to the situation in India can help but draw parallels with the Soviet Union, because I don't think there are any two countries in the world which are so multilinguistic, multiethnic, and multireligious," he said. "It's very interesting because both countries have chosen very different paths to create their own nationalism. You know, there was no such thing as Soviet nationalism, there was Russian nationalism. In India we did not even have in history anything akin to a Russian nationalism. . . . The challenge before both nations was to develop this nationalism. The Soviets chose the path of communism, ideology. We Indians chose a path which was a little less well defined, but a path of a constitution, a kind of liberal, multiethnic, multilinguistic kind of nation. So whereas the Soviet Union crushed all the languages in the republics, in India languages were encouraged. I think we went the other way to a fault."

The difficulty now, he went on, is that for the first time since India's independence, separatist insurgencies or other sorts of rebellious movements are raging simultaneously in a number of different places—not only in Punjab and Kashmir, but in several states in the northeast, pockets such as Gurkhaland—and there are even renewed stirrings in the Indian south.

"I don't think it's possible for any state to fight so many fires at the same time," Gupta said. "First of all, it bleeds you economically because it costs a lot of money to do this. Second, it creates a general feeling of cynicism that, you know, everything is up in flames, nothing is going to work out. Earlier, it was trouble in one part of the country. At least ninety-five percent of the people were able to say, okay, it's a small problem, so solve it. Today a lot more people—maybe thirty percent or forty percent—are either directly affected by the problem or witnessing trouble, and they are also watching the state's helplessness or the state's inadequacy. . . . In a poor society which has a lot of special social tension and discord anyway, militancy or rebellion can become employment, good business—and it also becomes a 'high.' "

As we talked on it became apparent that what gave Gupta hope, what made him in the end an optimist, was less his faith in the state's ability to transform itself than its track record of defeating insurgency even while proceeding from weakness. Through a shifting blend of brutality, patience, and federalist political solutions, not only India but Pakistan and Sri Lanka have—with the single exception of 1971—managed to hold on in the face of a mind-boggling array of separatist challenges. Occasionally it is the death squads that do the decisive work; more often some autonomy deal is eventually cut around the negotiating table. In these deals, the guerrillas are urged to form themselves into an ordinary political party and are given unbridled control over their regional patronage network. The guerrilla leadership is corrupted, the bubbling subsides, and the particular separatist challenge lapses into remission. Whether the best metaphor for this process is that of a cancer inexorably weakening the Nehruvian state until it dies or that of a long-lived body politic facing and defeating its own viruses remains to be seen. For now, while the cancer has its credible advocates, the big bets—indeed, nearly all the industrial and state wealth of South Asia—back the body politic.

Where the Nehruvian state seemed weakest, least able to assert itself, was not so much in Punjab and Kashmir. In those places, the forces of

insurgency and counterinsurgency stood in stark, often brutal, opposition, and so even a weakened state could muster impressive power on its own behalf.

But that was not the case in northern India, in the urban slums of Kanpur or Aligarh or Agra, the overpopulated heartland of the Indian body politic. In these places mobs of civilians, not organized guerrillas, mainly stirred the dust. The lines of opposition blurred, and the heavily armed servants of the state sometimes had trouble deciding which side they were on.

11

Riding the Tiger

All roads take us to God.
—*Lal Krishna Advani*

We had been searching all morning for the Man Who Kept the Crows. We found instead his grandson, Somnath Viyas, a gray-haired retired schoolteacher with a master's degree in political science who lived in a tall stone row house in a crowded, damp square in central Varanasi, one of India's holiest cities.

North India was smoldering again. In Varanasi, Kanpur, Aligarh, Lucknow, Agra—dense cities of more than a million people each—edgy mobs of Hindus and Muslims roamed the streets. In sudden bursts of fury they fought pitched battles with rudimentary homemade pistols, country shotguns, knives, gasoline grenades, and spiked sticks. Local politician-preachers led the mobs on processions into the slum quarters of their enemies to chant provocative slogans. Among the mobs stood battalions of paramilitary security police, dispatched by New Delhi to restore order in India's northern heartland. But the police were mainly Hindus and reluctant in this emotional, polarized climate to fire on their own, so they tended to restore order by standing in front of the Hindu mobs and shooting at the Muslim mobs. This understandably enraged the Muslims further. And if you were angry, you could do a lot of damage in these slums. The alleys were no wider than a car and were smothered by four- and five-story brick and concrete buildings of haphazard design whose

jumbled architecture provided cover for sudden strikes and quick escapes. Hindus and Muslims lived literally on top of one another in the mixed quarters. When the lines of battle were drawn, it was sometimes necessary for families to move their belongings out of one building and into another nearby so as to put themselves on the proper side. These makeshift religious lines would spring up overnight in a troubled slum and were referred to universally as the "Indo-Pakistan border" in a harkening back to the terrible religious strife that accompanied Partition. As the lines settled and the residents prepared to fight, you could see old women in the dirt alleys hauling goats and burlap sacks on carts across the street to join relatives on the other side of the "border." Then, usually in darkness, the fighting would begin. Once, in Kanpur on the eve of a battle, I saw young women walking from door to door to hand out women's bracelets to teenage boys who they felt had shrunk from the fight in a previous riot—the bracelets were meant to shame the boys into fighting harder this time.

The rhetorical, nominal cause of these riots was a continuing national dispute over religious places of worship. A swelling right-wing Hindu revivalist movement in India had identified some three thousand Muslim mosques and burial grounds that the Hindu nationalists said had been unjustly constructed centuries before on the sites of Hindu temples. (There are about one hundred million Muslims in India, or about 12 percent of the population. Some are the descendants of precolonial invaders; most are descendants of impoverished low-caste Hindus who converted to Islam in the old empires to seek opportunity.) The Hindu revivalists had targeted three such usurping Muslim mosques which they said had to be torn down or moved and replaced with Hindu temples.

One mosque was in Ayodhya, the supposed birthplace of the Hindu god Ram, or Rama. Late in 1992, a vast mob of politically organized hard-core Hindu militants swarmed over the seventeenth-century Ayodhya mosque, smashed it with hammers, and tore it down, stone by stone. This stunning act of intolerance ignited vicious slum riots across India. Hundreds died, mainly Muslims. A sect of Hindu fanatics in Bombay launched a pogrom against Muslims in the city's slums, burning down houses, setting victims on fire, stabbing people to death with crude knives. Religious violence, even on this terrible scale, is not new in India. But there was something about the destruction of the Ayodhya mosque, which the government had tried and failed to preserve, that seemed

unusually ominous and demoralizing to many secular-minded Indians. Although it was possible to understand the Hindu revivalist movement as a product in considerable part of the most transparent and artificial sort of political manipulation, the hatred and destruction unleashed in the squalid lanes of Ayodhya late in 1992 could not be so easily explained. All the mustered power of the Indian state had failed to stop what law and common sense decreed an illegal act. If that sort of Hindu militant street power represents a vision of India's future, the implications are almost too chilling to contemplate.

The Hindu militants' determination to destroy mosques will not stop at Ayodhya. On the short list of targeted Muslim places of worship are a mosque in Varanasi, site of an important temple to the Hindu god Shiva, and one in Mathura, which Hindus believe is the birthplace of their god Krishna. The campaign to replace all these mosques had begun in Ayodhya, cynics said, because Ram was the most popular god in the north Indian electoral heartland, and thus a campaign on his behalf would be the most politically useful to the Hindu preacher-politicians. Local religious riots generated by the campaign had their own peculiar dynamics. But they were linked to the broad, swelling national campaign by the Hindu revivalists to reassert Hindu prerogatives and to take revenge for alleged injustices perpetrated by Muslim rulers in precolonial times. After Ayodhya, where this will lead is uncertain.

The history involved is the kind you could bump into unexpectedly all over South Asia: mythical, preindustrial, emotional, vivid, manipulated, and above all, alive and well in the imperatives of ongoing violence. It was not the history of Nehruvian facts and textbooks, of five-year plans and bureaucratic commissions, but rather of ancient storytellers and demagogues. Some of the history was true, some of it was not, but the surrounding public debate rarely focused on the difference. The Hindu revivalists as well as their opponents in the Muslim clergy needed history desperately to justify their present battles, so they took what they could find in the texts and blithely made up the rest.

We were anxious to hear a dose of this mythmaking firsthand, in the hope that it would help to explain, at least in part, why so many Indians were fighting and dying over places of worship. My researcher, Rama Lakshmi, and I embarked on a winding tour of North India, stopping in city slums to watch the riots and visiting the sites of disputed mosques and temples to talk with local preacher-politicians about their causes, their

faiths, and their versions of history. In teeming Varanasi, we were told that the Man Who Kept the Crows, a local Hindu archivist and activist, had all the answers. It turned out, actually, that the Man Who, etc., was long dead, but his grandson Somnath Viyas was very much alive, and while he did not claim to have any answers at all, he did urge us to listen carefully to his story, which he felt would unveil the origins of religious violence in India's religious heartland.

Across from Viyas's sheltered front porch where we sat one misty morning to hear his tale rose the whitewashed walls of the Gyanwapi, or "Well of Knowledge," Mosque, a seventeenth-century Mughal structure surrounded by clusters of Hindu temples. The mosque's minarets competed with conical temple domes, including one of shimmering gold, for dominance of a dense skyline. Barefoot Hindu pilgrims with painted faces, ragged beards, and spindly legs splashed through puddles in cobblestone lanes. Perhaps thirty yards from the mosque's walls was the reputed Well of Knowledge itself, a dark hole into which one could not see very far. Tape-recorded Hindu chants and religious folk songs screeched from a multitude of speakers. Our host, Viyas, summoned a rope cot and a small straight-backed wooden chair for us to sit on. Then he began the story of the Gyanwapi Mosque, and how thousands of human corpses supposedly came to lie buried beneath it. As he spoke, Viyas acquired the flowing, rapturous voice of a storyteller, but also, at times, the halting manner of a rational man forced to recount a particularly bizarre dream.

This ambivalence, it seems to me and to many secular Indians, is the essence of religious history as it is mustered and manipulated in the present volatile climate: it is the point of departure from the rational to the irrational. The way history is seen—something different, to be sure, from what history may actually be—is the source of the distortions that religious-minded politicians find necessary to organize violence.

Viyas began that morning with what he knew was true: a 1929 court case that landed in steamy summer on the desk of a British colonial officer in Varanasi in the last days of the British Empire. The plaintiff was Viyas's grandfather (the Man Who Kept the Crows, so named by his neighbors and so known today throughout Varanasi for his habit of feeding local birds). One day, Viyas watched a party of Muslims carry a corpse to the Gyanwapi Mosque for burial. They dug a grave, recited prayers, and lowered the body. Grandfather Viyas was appalled—there was supposed to be an informal treaty in place between local Hindus and Muslims under

which the Muslims had agreed not to bury their dead at the mosque in exchange for permission to conduct regular Friday religious services. Introducing burials was an affront and a provocation, Viyas thought, so he filed papers with the British, seeking an imperial injunction to stop it.

Here we can imagine the beleaguered district magistrate, some middle-class Welshman far from home in service of the king, whose name is today only vaguely recalled by Varanasi locals. The magistrate's primary job was to prevent rioting. The petition before him urged that he stop the Muslim burials at Gyanwapi as a means to this end. An easy call—petition granted. But now the Muslims were affronted, and they filed their own petition against the magistrate, the secretary of India, and the British Empire. Their argument was that in the sixteenth century, the precolonial Muslim emperor Aurengzeb, and heir to the Mughal Muslim invaders of India, officially granted Varanasi Muslims the right to offer prayers, including burial prayers, at the Gyanwapi Mosque. Moreover, the mosque was at present in the possession of Muslims, so they had the right to do whatever they wished within its confines.

The British magistrate now felt that he had a potential religious brawl on his hands. Accordingly he stepped up to the best traditions of British imperial mediation. He consulted lawyers and preachers and community elders. He received long petitions and recitations of precolonial historical disputes. Among the evidence he considered was a lengthy petition submitted by a Hindu historian from Orissa who claimed to have examined archives in London and to have discovered there letters from provincial princes to the seventeenth-century Muslim emperor Aurangzeb which made clear the Well of Knowledge's true history.

According to this (Hindu) version, a modest Hindu temple was erected on the site of the Well of Knowledge at some point back in the misty recesses of the tenth century or earlier. Local Brahmin preachers, or pandits, maintained the temple, performed the religious rituals, and otherwise offered themselves up as fonts of spiritual wisdom to the local Hindu community. Then harmony was disrupted by hordes of invading Afghan Muslims who poured into the Gangetic plains from the Hindu Kush mountains to the west. In the suspiciously poetical year of 1111, a local Muslim warrior-prince by the name of Qutubuddin Aibak, the general of an Afghan king, smashed the Hindu temple at the Well of Knowledge to prove the superiority of his faith and his tribe. (The date of 1111, at the least, does not add up, since Aibak was not active in north India until the

last quarter of the twelfth century at the earliest. But Viyas and his intellectual brethren prefer numerology to fact.) The temple, in any event, lay in ruins for several centuries.

In the suspiciously poetical year of 1555, a Hindu pandit by the name of Narayan received permission from the Muslim emperor Akbar to rebuild the temple. Emperor Akbar's relatively pluralist religious outlook, which he acquired somewhat later in his reign, has made him a popular icon of recent Indian historiography. Narayan persuaded Akbar to authorize a new temple because northern India was suffering from a terrible drought and the pandit felt that if the Hindu gods could be assuaged, rain would fall. Akbar, perhaps concerned about the food riots that routinely accompanied drought, apparently considered this a reasonable hope, so the temple was reconstructed and the rain-inducing rituals were duly performed. Lo and behold, the rains came, and as our storyteller, Viyas, said, "It was a very good rain and all the farmers were very happy."

Akbar, being mortal, passed on to the great beyond, and two generations later the evil emperor Aurangzeb took the throne. In Hindu historiography, Aurangzeb is the malevolent "fundamentalist" opposite of the pluralist Akbar. As Viyas put it, Aurangzeb was "a very staunch Muslim and a blind follower of Islam who killed his three brothers, imprisoned his father and sister, and took the rein of administration by dint of cruelty and force and violence. He declared, 'I do not recognize any religion in India but Islam. It will be the state religion of India.' " Aurangzeb's representatives in Varanasi asked His Exaltedness what, specifically, they should do about the rebuilt Hindu temple at the Well of Knowledge. According to the letters supposedly dug up at the London School of Economics, these local Muslim warrior-princes accused the temple's Hindu preachers of engaging in idolatry and "wicked sciences." In possession of these accusations, Aurangzeb ordered that Hindu teaching centers be demolished and replaced with Islamic schools that would instruct the populace in Persian and Arabic. To carry out his order Aurangzeb dispatched to Varanasi his greatest and most terrible general, Khala Pahar, or Black Mountain.

Black Mountain, Viyas told us, "was six feet tall, black in color, and rode a black horse. He was a Brahmin from Bengal. He commanded a great army in Aurangzeb's service. Aurangzeb had given him two or three Muslim ladies and made him a general. Since he was a Brahmin, he knew where all the money was kept at the temples. He destroyed all the temples he could find. Wherever a temple was destroyed, Black Mountain

was there." In 1669, another year with a certain ring to it, Black Mountain supposedly arrived at the outskirts of Varanasi. Local Hindus rallied to battle against him. They fought for up to ten days. But Black Mountain had in his arsenal cannons of some sort, or so the story goes, and with this superior weaponry he overwhelmed the defenders.

As the evil general neared the Well of Knowledge, the temple's Hindu priests prepared for their fate. Among the valuables in their possession was one of the most spectacular jewels in all of India, an emerald in the shape of a Shiva lingam, or phallus, a symbol of the creator-destroyer god Shiva's potency. The emerald phallus had been shipped secretly to the temple by the king of Kota, who feared that if Aurangzeb found it in the Kota court, he would steal it. Now, as battle raged in Varanasi, with thousands of Hindu fighters falling bravely before Black Mountain's cannons, one of the Hindu priests, Sukhdev Viyas—ancestor of the Man Who, etc.—gathered the glistening phallus into his robes and, just as enemy soldiers reached the temple, leaped to his death down the Well of Knowledge. The next day, amid the smoldering ruins and scattered corpses wrought by Black Mountain's triumph, Viyas's corpse was pulled from the well and cremated at the holy ghats on the banks of the sacred Ganges River. Viyas's bereaved widow hurled herself onto the burning funeral pyre, performing the traditional suicidal act of *sati*. But the emerald phallus was never found. It was presumed to have washed into the Ganges.

In the aftermath of this terrible battle, Black Mountain's lieutenants constructed a Muslim mosque on top of the ruins of the former Hindu temple—the same Gyanwapi Mosque visible from the Viyas's front porch today. Portions of the old Hindu temple were used in the walls of the mosque—indeed, Hindu carvings are still visible in the mosque's walls—to emphasize the Muslim emperor's triumph. Ten to twelve thousand dead Hindus were supposedly buried beneath the mosque, their bodies rotting symbols of the futility of resisting Islam. "Today," Viyas told us, leaning forward solemnly toward the mosque, "if you removed the stone and dug four to five feet, then you would get some portion of a dead body."

For more than a hundred years afterward, chastened Varanasi Hindus worshiped modestly at the surviving Well of Knowledge and at a few trees surrounding the new, dominant mosque. Then, in the suspiciously

poetical year of 1777, in a kingdom far away, a princess named Ahiliyab-hai had a dream.

In her dream Ahiliyabhai swam in the water. A mysterious voice said, "Come and take me." When the princess awoke she went bathing in the Narmada River, which ran through her kingdom. There, as she swam, naked, a Shiva phallus "came into her lap," as Viyas put it. It was not the missing emerald but it was nonetheless an inspiration. Ahiliyabhai trav-eled to Varanasi and decided to erect a Hindu temple to Lord Shiva on the site next to the Well of Knowledge Mosque. She studied the designs of the previously smashed Hindu temples and authorized one of her own with a golden roof. For the gold she turned to Ranjit Singh, the rich Sikh ruler of Punjab, who owned seven gold mines and who sent the requested roof on a white mare he had bought from the emir of Saudi Arabia.

Inspired by the rebuilt temple, mobs of local Hindus broke into the Gyanwapi Mosque in 1810 bearing pictures of Lord Shiva. Muslims moved to defend the mosque and a riot ensued. British soldiers charged in with their rifles, shot dead a few stragglers, and finally bought peace by asking the Hindus to carry their garlanded pictures out of the mosque to the young trees beside it.

Thus the present scene in the crowded square around the Well of Knowledge in bustling downtown Varanasi: on one side the dominant seventeenth-century mosque with its painted minarets, on the other the conical, glistening dome of the Golden Temple, and in between a few old shade trees garlanded with flowers and photographs. And, milling around, a lot of young Hindus and Muslims with grievance on their minds.

Back now to 1935 and our beleaguered British magistrate at his desk piled high with petitions, not least among them the carefully scrawled Hindu accounts of this epic history. The colonial magistrate read the material, consulted Varanasi elders further, and decided somewhat wearily that the best he could do was to preserve the status quo. He formally ordered the Muslims to stop burying their dead at the mosque and instructed the Hindus to leave the Muslims alone. This peace lasted two decades. "It was a sound sleep," Viyas told us.

Then the Hindus awoke. A Hindu revivalist political party, in posses-sion of the scrawled "history" of the Well of Knowledge, organized a campaign to tear down the mosque and shift the princess's temple to the proper site. Thousands of Hindus flocked from all over India in 1958 to

demand redress. Local Muslims, deprived in independent India of both Mughal emperors and British arbitrators, shrank from a major confrontation, but scattered riots ensued nonetheless. Prime Minister Nehru sent in the troops just as his British predecessors had done. Thousands were arrested and jailed.

In search of a solution, Nehru invited a delegation of Varanasi Hindu leaders to meet with him in New Delhi. Viyas, then a young political science graduate, went along. He met with the secularist founder of the Indian nation-state in Teen Murti House in the capital.

"Nehru said, 'You have been waiting several centuries, I think. You can wait one or two centuries more,' " Viyas recalled. "He said they were trying to establish a good local administration and the administration would decide the matter. 'I will not touch it,' he said. It was good advice. He was a great man. . . . Ever since, I have kept the position of this place, this house, for liberating the mosque. Whether that comes today or later, I can't say. But I am a peaceful man. I want the liberation in a good way, not a bad way. I do not want bloodshed. Now, I cannot stop any Hindu political party. They will do what they like, but my position is this: no bloodshed. It should be done by conquering the hearts of the people. When many Hindus come here and see the ruins of their temple, they feel very much aggrieved. This is the curse of the Hindus."

We left Viyas in this mood and traveled back through the congested, partially curfew-bound streets of Varanasi and the blackened residue of fires set during recent Hindu-Muslim riots.

We were curious above all about what Varanasi's Muslims thought of this strange, vivid history. That night, we drove after dark into the Muslim quarter—recognizable by the tanneries and butcher shops, businesses essential to the Indian economy but anathema to vegetarian Hindus—to visit Naseer Benarsi, an eighty-five-year-old poet and local Muslim spiritual elder. We sat on sofas in his cramped living room and drank tea. Benarsi recited poetry and spoke at length about hearts broken by religious violence. Then he got around to history.

"A wrong done is always a wrong done, whether it is by Aurangzeb or by his father," he said. "It will always remain a wrong. But we were born in this land. It is now five hundred years after the event. I can say that if I had lived in Aurangzeb's time, I would have resisted his armies. But since I was not alive at the time, why rain on me? If the Hindus go on breaking mosques for their revenge, how long can Muslims keep that

need for retaliation inside, sitting with their hands folded? The Muslims know that the longer they wait, the worse it will get. They feel the need to strike back. As far as I'm concerned, I hope there will be an amicable solution. Everybody realizes that through this issue of religion, much damage can be done. We've always had warriors."

The next day, in Lucknow, we met Shah Syed Fazal-ur-Rahman Waizi Nadvi, the preacher of that city's Tilewali Mosque, one of the two thousand disputed Mughal structures on the hit list of Hindu revivalists. I asked about the story of the Gyanwapi Mosque in Varanasi and suggested that the version of history we had heard provided useful propaganda for the Hindu activists.

"There is another history," he replied. "There was another history that was written in Orissa by a Vishwanath. He argued that the temple at the Gyanwapi was not demolished by the Muslims. He said it was a raja's private Hindu temple and that a priest at the temple started stealing and embezzling. So the raja got rid of the priest and gave the land to the Muslims. It was a tradition for Hindu rajas to give land for mosques. It happened frequently. People are always abusing Aurangzeb and calling him names but this man built so many temples. There is no evidence for this battle in Varanasi. It is all propaganda. There are not documentary cases. Not only are there none, the story is impossible. Demolishing a temple is strictly prohibited in Islam. It never happened anywhere in India. You might have a colony of Hindus who converted to Islam and voluntarily changed their temple into a mosque. That is something different.

"The problem here is not history. The problem here is that Hindu politicians want to unite Hindus, and they can't see any other way to do it. Hindus are fractious. They are divided by castes and subcastes and it is difficult to find a theme for political unity. So these new politicians use this propaganda. . . . The people who are talking in this language—it's a handful of them, politicians mainly. The ordinary Hindu understands us and says, 'You might have been foreigners at one time, but whenever there were revolts or independence movements, you fought with us.' These Hindu leaders want to make us into aliens because it's the only way they can unite the Hindus. The Muslims are both afraid and angry. I am personally scared that we can't take this too much longer. In Kanpur thousands [of Muslims] came out into the streets, unarmed, and said to the police, 'Kill us in the streets.' I'm frightened that Muslims will now

take up arms and call for liberation like the Sikhs in Punjab. I'm frightened they will start to fight back with weapons. If it does go that way, it will be the end of the country. The country must go on with its secular foundations. What does an ordinary Muslim want? He wants to live peacefully. This new trend of religious violence is like a flood. When it comes, it takes everything—houses, people, everything. And when it recedes you will see only corpses and ruins."

We met a Hindu political science professor, another teacher of young minds. His name was Suresh Awasthi. He complained that Muslims were breeding faster than rabbits and that if they were not stopped they would soon dominate Indian society. For this reason among others, it was essential that Muslims renounce their imperial history, own up to their past religious and political atrocities, and make restitution to the Hindus. The reconciliation of history was everything. "This cultural question is essential," he said. "If they will just accept a history that is not the history of Muslim invaders, then they will have accepted reality—that Islam is not supreme, the Indian nation is supreme. We want this psychology to be changed. And there is a religious aspect to this. When family planning is pursued among the Muslims, they say it is un-Islamic. They put their religion above the needs of the nation on the family-planning issue. When they return to us these religious places, they will understand that their religious leaders have misguided them. . . . The Muslims don't want to face the facts of history. They want to change history to suit them."

———

Such is the language of religious violence in India: hot, intolerant, very much of the present, and yet woven from fragments of history and myth. Hindus twist and exploit the history of Muslim invasions; Muslims claim amnesia. Essentially irrelevant are the lost factual details, such as those concerning the dispute over Varanasi's Well of Knowledge—there are very few reliable records for an objective historian to work with, even if he or she thought objective history would be believed. What matters today is that India's precolonial history included enough religious wars, invasions, conquests, and appalling acts of slaughter and triumph to justify the anger of anyone who wishes to define the future by the past.

Since independence, the competing alternative in India has been to jettison the strife-torn past for the more appealing, secularist myths offered by the modernizing Nehruvian state. But as the Nehruvian state's

ability to govern effectively has declined, so has the binding power of its myths. As the journalist Ned Desmond has pointed out, it was Nehru himself who helped to create India's postindependence secular version of history in the seminal work he penned in prison, *Discovery of India.* In this rambling tract, which used history and myth to rally Indian nationalism against British rule, Nehru "created a fable that celebrated the achievements of Mughal emperors and [Hindu] maharajahs alike, playing down the ceaseless conflict and fratricide" while at the same time overemphasizing, for Nehru's own purposes, the history of emperors with a "protosecular outlook, or at least a strong impulse to harmonize contending religious forces within their empires."

Nehru's vision prevailed when the British withdrew. But India's Hindu revivalists and nationalists, as Desmond wrote, have long harbored a less idealized version of history in which India looms "not as a record of proven and varied cultural achievements but as a blood-soaked battlefield on which the two main contenders, during several centuries of conflict, were Hindu civilization and Muslim invaders. Hindus, they argue, were the chosen people of the subcontinent. . . . Muslims, in this account, were freebooters and religious fanatics who, arriving from Turkey, Afghanistan, Persia, and Central Asia beginning in the 11th century, shattered Hindu society, broke temples, forced conversions at swordpoint, and imposed an alien culture. Justice demanded that the glory of past Hindu civilization be restored as the basis of Indian political identity, and all the followers of 'alien' traditions on the subcontinent, especially Muslims and Christians, must bend their knee to the Hindu order, and forget the special privileges Nehru granted to them."

In South Asia, past, present, and future bleed into a swirling pool. In the two decades between 1962 and 1981—during the long, ponderous rise of the Nehruvian state—4,770 people were officially recorded as having died in India's religious riots. But during the 1980s and early 1990s, as the state began noticeably to decompose amid accelerating social change, the religious-violence death rate roughly doubled. Between 1989 and mid-1991 alone, 2,025 people were hacked, stabbed, burned, and shot to death in urban brawls between Hindus, Muslims, and Hindudominated security forces. On a per capita basis, the rise in the death toll is not so dramatic because the increasing number of victims is compensated for by the growth in the overall population—on a graph representing victims of religious violence since independence as a percentage of

total population, the line does not rise steeply during the 1980s; rather, the graph looks like a series of rolling waves, with the latest crest rising across the 1980s to the present day. Whether per capita statistics or absolute numbers offer the most useful way to think about the toll of religious violence is not, perhaps, the point. The point is that since 1980, the problem has been getting steadily worse.

Yet while the fact of rising religious violence was undeniable, what all this bloodshed meant and where it might lead politically were not so clear. Various defenders of the secularist state—whether nihilists in the security forces or humane adherents of the fading Nehruvian ideal—preferred to see the riots as a cyclical, manageable legacy of history, "a small ripple over the sea," as Indian prime minister P. V. Narasimha Rao put it. On the other side, various religious leaders, Hindu and Muslim alike, drew language from their visionary texts to describe the emerging conflict in apocalyptic terms. This view naturally contained an important role for the religious leaders themselves and ample motivation for their followers; thus it seemed self-perpetuating and potentially self-fulfilling.

India's Hindu leaders perhaps can be excused for thinking that rising religious violence in the streets and slums of north India during the late 1980s meant divine destiny was with them—after all, in India's national election of 1990, the Hindu revivalist Bharatiya Janata Party (Indian People's Party), or BJP, scored its most impressive political victory ever, winning the second-largest number of seats in the national parliament, behind Nehru's long-dominant, secularist Congress Party. The Hindu party's leaders marched in saffron robes beneath banners promising a return to mythical religious glory and (as they so frequently chanted) "Victory to Lord Ram!" Besides becoming leaders of the national parliamentary opposition, the revivalists also won control of the state government in Uttar Pradesh, the most populous state in the nation, the center of the Mughal Empire and widely seen as India's political heartland. Once in office, the Hindu preacher-politicians vowed to end the rioting that had charred the downtown slums of the largest cities, eliminate corruption in all its forms, and to conjure up a temporal, political paradise.

Predictably, what the preachers mainly did instead was to ensconce themselves in the privileged offices vacated by their secularist predecessors, ride about in chauffeured Ambassadors, settle with their families in state-subsidized bungalows, and begin manipulating the patronage networks of state employment and business licensing that are the key to

political prosperity. Struggling for control of these scant but precious state resources, the Hindu revivalists divided themselves quickly into bickering subfactions just as their secularist predecessors had done. If there had been no established democracy in India, presumably the preachers would have had the foresight to declare a long-lived dictatorship of the clergy and thus would have bought some time to enhance and divvy up the spoils of office. As it is, however, the preacher-politicians are accountable every five years to the electorate, and in Uttar Pradesh they faced the daunting prospect of explaining to the electorate why Uttar Pradesh does not very much resemble heaven. The devastating attack on the Ayodhya mosque can be seen as one answer to this predicament: by defining their politics in the angry streets, the Hindus dodge responsibility for their failures in office. While it is debatable whether, in Ayodhya, this was a deliberate strategy by the senior Hindu movement leadership or a scrambled reaction to events beyond their control, the result is the same either way. After the destruction of the Ayodhya mosque, the Hindus were dismissed from government in Uttar Pradesh and many were locked up temporarily. Now they are free to wage the politics with which they are most comfortable and at which they are most competent: street demagoguery.

A Westerner may find it difficult to resist being seduced by the spectacle of South Asia's politicized faiths—the Hindu shock troops with their painted faces and thrusting tridents, or the white-bearded mullahs leading great crowds to burn their enemies in effigy (and sometimes in the flesh). But ultimately, what is so interesting about South Asia's modern politicized religious movements is just how ordinary their leaders really are, how easily they are subsumed by the public culture of patronage, clan, graft, and manipulation.

This is another trick the secular, socialist Nehruvian elite learned from the British imperialist: how to buy off your opponents by tempting them to become more like you. Among the recent revolutionary claimants to South Asia's future, be they Marxist or separatist or religious, only the most pathologically committed—Wijeweera of Sri Lanka's People's Liberation Front, for example—have proved able to resist this sort of temptation extended by the mothering, smothering state. And these exceptions, by the very extremity of their actions, defeat themselves by inviting the state's full wrath and violence, which ultimately is backed by a public consensus that a revolutionary as extreme as Wijeweera simply does not

understand how the system works, and thus cannot have the greater good at heart.

Of course, this process of counterinsurgency depends fundamentally on democracy and a functional state. Without the authority that even a wounded democracy provides its elected elite, and the chances a democratic system offers to reslice the state pie, an inexorable momentum can shift to the insurgents, as the British colonialists discovered with the Indian independence movement in the 1930s and Pakistan's generals rediscovered in 1971 with Bangladesh's Sheikh Mujib and in 1989 with their own Benazir Bhutto.

In the present cases of Hindu revivalism in India and Islamic radicalism in Pakistan, the doctrines of the religious insurgents have been around a lot longer than Maoism, Bengali nationalism, or even democracy, and so the attached popular emotions are easier to exploit by conjuring myths such as the legend of the Gyanwapi Mosque. Yet South Asian rulers have been buying off and fobbing off religious radicals for a lot longer than they have been coping with vicious Marxist revolutionaries or beautiful, debonair democrats, so the state's keepers are considerably more skilled at achieving their goals. From the standpoint of a counterrevolutionary, the wonderful thing about religion is that anybody can claim to have it.

India could learn about this from Pakistan. To preserve and protect themselves against the international tide of Islamic radicalism symbolized by the 1979 Iranian revolution, governments in Pakistan have made a virtual science out of appropriating symbols of Islam—Benazir with her modest scarves, Zia with his public lashings and executions—so as to deprive the radical clergy of the symbols' political power. The long self-appointed rule of an Islamic middle-class army in Pakistan has further undermined the clergy's political power—the debate over Islam and politics has taken place within the Pakistani state's structures, rather than as a confrontation between governments and outsiders. At the same time, sufficient public and political capital has been poured into the mosques to ensure that a majority of clergy come to regard national religious revolution, with all its nasty ferreting out of heretics, as a potential lifestyle inconvenience. There is a legitimate question whether Pakistan's internalization of religious politics has carried too high a price—some argue that it helped push the country toward its 1971 breakup by institutionalizing unresolved, competing demands about ethnic and religious identity. But

in the present day, the trick looks to have been more successfully played by the full range of Pakistan's politicians than by India's.

In India, the government's relationship with the Hindu clergy and its political allies has been similar in a few ways but far less complete. Troubled secular politicians presiding over the Indian state apparatus since Nehru's death, such as Indira Gandhi and her son Rajiv, have periodically "played the Hindu card," as the Indians put it, by rushing to and fro to deliver prayers at Hindu temples in advance of an election. (By most accounts, Indira is regarded as a true religious believer, Rajiv as more of a political opportunist.) But both Gandhis were less attentive over the years to seducing and buying off the hard-core networks of Hindu radicals centered around the Rashtriya Swayamsevak Sangh, or RSS, a secretive network of right-wing Hindu nationalists. The Gandhis felt they had no need to bother about the RSS. Although its roots date to the 1920s, for most of the time since then, the RSS has been a small, marginal, and popularly abhorred political force. But in the late 1980s, as the Nehru-Gandhi dynasty tottered and the political economy it built foundered, the RSS and the political party it created, the BJP, at last came in from the wilderness. Indeed, they thundered to center stage in Indian politics and society, preaching their sermons and chanting their chants to large and enthusiastic crowds. They stirred mobs of Hindus to hit the streets in northern cities, attack disputed mosques with hammers and sticks, and punch it out with their Muslim neighbors with greater enthusiasm than before. On this wave of brutal violence the BJP rode to sudden and unexpected political influence, promising to tame the very destructive forces of religious violence that they had helped to unleash. "Riding the tiger" is what the Hindu radical leaders call their political art.

The tiger's ferocity may arise in part from the subcontinent's storied past of religious war and conquest, but its present bite comes, too, from contemporary competition in a society where the established Nehruvian order is under pressure from many sides. Just as during the medieval period Islam and Hinduism provided a language and mythology that galvanized rival interest groups to battle over decidedly earthly matters of conquest and power, so, too, in the 1980s and early 1990s, religion has become one organizing principle in conflicts that are not by any means confined to spiritual disagreement. Again, Desmond's summary is cogent. On his list of factors feeding the outburst of Hindu nationalism in the late

1980s he includes the rising prominence of Indian Muslims in urban centers, especially after many of them returned with bundles of cash earned while working as laborers, engineers, nurses, hoteliers, and drivers in the rich Arab states around the Persian Gulf. At the same time, he writes, "India's rate of economic growth nearly doubled, creating a new consumer economy. . . . India's middle class was no longer an elite, Westernized group, as it was at partition, but a highly acquisitive, anxious class whose members only vaguely comprehended the point of secularism while very sharply feeling a grievance against any group with a supposed special status—especially Muslims."

In some respects the problem is not that the postindependence Nehruvian elites in South Asia did too little to foster mobility beneath them, but rather that they did too much, raising expectations the state could not fulfill. India's Hindu movement seems in many ways an example. One of the credibility gaps the Hindu revivalist BJP had to overcome as it bid for power in the late 1980s was its reputation as the political party of urban Hindu petty traders, an enterprising but acquisitive class dismissed by the older Nehruvian elite for their notorious love of money. Yet it was precisely this affinity for traders and trading that helped to attract many of India's emerging urban middle class to the BJP—these urban Indians were often capitalist in orientation and wished for a more stable, less corrupt polity than the secular Congress Party under the Gandhis could provide. The BJP promised to address these aspirations, and its coffers were showered with middle-class and industrial money to help extend the party's reach.

With success, the BJP has discovered a new predicament. The Congress Party, fractured but still clinging to power, has moved decisively to recapture middle-class loyalties by adopting free-market economic reform, long a distinguishing feature of the Hindu revivalist platform. This thunder-stealing by Nehru's heirs in the Congress pushes the BJP further toward obscurantist religious radicalism as a means of distinguishing itself from its rivals—mosque-breaking being a proven tactic along these lines. But this sort of persistent Hindu radicalism may in the future look all the more ridiculous to the Indian middle class when it sees the recently elected preacher-politicians rolling around in their state-sponsored chauffeured Ambassadors or doling out jobs and land through the Nehruvian state patronage networks. Yet whether the Hindu movement has in fact peaked depends partly on whether India's Congress government can

deliver to India successful reform of the bloated economy and of itself, a prospect no Hindu trader is likely to bet his savings on for now.

Apologists for Hindu revivalism employ the rationales of the failing Nehruvian state, or the injustices of history, or the modest programs of affirmative action granted to Muslims, or the yearnings of Hindus for a nationalism that will at last succeed decisively. But in the towns and cities the Hindu movement and its Muslim counterpart often tangle over far more pedestrian and nasty business: land-grabbing, business rivalry, extortion, and other enterprises of the criminal underground. Thug-politicians of familiar character and methods see religious revival as a new path to an old end.

I came across this in Hapur, a squalid, swelling market town on the road between Delhi and Aligarh. The first and overwhelming impression the city makes is of chaotic, booming commerce: tinkling bells of bicycle rickshaws, squawking motorcycle horns, belching water buffaloes, and singing pushcart vendors. Hapur is a subcontinental Dodge City—only it is not a lone bustling outpost on windswept plains but one of dozens of interlocking overpopulated market centers in the northern belt, where agriculture and industry have found prosperous intersections. Land prices have soared in the last decade, far outstripping inflation. Wheat, potatoes, shoes, cloth, machine and auto parts pour in and out of town on bullock carts, camel carts, motor rickshaws, rusting flatbed trucks, and towering ten-ton Tatas. With the goods come people, villagers migrating temporarily or permanently from the countryside in search of work. Two thirds of the population is Hindu, one third Muslim. They jam into tenements with relatives or pitch tar-paper shanties on the edge of town. Through this scene wander the usual array of fast-buck artists: property dealers, labor contractors, wholesale traders, insurance salesmen. Some have inherited their trade from earlier generations but many more are striking out on their own, pushing into neighborhoods and businesses where they have not been before. In the moribund Indian political economy, I tended to view this sort of commercial trail-blazing as heroic, since it was the key to job creation and rising incomes, and potentially to national upliftment. But, as a thirty-two-year-old property dealer named Saleem Ahmed discovered, it can bring a businessman face-to-face with strange and dangerous forms of competition.

I went to Hapur initially because of a snake. The Delhi papers had made a celebrity of a five-foot black cobra who started a Hindu-Muslim riot by

slithering into a peepul tree and nesting in its leafy branches. The snake's arrival, which occurred auspiciously at the start of a Hindu religious snake festival in an impoverished quarter of Hapur, prompted an outpouring of Hindu religious fervor. Egged on by local preacher-politicians who drove about with leaflets and megaphones to herald the snake's appearance as a miracle, thousands of Hindus poured from their homes and worshiped for days at the peepul tree. They threw money and jewelry at the snake, laid out bowls of milk for it to drink, chanted and sang religious songs. The preacher-politicians said that the snake was Lord Shiva incarnate and that he wanted a temple built at the base of the peepul tree. Preparations were made and garlanded idols duly placed beneath the snake's nest. But residents of a Muslim slum fifty yards down a dusty lane objected. When the police, attempting to enforce the Muslims' legal rights, ordered the idols and temple paraphernalia removed from the peepul tree, the Hindus rioted. In bursts of rage, knife-wielding mobs raced into the Muslim quarter and stabbed anyone they found on the streets. At least half a dozen Muslims died. A few Hindus also were killed when the police, facing down the mob, lowered their rifles and opened fire.

The snake was certainly a catchy angle, but to a skeptic concerning religious miracles, what seemed more pertinent was the question of land. This is what Mark Fineman of the *Los Angeles Times* and I began to ask about when we arrived to examine why the snake riot had occurred.

Hindus who lived in the brick tenements around the peepul tree said that the land where the cobra appeared had originally been owned by the Patwaris, a local Hindu trading family. The vacant lot at issue was not much to look at—an acre of so of half-flooded swamp at the intersection of dirt lanes surrounded by teeming, teetering slums. Nonetheless, the lot would fetch serious money in a town like Hapur. It had been empty for many years; nobody in the surrounding slums was quite sure why the Patwaris had sold it. But they had the impression, imparted by the Hindu preacher-politicians on loudspeakers during the snake's miraculous appearance, that the Patwari family had always intended to build a temple on the site but just had not been able to get around to it yet. Thus the snake's appearance during the recent Hindu festival had confirmed that a temple on this land was ordained.

In fact, the Patwaris had no such plans, or so said Anil Kumar Patwari, who turned out to be a young, enterprising wholesale trader who specialized in shoes. In his shop half a mile away he explained to us what had

happened. Patwari had inherited the peepul-tree lot from his parents and had sold it five months earlier to raise capital for family businesses, which he said were expanding rapidly because of a general economic boom in Hapur. The buyer was Saleem Ahmed, a Muslim property dealer who intended to subdivide the land and resell it as building lots to Muslim families and businessmen. Patwari said it never occurred to him to be concerned that the buyer was a Muslim. "I believe in living peacefully with everyone," Patwari said. "I'm just sitting here in my shop—I have no concern with all this religious feeling. I did it just for the money. We got six hundred twenty thousand rupees [about $22,500] for it. All this business about a temple is just a week old. Nobody talked about a temple on that land. This is just in the last week. The snake did not just suddenly appear. This was all stage-managed. A local snake man got the snake and the people put it there because they wanted the temple."

So the people, or their local Hindu preachers, invented their desire for a temple in order to prevent Muslim businessmen from encroaching on their neighborhood? And they brought out a snake in order to stir enough Hindu fervor to accomplish this?

"This is obvious," Patwari said. "Everybody is talking that this is the real reason for the riot. The plots have already been sold by Saleem to different Muslims for building. The Hindus and Muslims live opposite each other in that neighborhood. The Hindus fear the road will be blocked by the Muslims and the entry to their area, to their shops, will be blocked. The only way to prevent this is with the temple."

At the Hapur police station, as we sat on lawn chairs arranged on carpets in the sun, police superintendent Rajesh Kumar Lai said that this analysis sounded about right to him. "The Hindus were of the view that if this land was sold to Muslims, they would come near to their community and their Muslim colony would expand. There was a fear that if they expanded, there may be problems later on. That was the reason this whole thing developed. . . . It was basically a land-grabbing process.

"About a month ago, they decided to put a photograph of Lord Shiva on that tree and they started worshiping at that place. They formed a temple committee and started negotiations with Saleem and other Muslims. The Muslims were of the view that if a temple was built, that would be a cause of dispute and problems in the future. The administration tried to mediate and find a peaceful solution. Our administration initiated measures to attach the property so nothing could be done on that

place—to defuse the situation. Nobody could build anything at all. But the Muslims obtained a stay on our order in court. This meant they could build.

"Right afterwards, a big snake appeared—a cobra. It had no fangs and it was blind. It is said that it was purchased for three hundred rupees from a snake charmer, purchased by mischievous elements. It was told to the public—in the form of pamphlets and speeches also—that Lord Shiva had appeared in the form of a cobra. That snake was put near the tree and the information went around that this place is now more holy because Lord Shiva decided to appear as a snake. People here are very simple. In their belief in God, their fear of God, they were carried away. Large groups came with folded hands to see that snake. A feeling of resentment, fear, and panic developed among the Muslims.

"The next day, a wall was broken near the tree. There was tension in the air. Rival crowds, very agitated, chanting slogans, roamed about. Local police officers tried to cool the feelings. We tried to negotiate the matter. There was a meeting in which myself, others in the administration, and representatives of both parties talked. Different peace-loving people of the area, responsible persons, were called. They decided in the interests of peace and harmony to remove some of the objects from the tree. Meantime they were negotiating for the land also. Plus they were requesting the Muslim fellows that they should be allowed to construct a *dharamsala* [religious hostel] in that area. Initially the Muslims agreed to this. But later on, when measurements were done, no land was available. When no extra land was available, the negotiation failed.

"The snake itself tried to run away several times. But the Hindu leaders did not let it. The snake was their money-earner. The snake brought the people.

"A few days later, we called the Hindu leaders. They said, 'The situation is beyond our control. We cannot remove those idols.' We requested them to take these things away amicably, on their own. This they would not do. They resented it. As a strategy, men went indoors and they sent their ladies outside. The women surrounded the tree and started worshiping and singing. On the other side, the Muslims were also collected. It appeared there was a chance of a clash between the two communities. So we decided to remove those photographs and idols from the tree. The crowd started to throw stones. It was coming from all around—except from the Muslim side. When the stones started coming, the ladies went

home. We lathi-charged [attacked with sticks] first, then fired tear gas. They went onto the rooftops and started pelting stones and country-made bombs. They started firing country-made pistols. They set one Muslim shop ablaze. We were almost cornered. We did not want to use bullets. It's a last resort. But more and more our efforts failed. . . . The bombs started falling on us. We were injured. There was no option but to use firearms.

"Even then, they were crazy. They kept on throwing things. It was surprising. That was because of their heightened religious feelings. They were ready to sacrifice themselves. Those who started this—their motive was land-grabbing by exploiting religious feelings. Finally, the firing controlled them. The dead and injured were sent to the hospital.

"Taking advantage of this firing, the snake vanished in thin air. The snake has taken its toll. The snake is gone."

I was curious about what Saleem Ahmed thought of all this. We wandered around the Muslim quarter asking about him and eventually he turned up. He was thirty-two years old, a father of four, mild in demeanor, subdued about all that had arisen from his land deal. In fact, he said, the peepul-tree deal was the first land transaction he had ever attempted. He had decided to move into real estate because his other business—fertilizer—was doing well and throwing off surplus cash. By subdividing the land he bought from Patwari, Ahmed cleared a quick 120,000-rupee profit. He said that after he sold the land, the first he heard about the plans for a temple was when a local Hindu leader approached him, explained that religious idols had been placed in the peepul tree, and demanded 20,000 rupees to remove them. Ahmed said that when he refused to give in to this extortion, the business with the snake miracle began.

I asked Ahmed how he felt about the real estate business now that he had gotten a taste of it.

"I wish I hadn't gotten into this entire affair," he answered. "I hate this job. There's a lot of antipathy toward this kind of businessman. The money I made was of no value. . . . I'll go back to my other trade now."

I thought for days afterward about Ahmed's demoralization. On the one hand, it seemed to me inauspicious for India, because the enterprise of millions of Ahmeds is the tide on which India's political economy rides. Obviously, he and his Hindu and Muslim brethren will do better for themselves and better for their country—create more jobs, create more income—if they can buy and sell their property and trade their shoes in

an integrated economy, one that is not Balkanized by the shifting, imaginary Indo-Pakistani borders that spring up in the northern industrial towns and cities in times of religious violence.

But there was another way to view Ahmed's predicament. In his property deal around the peepul tree, he had rediscovered to his chagrin a code of community that South Asians have lived by for centuries. These communities are defined not only by religion but by ethnicity and tribe and clan. When they compete as loose-knit groups in a dynamic political economy, the result is by no means limited to bloodshed. The communities also provide creative, collective backing for the understandable and necessary desire of poor people to become rich. Through this process, a larger, more egalitarian nation-state can arise. And if the Hindu-Muslim divide offered a sometimes dispiriting example of this kind of conflict between South Asian communities, there was related conflict under way in boom towns like Hapur that seemed to contain more cause for optimism: the struggle among castes.

12

Inside Out

"Servants are thinking too much," that is still a common phrase that you hear around the house.

—P. Murali Gopal

I do not know the name of the man I admire most in India. He may have left a business card but I did not retain it.

He showed up unannounced at my front door in New Delhi one afternoon in the midst of the 1990 caste riots. An affirmative action plan promising reserved government jobs to a wide tier of India's lower castes had sparked a violent reaction in the north. Mobs of upper-caste university students fearful of losing opportunity through reverse discrimination roamed New Delhi's wide avenues, trashing cars and grocery stores stocked with smuggled imports from the West. Lower-caste students and farmers staged their own demonstrations, battled with police, and erected makeshift roadblocks on the highways out of the capital, where they burned buses and pelted cars with stones. Hysteria about the riots and the divisive consequences of affirmative action sang daily from the Indian national newspapers, which are owned, edited, and written by members of the upper castes. Fueling the apprehension was a spreading wave of ghoulish self-immolations by aggrieved upper-caste teenagers and pre-teens. The burnings had been sparked by Rajiv Goswami, an obscure, quiet upper-caste student at Delhi University who stood one afternoon on the perimeter of a street crowd of chanting protestors and then, in circumstances which remain unclear, doused himself with kerosene and set

himself alight. Soon Goswami, wrapped in gauze and fighting for his life in a New Delhi hospital, was being hailed as a tragic but noble paragon of self-sacrifice in a worthy cause, namely the development of a society based on "merit," not caste or feudal identity. Seeking to emulate Goswami's reputation, and perhaps to resolve troubles unrelated to political dilemmas such as affirmative action, dozens of other upper-caste teenagers in New Delhi and elsewhere began to soak themselves with gasoline and set themselves on fire. Panic and dread spread among parents of the upper-caste urban middle class—accountants, clerks, bureaucrats, and businessmen born to social privilege but struggling under varied pressures in an increasingly competitive political economy. In my neighborhood, which was dominated by such relatively wealthy but insecure households, parents kept a sharp eye on their matches.

In this atmosphere I opened my door and stared in disbelief at a smiling young man on my front stoop who clutched a cigarette lighter, a bottle of kerosene, and a fire extinguisher. He was perhaps twenty-one, clean-cut, dressed in pressed slacks and a knit shirt. He announced that he was a salesman, appointed representative of the finest manufacturer of fire extinguishers in India. He said that if I would spare a minute of my time, he would provide a demonstration that would not only amaze me but would convince me of the immediate need to stock my house with his fine safety products.

"Sir," he asked, "shall I set myself on fire?"

As he began to pour kerosene onto his forearm, I recovered my voice in time to object. I noted that as a foreigner, I had no great worry that my children would immolate themselves over a caste-based affirmative action plan. But I did wonder whether this sales pitch was working very well elsewhere in the neighborhood.

"Business, sir, is booming," he answered.

I invited him in and asked about his background as he unpacked demonstration fire extinguishers and promotional videotapes. He said that he was lower caste by birth. His father was a peasant farmer who owned and tilled a couple of acres, meaning that he was better off than those at the very bottom of the rural ladder, the landless. Still, his parents had worked mightily and saved scrupulously to put him through school, he said. Now he was at university, an undergraduate in engineering. He hoped eventually to study abroad. Meantime, to earn money for school and to keep himself in style, he was moonlighting as a fire-extinguisher

salesman, tromping door to door through upper-caste neighborhoods, offering to rescue the privileged from themselves at twenty U.S. dollars a pop. It was a very good franchise, he said.

Though uncertain about the quality or utility of his extinguishers, I told him that I would buy three, strictly on the principle that such audacity must be rewarded if India is ever to realize its ambitions. I think the salesman wasn't sure what I was talking about, but he remained polite enough, no doubt on the principle that the money of lunatic foreigners was just as good as the money of frightened Brahmins.

I tended to invest my hopes in such quixotic characters because otherwise it would be easy to give in to despair about the legacy of feudalism and caste in South Asia. Even in Pakistan and Bangladesh, where casteless Islamic ideology has helped to decouple feudal economic arrangements from spiritual tradition, the old system clings to the land like glue, trapping all sorts of ambitious people in place. The system finds a thousand ways to perpetuate itself, including forms of religious sanction, as in the exploited tradition of living Islamic saints in the Pakistani countryside. As with race in America, it is difficult to be certain when you care too little and when you care too much about feudal and caste discrimination. But if you believe in virtually any version of the egalitarian ideal, and if you confront with open eyes what this discrimination means in South Asia today and how it operates, the enormity of the problem can be staggering.

In India, ancient caste identities remain very much alive, despite the determined efforts of Nehruvian policymakers to kill them off. If you could produce a satellite photograph of India with different colors marking the prominence of different castes, the result would be an indecipherable patchwork. There are thousands of castes and subcastes sanctioned by Hinduism as divinely ordained earthly stations from which one cannot escape except through death and reincarnation. Some castes are large, such as the superior Brahmins or the inferior untouchables, but even these have regional subdivisions notable as much for their differences as for their shared status. Other castes are tiny groups, confined to a single clan of artisans or laborers in a single village. The overall stratification is roughly symmetrical. About 15 percent of India's population are reckoned to belong to the upper castes at the very top. About 20 percent belong to the very lowest castes or to oppressed indigenous tribes at the very bottom. (Untouchables are in this group, though technically they are

not a caste at all, but a spiritually homeless group of "outcasts.") This lowest tier is designated by the government as "scheduled castes and tribes" and has been targeted in various affirmative action programs since just after independence. In the middle, some 65 percent of the population belong to what is known these days as the "other backward classes," lower and lower-middle castes and minorities such as Muslims and Christians. Within this grouping are some clans that have done very well since independence, some that have done very poorly, and some that have simply remained in servitude to their landlords. It was a doomed attempt by India's crusading prime minister V. P. Singh to initiate for these other backward classes a new, sweeping affirmative action plan in public employment that sparked the caste riots of 1990, including the upper-caste self-immolations that brought the fire-extinguisher salesman to my door.

For decades now, South Asian politicians and activists have been attempting sporadically to untie the hierarchical binds of history, religion, and culture through land reform legislation, speeches, symbolic acts, marches, electoral campaigns, industrialization plans, welfare programs, and government hiring schemes. Many of these efforts reflect the noblest aspirations of the Nehruvian state: social mobility and an end to caste distinctions through universal education, full employment, widespread health care, and a benevolent, leveling bureaucracy. That Indian society continues to honor these ideals is evident in the way it can still be shocked by dramatic instances of their breach. Indian newspapers, magazines, and video news programs controlled by the upper castes report regularly and prominently on the continuing murder, rape, and arson attacks carried out in the countryside by upper-caste landowners against the lower-caste landless. But often implicit in such reporting is the idea that these cases are archaic exceptions, abhorrent to the enlightened sensibilities of the cities, where castes and creeds mix freely and can stake their claims to the future. What the opinion-making upper-caste elite does not often wish to reckon with is how the Nehruvian state itself has been constructed to preserve caste roles—and especially in the cities. Too often what the state has created is not a level playing field but a series of interlocking, competitive clan- or caste-based mafias—vote banks, as they are called by Indian politicians—where the organizing principle is not merit but patronage. And patronage flows not only from the state machinery but from the advantages of birth. Upper-caste networks are enriched and often protected from challenge by inheritance of land and state-sanctioned

business franchises obtained from the precolonial princes, and later, the British imperialists.

The independent Indian state has partially undermined the strength of upper-caste networks. In the cities and in such institutions as the bloated military, old caste and feudal identities are dissolving. A younger generation is rising with attitudes significantly more egalitarian than those of their parents and grandparents. New lower-caste mafias have attached themselves to the state, mainly through affirmative action and electoral politics, and have built up their own networks of patronage and wealth, lifting some of their members to new social and economic heights—in some cases, even overthrowing local upper castes who used to hold them down.

Yet progress toward the creation of a casteless society has been much slower than the Nehruvian idealists promised. One bit of anecdotal evidence was what Indians would say when I asked whether the old caste and feudal identities really made any day-to-day difference in their lives. I asked this question of hundreds of people in cities, towns, and villages. Almost invariably, those of high birth said that feudal and caste origin mattered less and less in swirling, modernizing South Asia. Younger Brahmins and Rajputs would say that they had lost their parents' ability to determine the caste of a stranger with a few subtle, well-chosen questions about family background. But not once did a person of low birth tell me the same. They knew exactly how to determine the caste of a stranger and did so regularly; to them, caste and feudal identity made all the difference in the world.

It was not difficult to see why, even within a square mile of my supposedly exclusive neighborhood of "luxury" concrete-block three- and four-bedroom homes inhabited by upper-caste Indian bureaucrats and multinational businessmen. Just a few hundred yards from my driveway, on a sheltered hill up a dirt alley, lived a colony of untouchable "ragpickers" who made their living from the refuse of the Delhi rich. Their small compound, perhaps two acres square, consisted of a dozen low tar-paper shanties; a "school" constructed from a canvas canopy, rope, and wooden pegs; and heaps upon heaps of steaming, stinking garbage, which the residents collected, sorted, and sold off to Delhi scrap dealers. Flies and mosquitoes swarmed through the colony, far outnumbering the residents. Unwashed, unclothed children chased one another through the trash as their parents squatted beside the great piles, picking and sorting. In

economic terms, the ragpicking colonies—there are scores of them nestled into major cities—are carefully integrated into urban life. They serve as partial substitutes for municipal garbage collection. There is little public refuse collection in India, in part because there is little household waste that the larger economy wants to dispose of entirely. One man's scrap is another man's house. One man's newspaper is another's shopping bag. One man's lawn trimmings are another's donkey feed. Ragpickers are intermediaries in these recycling transactions. But while they operate in a market-based, cash-driven subeconomy, they cannot be thought of as free agents. The roles they played centuries earlier as bonded, landless peasants in the rural villages many of them now play again in the new cities, despite the job set-asides and education schemes that have brought a relatively small number out of the trash heaps and into the dimly lit offices of the bureaucracy. The exploitation these urban untouchables face today is more complicated than it used to be, but to the ragpickers themselves it does not seem different because it arises not merely from poverty but from the stigma of low birth.

I drove up to the ragpicking colony one afternoon and sat on rope cots with a dozen residents to talk about caste and politics. Surely, I argued to them, despite the timeless degradation and poverty, there were scraps of progress here in the colony as well—the school provided by the government, for example, or the fact that they had escaped from the isolated oppression of the villages to a city where they could better protect themselves and their children. Didn't it seem likely, at the least, that some of their children's children might find a way off these heaps, propelled in part by the hard work and willingness to migrate of their courageous grandparents?

But it was difficult to find anyone who held this view. They understood my argument well, they wrestled with it privately themselves—they just did not believe it.

"I've been here since 1974," answered one emaciated man, Om Prakash. "I haven't seen anyone rise out of this. We have all stayed poor. Not a single person has become big. We only watch after our own children. I had a brother, he came to New Delhi and did a bachelor of arts degree. Now he's back in Haryana working as a ragpicker. This is the place for us. We can't get out of here. We hope and we try. There's always hope, but we never reach anything. I'm sure my grandfather hoped, too. Even

if I work hard, if I go forward one step, there are ten people pushing me back again."

A few hundred yards from the ragpickers' hillock lies the rutted entrance to an even more oppressive world: a colony of stone crushers. I first noticed them while landing at New Delhi's international airport. In certain air traffic patterns, the planes sweep low over a vast scarred landscape of eroded red clay rock quarries just outside the airport grounds. If you peer down carefully into the pits, you can see small bands of shirtless men and scarved women and even children smashing rocks by hand with picks and axes. In summer, they do this work in temperatures of up to 120 degrees or more. There are about five thousand of them, mainly landless untouchables from neighboring, drought-stricken Rajasthan who are collected by unscrupulous labor contractors, forced into debt, and then set to work in the quarries for decades, even generations, until their loans are repaid. The workers live in shanty colonies on the rim of the pits. Shortly after dawn each morning they carry their picks and sledgehammers on their shoulders down into the quarries and begin smashing against the walls. When piles of rock accumulate at their feet, they lift the stones and hurl them into flatbed trucks that arrive to haul the rocks away. A family earns about $1.50 per truckload at present exchange rates, after commissions and expenses deducted by the quarry owners. On a good day, a fit husband and wife working hard together can fill two or three trucks. The pits are divided up among families until all the stones on a given wall are crushed. Typically, a single family will smash rocks on the same wall in the same pit for seven years or more, day after day. Sisyphus could not have known worse than this.

Before climbing down into the pits one day to talk with the crushers, I visited the manager of the quarry "labor society," which skimmed a percentage of the crushers' wages and in theory invested the money in housing and water. We talked for a while about how the quarry system works. I asked casually why all the crushers were either untouchables or tribals. "It's the nature of the work," the manager answered, laughing. "You wouldn't expect a Brahmin to come and do this, would you?"

God forbid. Wandering that afternoon from pit to pit, dodging stones as they fell from hammers, I asked the crushers whether any of the Brahmin-born, socialist-bred labor organizers or politicians who lived in the big flats and houses just a few hundred yards away had ever accom-

plished anything for them. Nobody shied from the opportunity to complain.

"In the morning, you can't work because of the heat and at night you can't sleep because of the mosquitoes," said Lal Chand, squatting on a pile of rocks in the shade. "We've got no electricity. The nearby slums have electricity, but we don't. There are all sorts of people who come here and say you will get electricity. They want something from us—votes, money—then they go away. Nothing changes. They tempt us with a lot of things, but then they disappear." He has been crushing rocks for six or seven years, he said. I asked Chand how he occupied his mind while swinging his sledgehammer. He said mainly he thought about riding the bus to buy liquor and get roaring drunk in Haryana, a journey he could afford to undertake about once every twenty days.

In a neighboring pit I found a young, attractive, muscular married couple, Choti Devi and Bahwaral Lal, rhythmically hacking at a wall and loading a truck with stones. They were born and raised on the rim of the quarry—their parents work in the same pit—and were married fourteen years ago, when he was twelve and she was eleven. They have two sons, two daughters. They have been chopping at this same wall for ten years.

"I keep thinking about food all day—that's what makes me work," he said, glistening with sweat.

"What about your kids—will they do the same job?" I asked.

"My son will do the same thing," she answered, hoisting stones to her head and heaving them into a parked truck. "I'll send him to school, but there's never enough money, so he'll do this as well. This work is nothing difficult. I have the strength."

"What's so special about kids?" her husband asked, smashing stones for Devi to lift. "I was a kid and I did it. If there's no alternative, why not? I studied math and science, but now there is no alternative."

"He gets mad in this heat," said his wife. "Two years ago he got mad and ran away. We both blame it on the heat. We've got to live this life. If we fight, it's because of the heat. We've got to take our anger out on somebody."

"It helps when she comes and works," he said. "It helps a lot."

I asked about New Delhi's various labor organizers and socialist activists. What did they think of them?

"They come and tell us to become one," he answered. "How can

laborers become one? We've got pressures from the masters. If we get into the union, we'll lose our jobs."

"What worries you the most?" I asked.

"Tuberculosis."

Silence. Then the rhythm of hammers on rocks, rocks falling on rocks, rocks landing in trucks. A jet flew overhead, banking low on approach to Indira Gandhi International Airport. I asked Lal what he thinks about when he sees the planes.

"We want to go there," he said, stopping now to lean on his pick. "I feel angry when I see them. They're looking at us. Even I want to fly. I want to sit on an airplane and see the world."

"Perhaps it will happen," I mused, foolishly.

"The only time I'll fly from here is when I quit the world," he answered.

Caste discrimination and bonded labor contravene the laws of independent India, but the state bureaucracy and its business auxiliaries, dominated by upper castes, have a common financial interest in ensuring that the old codes are preserved. The quarries by the airport, for example, are regulated by a typically obscure public sector outpost, the Delhi State Mineral Development Corporation, whose managing director is a senior member of the elite Indian Administrative Service. Some months after I visited the stone crushers, a friend put me in touch with a senior engineer in the DSMDC who was willing to explain in detail how the system at the quarries worked. We met for lunch in the air-conditioned dining hall of the India International Centre, a favorite watering hole of the federal bureaucracy. Sipping his soup, my informant explained that he had tried a few years back to attack from within the corruption and Byzantine side deals that helped keep the quarries' five thousand untouchable crushers in a state of virtual slavery. But he had now given up. The system was too calcified to be changed from the inside, he said.

The crushers are recruited in groups of ten or twenty from villages in Rajasthan and Uttar Pradesh by local upper-caste landlords or by lower-caste emissaries of the landlords, my informant began. The recruits are provided with advances of five thousand to ten thousand rupees by a labor contractor, who takes them to the mines, arranges a shack, and allocates a pit. Few of the recruits appear on the books of the regulatory agency because petty contractors—to hide the degree of exploitation—load the official labor lists with false names and then employ twenty or

so of these recruited untouchable crushers to work under each false name. DSMDC officers stand each afternoon at the gate to the quarry and skim money from each truck driver as he leaves. This money pays the DSMDC salaries and sometimes even produces a small profit for the government. Private companies licensed by the DSMDC to produce the stone within the quarry grounds pay the DSMDC bureaucrats additional money to manipulate supply and market conditions—for example, by keeping a competing quarry closed for purported safety violations. For these payments, bureaucrats auction their services to the highest bidder and do very well. Posting at the DSMDC is usually for one or two years on a rotating basis, so the bureaucrats who land there "feel that if they don't make their money now, they will be transferred to some ministry far from the action, and they will never get rich," my informant said. Everybody is on the take, some for large amounts, some for small. He estimated that in the previous fiscal year a senior IAS man at the corporation earned ten million rupees in payoffs, less kickbacks to politicians. Moreover, there is very little chance of getting caught. Tax collectors are brethren in the federal bureaucratic service and know that their turn to get rich will come, he said. They tend to be from the same upper castes and sometimes from the same regions. Their sense of collective loyalty is augmented by the shared experience of elite federal service. All the payoffs that bind the group are handled in cash. Members of parliament support the networks because the stone crushers form a vote bank that can be loaded into trucks and taken to voting booths or political rallies on demand—the crushers welcome any break from the pits. Most of the politicians who run this particular quarry by the airport are members of the Congress Party, he said, although lately there have been some defections to rival parties. It makes no difference what party they belong to, aside from the potential problem of excessive competition between political rivals, he added.

He had been working in the bureaucracy for twenty years. I asked how things had changed. He said these structural problems had always been present, of course, but that it had gotten markedly worse when Indira Gandhi came back to power in 1980. Her son Sanjay built a network of mafia goons who propped Indira up and helped finance her comeback. It grew worse and worse through the 1980s, he said. A few years ago my informant had a moral epiphany, as he described it, and announced upon being transferred to a mine in Haryana that he would not take any money and would properly enforce all of the federal wage and labor laws. His

colleagues arranged to have him transferred out within six weeks and concocted paperwork "proving" that he was the only one in the whole system taking money illegally. They said they would ruin his career if he persisted with his quest, he said. So now he collects a monthly salary of eight thousand rupees and does nothing. "We need discipline," he was saying by the time the coffee arrived. "We need a Stalin. Only that will save us." He wasn't smiling.

The nexus of politicians, bureaucrats, industrial barons, petty contractors, union bosses, and indebted laborers that my informant described at the quarries is too often typical of the structure of Indian public enterprise. In Bihar are the coal gangs, in Maharashtra the sugar barons, in Uttar Pradesh the tyrannical carpet bosses, in Assam the tea gangs, and on and on. These structures can be dynamic because there is intense and sometimes violent competition for control of the wealth that flows from the core enterprises. But this competition generally occurs across a relatively narrow social band and has proven too heavily dependent on protection and subsidies from the government to be sustainable in the long run by the heavily indebted state.

The roots of this mess are in the land. The eclectic, exploitive, often caste-based arrangements that have grown up around many of the public-sector enterprises reflect similar arrangements that have evolved in the countryside during the last several centuries. The rural structures of South Asian feudalism are diverse because the history of empire, war, and conquest on the subcontinent produced different results in different areas. Not even the British could impose a uniform system, and they changed their minds several times about what was the best way to hold the indigenous population in check. But they did introduce the idea of private property to India. When the British first arrived in the eighteenth century, there was confusion about who actually owned the land that is today India, Pakistan, and Bangladesh. This question was not merely academic, since if they wished to control India, the imperialists needed to understand who else claimed to own it and how they might best be paid to keep quiet. Lord Cornwallis, a witness to the recent British calamity in America, devised the "Permanent Settlement" in much of what is now northern India. The settlement recognized the landlords and local rulers as owners and required them to pay a fixed sum annually to the British government; because their taxes were fixed at a flat rate, the landlords could make loads of money if they improved productivity, and many

promptly did. Cornwallis thought this might head off the revolutionary violence he had encountered in America by providing an intermediate, indigenous class a stake in the empire. But this didn't work very well, in part because the landlords merely exploited more vigorously than before the farmers below them. So by the nineteenth century, when the British conquered Maharashtra, the colonialists were experimenting with more utilitarian systems, which recognized small peasant farmers directly as the owners of the land. This helped to create a class of relatively rich small farmers, who then exploited vigorously the landless below them on the caste totem, particularly the untouchables.

The Congress Party was initially the party of wealthy Indian landlords. Later, under the leadership of Gandhi and Nehru, and influenced by such diverse twentieth-century events as the Bolshevik revolution and Franklin Roosevelt's New Deal, it adopted a radical agrarian line. Within the party and the Muslim League, however, egalitarian ideas were slow to take hold as different classes of landlords battled with each other for influence and control of the prospective spoils of independence. The short version of this long and complex struggle is that while the founders of the Nehruvian state permitted and sometimes encouraged gradual change in the countryside—and in a few regions threw out upper-caste landlords to replace them with middle-caste peasant farmers—by and large they promised much more land reform than they actually delivered. In places like Maharashtra and Gujarat, middle castes prevailed, sometimes on their own and sometimes with help from the state. But in the northern heartland, as the land reform specialist Arvind Das put it to me one afternoon in New Delhi during a helpful tutorial, "a lot of legislation was enacted and very little was implemented." In part this was because when the government passed reform laws, it provided long waiting periods before the laws took effect. In this interregnum, landlords juggled land records, allocating plots to fictious names, dead relatives, dogs, cats, and actual sharecroppers while retaining firm control themselves.

Das estimates that in a state such as Bihar, albeit an exceptional place where the most vertical forms of feudalism remain intact, there are perhaps two hundred landlords who control more than five thousand acres each—enormous estates in such a fertile, overpopulated region. His assessment is that the richest of these landlords owns about thirty-three thousand acres, all controlled through fictitious records. Most important, such empires can be preserved only by integration with the structures of

the Nehruvian state. The Bihar landlord with the estimated thirty-three thousand acres has achieved such influence through a son-in-law who is a senior bureaucrat in the Indian Administrative Service, a daughter who is a Congress Party member of parliament, and three grandchildren who are members of the IAS. "In this system, the person with investments and money puts it into his son's education toward getting a government job," Das explained. This preserves and extends the family empire into new areas, such as public-sector businesses. Since the bureaucracy controls the economy, those with resources compete to control the bureaucracy. Extreme cases of landlords who may control thousands of acres are very rare, but the principle holds nonetheless for landlords who hold smaller but relatively sizable tracts of fifty to one hundred acres.

In Bihar, especially, the competition is sometimes expressed in persistent small-scale wars. Upper-caste landlords have formed private armies to defend their land from rivals, including middle-caste peasants and low-caste leftist revolutionaries, known as the Naxalites.

During the most intense caste conflicts of 1990, I flew down to Bihar's capital, Patna, and drove out with a local crime reporter to talk with an upper-caste warlord about his prospects. We rattled over pitted and unrepaired roads and crumbling bridges through eroded land to a small village named Pauna. At sunset, the warlord arrived in a sputtering Ambassador with a band of bodyguards who wore bright red scarves and carried double-barreled shotguns. This self-styled Rajput general, Shivaji Singh, sat on a rope cot as much of the village population gathered to listen. "The situation is rising beyond tolerance. Any time the tension is going to break," he said. "For the last ten years we've been fighting these Naxalites and these backward-caste armies. Eighteen from our village have died, six from my own group. If this tension continues, in the future it will be much worse than ever before."

"Will there ever be a time when caste is not important in India, when it will not so sharply define people's lives?" I asked.

"No such time will come," he said. Then, pointing to the night sky, "It will take as long as it takes you to count all the stars in the sky. The upper castes have been preserving their land and their possessions. The backward castes have been doing the same. Among the backward classes, there are two sections—those with land, and those without. What has happened is that the poor landless laborers still believe that the upper castes are their enemies, not the rich leaders of their own castes. . . . There

is no way out. I know I won't win because they are greater in number. But I have no choice but to fight, so I will fight."

A paradox of continuing feudal and caste conflict in South Asia is that where the Nehruvian state is especially weak—such as in Bihar or Pakistan's southern Sind province—feudal rivals tend to take matters into their own hands, battling with weapons for control of land or criminal mafias. But where the state is strong, the power of those in charge too often institutionalizes caste-derived hierarchies, which encourages losers in the competition to resort to violence against the state. At the same time, the central role of the state—whether it is the bureaucracy in India or the army in Pakistan—convinces many involved that possession and abuse of the state apparatus is the key to ultimate victory.

South Asia's free market reformers today are attempting to alter the basic terms of this competition by asking the Nehruvian state to dismantle itself, to ease itself out of the center. But the reformers know that in the process, the state must provide peaceful and stable mediation of ongoing emotional, often violent, caste and feudal disputes. If, under the guise of free market ideology, the state merely leaps off the stage and hands the existing political economy to upper-caste brethren in narrow, private transactions, leaving the "backward classes" to find opportunity on their own, the eventual result could be disastrously inequitable. Optimists in India pin their hopes on the strength and caste pluralism of the new urbanized, consumerist middle class. Optimists in Pakistan are a little harder to find.

For reasons that perhaps he alone considers noble, former Indian prime minister V. P. Singh offered an awkward quota-based form of this necessary state mediation in August 1990, when he proposed to implement the affirmative action and government jobs plan known as the Mandal Commission report. It was a minor disaster, and not only because of the riots and self-immolations it provoked. Singh is a peculiar politician. The upper-caste son of a feudal raja, he embraced socialism, toiled in the bowels of the Congress Party, developed a reputation as an enemy of corruption, then broke with Rajiv Gandhi and won the prime ministership at the head of a loose coalition on a platform of clean government. Some of the upper-caste establishment supported his original campaign because they, like the urban middle class, yearned for clean administration and checks on the Congress Party–sponsored public-sector mafias. But they hardly expected Singh, one of their own, to attempt a caste revolution by

administrative fiat. Singh who had made no great issue of caste quotas earlier, apparently seized on this idea mainly out of tactical necessity; his coalition was falling apart and he needed somehow to galvanize support from the vote banks of "other backward classes." Afterward, he made a virtue of political necessity and stuck with his new "principles" through a long and steady political decline.

What seemed most interesting about the caste riots Singh provoked were the attitudes of the university students on the barricades. This was the Indian generation poised to inherit the state, and it seemed utterly at odds with itself—as evidenced not so much by the violent, transitory conflict in the streets as by the students' divergent views of what the egalitarian ideal meant to the future of South Asia. The upper-caste students demanded unfettered opportunity. The lower-caste students insisted on a chance to exploit the state.

In the midst of the riots I went to Delhi University to talk with lower-caste students about their predicament. I sat with groups of four or five in the damp student hostels and debated for hours. My argument usually was that by concentrating so heavily on access to the government bureaucracy, they were not going to turn society inside out but would only ensure that power and wealth remained in the form of an inverted cone—and the cone would shrink in volume as the state continued to decline. Their quick response was that they and their families had lived outside the state apparatus for centuries in conditions of overwhelming poverty and injustice. Now that they had the chance, they wanted in.

"The whole system works on this fact, the dominance of the civil service," said Suraj Yadav, eldest son of a lower-caste peasant farming family in Bihar. "When one goes to officialdom, one gets the feeling of what the system really is. These are the lucrative jobs, and naturally one aspires to the best thing. They are the best in terms of the privileges and the prestige one enjoys. . . . By giving [government job] reservations, the way Indian society functions, the benefits will percolate more quickly. There will be a check and balance."

I asked what his parents expected of him. He was the first from his family to make it to college.

"I MUST get into the civil services," he said. "I have felt that this bureaucracy is dominated by the same feudal class, the people who have been ruling Indian society all along. I want to root out the nepotism. There is this perpetuation of economic resources between the bureau-

cracy, which is upper-caste-dominated, and the politicians, also of the upper classes."

"But isn't your plan just a substitution of a lower-caste mafia for an upper-caste mafia, rather than a changing of the system to reward merit and create prosperity?" I asked.

"I didn't say I would replace the system," he answered. "I cannot overhaul the system overnight. Suppose I go into the private sector, the question is, who will I be serving? The same feudal class. I won't be allowed to flourish because of the bureaucracy's hold over the private sector. Suppose I go into contracting—they simply will not give me the licenses."

"But isn't that an argument for dismantling the bureaucracy and perhaps having a system of job and school reservations based on economic need, not caste identity?"

"The idea that India would be a casteless society under such a system is nonsense," he answered. "The reservation policy is not meant to eradicate poverty. It is meant to correct past wrongs and to create a better future. The purpose is to create social justice."

"But doesn't the emergence of a new middle class in the cities, however tentative, suggest that in time, if you just let free market prosperity take root, these caste and feudal arrangements will start to dissolve?"

"There is a middle class coming up, but the caste system is not breaking up," he said. "Where caste is breaking down is where the government reservations policy has already succeeded—as in the south of India."

A lower-caste friend of Yadav's from Bihar, Praveen Chandra, chimed in, asserting the primacy of social mobility through government jobs. "When this man from a lower class is sitting down next to you at the government office, who will you now hold in contempt?"

I heard the answer to precisely that question a week later when I invited three upper-caste student leaders from Delhi University to my office. They turned up in stone-washed jeans, preppy knit shirts, and tennis shoes. They were passionate about the idea of a casteless society organized on principles of markets and merit. But their idea about how to help those on the bottom compete as equals seemed infused with condescension.

"It doesn't make sense that after centuries of oppression, just by giving them a job, their self-esteem is going to go up," said P. Murali Gopal to my suggestion that a government jobs plan, however flawed in principle,

might be a useful way to create rapid social mobility. "There is a lot of discrimination, yes. You see harijans [untouchables] being burned. These things are still there among the educated. These are the attitudes that we got from our fathers and we want to change that. We don't burn harijans or go about raping their women, but yes, it's still there. . . . But there will be a backlash from reverse discrimination. Even now, in government offices, even with senior officials, when you hear them talking about their scheduled-caste colleagues, it's very humiliating. There's no acceptance. When they see this chap, how are they going to think of him if they are victims of reverse discrimination?"

"What comes to everybody's mind is that these people have what they have only because of reservations," added Subodh Marwah, who was dressed in Adidas high-top basketball shoes and a Ralph Lauren polo shirt. "It is coming out that we are talking very negatively about the backward classes. But what my father's generation believes is not what we believe. We have to have every kind of person to make the country move. My father's generation talks as if when a person reaches a certain intellectual level, he can't move down to do these other kinds of [menial] jobs. So if the servants moved up, we would be stranded without any help. We think this school of thought is wrong. We want them to come up, but not at our expense."

"As thinking people, we realize that job reservations are giving the lower classes false dreams that they will not get," said Ajay Khanna.

"I go back to my village and see the ayah [nanny] that took care of me when I was born," reflected Gopal. "For her, nothing has changed. It's so sad."

"It's the politicians who are fooling us," said Marwah.

It is that, or it is the upper castes who are fooling themselves.

13

Secret War

So we are as good or bad a civilized nation as anyone living in the West because, when you carry out this sort of operation, it has a double edge.

—*Retired Pakistani Brigadier General Mohammed Yousaf*

Just west down the Grand Trunk Road from Rawalpindi, in a flat expanse of agricultural fields, railroad tracks, hand-painted billboards, ramshackle food stalls, and muddy market junctions, there sits a walled compound that was for most of the 1980s the Afghan operations headquarters of Pakistan's Inter-Services Intelligence agency. No signs or uniformed pickets identify the complex. In the chaos around the Pakistani Grand Trunk, the trucks this ISI compound disgorged and received each day passed largely unnoticed. Four to five dozen of them departed each morning between five A.M. and noon. The commercial license plates tacked to their rears were false and frequently changed. In their locked cargo bins rattled Chinese-made long-range rockets, or Soviet-made rifles bought from the Egyptians, or American-made antiaircraft missiles, or Italian-made antitank weapons, or British-made limpet mines, or even on occasion Argentinian horses and Texas mules shipped across the Atlantic by the CIA to slog through the rugged, treeless Afghan mountains in service of the mujaheddin.

The trucks crossed the ISI compound gate singly and at carefully planned intervals of five or ten minutes, then turned left on the highway to Peshawar, weaving among the elaborately painted commercial trucks with their singsong horns, the speeding Japanese compact cars, the bull-

ock and mule carts, and the scores of mustachioed male pedestrians in earth-tone salwar robes who loitered about the road with an air of general suspicion. Behind the wheels of the ISI trucks sat drivers from the Pakistan army's logistics command. They wore civilian dress, as did their shotgun-riding bodyguards. On the floor of the cab each team kept a single fully loaded assault rifle, a practice more discreet than that of some ordinary Pakistani drivers, who don't mind dangling their weapons out the window as they overtake bothersomely sluggish cars. In this state of preparation the ISI trucks rolled slowly to Peshawar, the dusty frontier town lodged against the hills beneath the Khyber Pass, on the Afghan border. Day in and day out for nearly a decade these trucks laden with weaponry rolled to Peshawar and then came back empty to Rawalpindi following an overnight stop, during which Afghan rebels backed by the CIA and ISI unloaded the goods into unmarked Peshawar warehouses. Throughout the enterprise the trucks encountered no Soviet agents or highway bandits or saboteurs, the man who ran the program, Mohammed Yousaf, later assured me. The drivers, he said, had but one vexing problem—road accidents. They kept smashing into the zippy Japanese compact cars or into other trucks racing down the highway. Once an ISI truck filled with a stash of weapons and explosives rolled right over an oncoming car and killed two of its occupants, who happened to be Pakistani army officers. Such events drove the secret agents at ISI headquarters to distraction. But there was nothing to be done but pay off or otherwise assuage the victims. If you want to run a secret war in South Asia, you've got to play it as it lays. This was something the CIA may have learned more quickly than the KGB.

Peshawar is where the British Empire in South Asia retreated when it was decided, following the massacre in the late nineteenth century of tens of thousands of British imperial soldiers and civilians at the hands of Afghan tribesmen, that it was not plausible to go any farther. A hundred years later on the western side of Peshawar, where the jagged mountains rise, you still get a sense of Afghanistan as a place unto itself. Geography is part of it—the way the Hindu Kush mountains (the name means "Killer of Hindus") form a wall around much of the country, and then walls within walls, dividing valley from valley and tribe from tribe. History is also part of it. Afghanistan has for centuries been a crossroads between East Asia, Central Asia, South Asia, and West Asia (as the Middle East is known on the subcontinent), and it has participated in more than its

share of wars for being situated in the crosshairs. In the Indian subcontinent's subculture of melodramatic machismo, you hear much idle boasting about which ethnic group is more sturdily martial than another, with the conventional prejudice, reinforced by British imperial policy, placing the Gurkhas and the Punjabis somewhere near the top of the heap and the talkative, erudite Bengalis somewhere near the bottom. One explicit premise of such chatter, however, is that the Afghans are a separate category because, after all, for them war is a kind of national sport. Afghans are justifiably offended by this line, but at the same time what nationalism they possess does arise in part from a shared pride in some of the very characteristics so frequently remarked on by the "three-feet-short" South Asians—especially the Afghans' record of being the only country in the region to consistently defeat foreign invaders who had superior arms. Underlying some of these generalizations is the obvious way in which preindustrial imperatives brim so much closer to the surface in Afghanistan than elsewhere in South Asia. In modern India, Pakistan, Bangladesh, Sri Lanka, and even in Nepal, imperial and independent states advertising themselves as the basis of individual political identity became well established after the eighteenth century. In modern Afghanistan no such state managed to endure and grow outside of the Kabul valley, where the country's seat of ancient kings is ringed by a forbidding wall of mountains. When a handful of Kabul conspirators who amounted to little more than an overambitious Marxist book club attempted through revolution to create and impose such an Afghan state in the late 1970s, all hell broke loose.

The depths of this hell were chiseled during the 1980s by the reigning quasi-imperial superpowers, the Soviet Union and the United States. The basic facts are by now well known, although the balance of moral responsibility remains a topic of contention for many of those involved. Part of the difficulty is that after Soviet troops withdrew from Afghanistan early in 1989 and the crumbled remains of the country began to fall in on themselves, a vigorous effort ensued to obscure and recast the origins of the struggle. One proponent of this version of history was Afghan president Najibullah, a high-school leftist revolutionary and former secret police chief in the days of the Soviet occupation who later projected himself as a moderate democrat and capitalist, a bulwark of secularism against a tide of mujaheddin Islamic radicalism. Najibullah will be remembered vividly by many foreign visitors to Kabul in the late 1980s because

in an effort to promote his new image—and, he said, to facilitate peace in Afghanistan—he probably gave more interviews to foreign journalists than any other head of state in the world.

Najibullah is (as of this writing, we still await, against all odds, the use of the past tense) a large, brutish-looking man with expressive eyes and a chilling belly laugh that erupts without warning. During his interviews, he sat across a shiny conference table with his hands folded and stared at you meaningfully—you felt he was measuring your ability to stare back. In three years, I must have seen him ten times in Kabul, and in each session I asked him what, exactly, he used to believe, back in the prerevolution days of secret Marxist study groups, Kabul University demonstrations, and liaisons with the attachés of the Soviet and East European embassies in the capital. And each time, he gave an answer such as, "The philosophies and ideologies have been put aside now. We have turned the page in a way that we face a white page and we are going to write new things. Most of the time we are not looking backward, we are looking forward."

In some ways, I thought, that was too bad, for what a time it was in Kabul in the late 1960s and early 1970s! In an isolated mountain capital, an island in a sea of feudalism and tribal superstition, a small band of Afghan university students, poets, self-styled intellectuals, and army officers—no more than a few thousand in all—conspired to change the course of their country's history. They met secretly at one another's houses, evading the security forces of the king, a tottering despot named Zahir Shah, and they read aloud from the texts of Marx, Engels, Lenin, and Mao. They plotted conspiracies and bandied about such grand phrases as "progressive democratic socialism" and "the dictatorship of the proletariat." The more noble among them thought about transforming backward, impoverished, unjust Afghanistan into a progressive, equitable society. For an explanation more illuminating than Najibullah's rehearsed amnesia, I went once to see Suleiman Layec, a founder of the Communist-style People's Democratic Party of Afghanistan and one of the country's better-known revolutionary poets. Layec sat in a spacious office in the central committee building of the PDPA; between murderous party intrigues, he was composing an epic poem on modern Afghanistan's history.

"In the sixties, when we were establishing our party, the cold war was at its climax," he said. "Every week in Africa and Asia a new country was

liberated and broke the pull of imperialism. In Africa, the anti-imperialist slogan was very strong. This was the theme of that period. Even at the United Nations people spoke of these things, and this slogan was very strong in confrontation with the United States. We had no experience of establishing a party. It was the first experience of Afghan revolutionaries. It was a political baby—it had to learn to walk. There is a poem that says a baby who has never learned to walk must fall a hundred times. That is our party."

I asked Layec how such a small group of people in Kabul could have tried to emulate the Soviet Union by embracing and enforcing revolutionary ideas—the liberation of women, the abolition of state support for Islam, the redistribution of land—that ran so completely against the grain of Afghanistan's religious and social history.

"You are in a progressive and industrialized country—for you, it is not possible to imagine," he replied. "In our program, instead of reality, we put the ideals. But it was impossible because the reality was something else. . . . We have a saying in Pushtu: 'The fire must be extinguished, even by urine.' People said, This despotism must be overthrown, even by these pathological revolutionaries. The Soviet Union, compared to Afghanistan, seemed a more progressive and industrialized society. It was several things—the mood of the time, the spread of liberation movements, and the moral feeling against the monarchy. Plus, there was this model which seemed so much further along."

The disaster these Kabul revolutionaries produced accelerated at blurry speed. In April 1978, a conspirator in Layec's party shot the current prime minister in the head and declared that socialism had arrived. But as soon as the party tried to implement its revolutionary reforms, the Afghan countryside revolted. This exacerbated rivalries within the party, and the first revolutionary president was suffocated with a pillow by thugs working for the second revolutionary president. The second revolutionary president was poisoned and shot to death by thugs working for the third revolutionary president. This was Babrak Karmal, who backed up his claim to be the lawful arbiter of socialism and progressive thought with several divisions of Leonid Brezhnev's Soviet army, dispatched in furtherance of the "Brezhnev Doctrine" of ever-expanding bolshevism. The war was on. In the decade that followed, an estimated one million Afghans died in fighting between Soviet and Afghan revolutionary troops on one side and the CIA-backed mujaheddin rebels on the other. Another five

million fled across mountains and deserts into exile in Pakistan and Iran. The greatest number settled in and around Peshawar, which became the principal staging ground for the mujaheddin as well as the forward logistics command post for the $2 billion "Reagan Doctrine" covert war program funded by U.S. taxpayers, supervised by the CIA from its station at the U.S. embassy in Islamabad, and managed day to day by Pakistan's ISI.

By the time I reached Peshawar in 1989, the place had the feel of a once-flowering city-state in a period of disillusioned, angry decline. The Soviet troops had left Afghanistan by then, retreating under mujaheddin pressure to the seat of a disintegrating empire. But the war across the Khyber was still grinding on, now pitting Afghans against Afghans in conflicts defined less by cold war ideology than by the old codes of tribalism, ethnicity, family, and faction. The causes were sometimes old and obscure but the armaments supplied by the CIA and the Soviets were new and exceptionally lethal. For this reason and others, the cold war images of Afghanistan propagated during the 1980s in the West, which portrayed the conflict as a kind of large-scale *Jonny Quest* cartoon, no longer seemed plausible. This had a demoralizing effect on everybody, including the Afghan mujaheddin leaders, who now tended to blame the CIA for conspiring to deprive them of final victory over their evil Communist enemies in Kabul. For their part, many of the official Americans involved were in a mood to take their toys and go home, but they were divided about whether this was tactically or morally correct in the circumstances. To questions about why the mujaheddin had not united in military triumph, as Western spies and policymakers had long predicted, the Americans tended to mumble clichés about ancient Afghan tribal feuds and said that while they hoped for the best, with the Soviets gone it was now up to the Afghans to sort things out for themselves. As the spies and diplomats squabbled, the committed flocks of Western philanthropists and freelance adventurers who once enlivened Peshawar with a strange pluralism began to disperse to more promising locations, such as Cambodia or Somalia. Attention in Peshawar now focused on problems that had been present all along but generally ignored. These included the oppressive puritanism of the Islamic radicals, the intolerant tendency of mujaheddin leaders such as Gulbuddin Hekmatyar to order assassinations of political rivals, the enthusiasm of some rebels and Pakistani government officials for heroin trafficking, the way the secret war had under-

mined Pakistan's fragile political economy by producing a million new heroin addicts and a subculture based on automatic weapons, and the way CIA-ISI manipulations had exacerbated divisions among the Afghans, producing an ineffective Peshawar-based mujaheddin leadership of Islamic hard-liners and royalist car dealers—a group often despised by the Afghan rebel soldiers who did the actual fighting and dying in the field. "Donor burnout" and "the Lebanonization of Afghanistan" became the new clichés of bar talk down at the American Club, a sunny watering hole outfitted with painted lawn chairs and a clay tennis court, situated near the walled suburban compounds of Peshawar's upscale University Town.

One visible effect of the secret war was the incongruous presence of late twentieth-century Western technology in a town that looked otherwise enveloped in nineteenth-century frontier ruggedness. That such technology was being imported in large quantities was no secret, since the CIA's covert aid program was debated openly in the U.S. Congress and many of its details were disclosed regularly by journalists quoting proud but anonymous U.S. government officials. But the scale of the technology involved, and how it was selected and employed, was not well known. In Peshawar you got startling glimpses of it. If you drove out rutted roads through mud-walled slums to interview a celebrated mujaheddin commander such as Abdul Haq, who had a CBS-affiliated television cameraman to handle much of his public relations, you were likely to spend as much time talking about the comparative features of Japanese and American lap-top computers as about the conduct of an anti-Communist insurgency. Every major mujaheddin party, and some minor ones, acquired from the CIA television and radio studios, which they installed in dilapidated Peshawar compounds and used to produce videotapes or audiocassettes advertising imminent victory. In these places, you would tromp up barren stairwells at the heels of a rebel in muddy boots and then be ushered with a sort of whoosh into a carpeted, dustless digital studio blinking with mixers, dubbers, and stacks of amplifiers. Young Afghan men with long beards, Islamic caps, and duty-free watches sat at the controls exuding the confident air of spaceship commanders.

Among the mujaheddin, ancient imperatives of status and prestige congealed around the new technologies. A commander was not a commander unless he controlled a stash of the most impressive stuff, such as the shoulder-fired, heat-seaking Stinger missiles, or the mortars that could

be targeted on enemy positions through a computer uplink to a U.S. Navy satellite. As with everything else, the Afghans insisted that they do things their own way, so their relationship with the technology seemed at times stubbornly idiosyncratic. They were often, not to put too fine a point on it, a little casual. The enduring image of a mujaheddin rocket attack on a government-held city was not of disciplined cadres studying targets through laser scopes but of a lone guerrilla nestled in a pile of rocks with his weapon pointed vaguely at the horizon, who then lit the fuse with the glowing ember of his hashish joint. This was the great charm of the mujaheddin. Their courage and determination—the qualities that defeated the Soviet Red Army—seemed innate, unpolluted by the savage, imposed disciplines of cult-revolutionary ideology or modern professional military doctrine.

Perhaps the best example of this was how the mujaheddin did not take the CIA anywhere near as seriously as the CIA took itself. Once I drove through the mountains from Peshawar into Afghanistan with a young mujaheddin who narrated casually how he had worked for a time as a CIA spy. The agency invited him up to the U.S. embassy in Islamabad, Pakistan, provided him with a briefcase-sized coded "burst communications" set, and asked him to send back reports from inside Afghanistan, on a salary of about one hundred dollars per month. My friend described how much fun he had learning to use the English keyboard, typing out his reports, hiding his communications aerial so that fellow mujaheddin would not see it, and then hooking up with the CIA's Islamabad embassy computer to dump his information. He typed up reports about battles, heroin trafficking, Afghan politics, whatever he came across. Later, as the CIA's budget for the covert war shrank and then disappeared, my friend was laid off. He talked about being a CIA spy the way a young American might talk about a job he once had flipping hamburgers at McDonald's— it was just one of those things you did for a living, and when it was over you moved on to the next. In his mind, it seemed to have nothing much to do with Western ideas of country, ideology, or treason. Those were matters that would be reconciled by the Afghans in their own time, in their own way.

But to many of the spies and bureaucrats who managed the war by remote control from Washington and Moscow, Afghanistan during the years of the Soviet occupation was an urgent abstraction. For a generation of Washington spies and planners, Kabul was the nexus of the final

struggle with the Soviet Union. Analysts and covert-operations specialists at the CIA in Langley, career diplomats at the State Department in Foggy Bottom, information and propaganda specialists at the U.S. Information Agency, and grand geostrategic thinkers at the National Security Council and the Pentagon devoted themselves to defeating the Soviet thrust into Afghanistan. Few of them actually saw Afghanistan, but as a place on a map, they knew it well. I remember sitting with a senior U.S. diplomat when he first arrived in Pakistan to help prosecute the drive for Kabul. To illustrate his points, he pulled out a colored, highly detailed Pentagon map of the Afghan capital and began sliding his fingertips across it—here's the airport, here's where the rebels are going to drive in from the east, here's the defense ministry, the presidential palace—and it was as if he were speaking of a city he had lived in for decades.

Western and Pakistani liberals frequently expressed contempt for the CIA's role in the secret war, sometimes on general principles and sometimes based on specific contentions that the agency's work produced more harm than good for the Afghans by promoting factionalism and Islamic radicalism. Some of this criticism seemed to me justified, and I spent much of my time in Afghanistan attempting to report on how the war no longer resembled a frontier cartoon, if it ever had. But it also seemed to me a little ridiculous to hold Washington spies and bureaucrats responsible for the historical Afghan inclination to divide and disagree. More than that, it seemed to me absurd to suggest there was moral equivalency between Washington and Moscow in the cold war's descent on Afghanistan. If you agreed that the spontaneous rebellion of a clear majority of ordinary Afghans against the tyranny of an occupying foreign army and its thuggish ideological agents in Kabul was justified and even righteous, then how could you be opposed in principle to providing the mujaheddin with the means to win, even if the effort required, as deputy ISI chief Yousaf said, double edges?

Initially, after the Soviet invasion of Afghanistan, President Jimmy Carter signed a secret presidential "finding" authorizing low-grade CIA assistance to the mujaheddin, mainly rifles and light weapons dating to the Korean War or earlier. The purpose of this aid was to promote "harassment" of Soviet troops by the Afghan rebels, reflecting the CIA's assessment that the mujaheddin could never win a war against the Red Army. This approach may have seemed pragmatic at the time, but in retrospect it looks deeply cynical. By the mid-1980s, as the Soviets

unleashed the full force of their arsenal in Afghanistan—including teams of specially trained Spetsnaz special forces, helicopter gunships, and "Omsk Vans," battlefield communications centers that intercepted mujaheddin radios and walkie-talkies and ordered immediate, violent air strikes in reprisal—the Afghan rebels were badly bloodied. As Vince Cannistraro, a CIA operations officer, put it to me as I was researching the history of the CIA's covert Afghan program, the earlier aid was "just enough to get a very brave people killed" because it encouraged the mujaheddin to fight but did not provide them with the means to win.

That began to change in 1985 when President Ronald Reagan, at the urging of a clan of politically appointed New Right activists in his administration, signed National Security Decision Directive 166, which authorized among other things "all necessary means" to aid the Afghan rebels against the Soviets. This led a team of Pentagon and CIA guerrilla-war specialists in Washington to unleash on the Afghan battlefield much of the U.S. military's high-technology arsenal and operational expertise. What Yousaf described as a "ceaseless stream" of CIA and Pentagon specialists flew to Pakistan's military airfield in Rawalpindi, parked their suitcases at U.S. embassy guest quarters and CIA safe houses in Islamabad, and then drove in civilian cars to the ISI compound on the Grand Trunk Road, from which the unmarked supply trucks departed each morning. The Americans brought with them detailed satellite photographs and ink maps of Soviet targets around Afghanistan. Soon the walls of Yousaf's office were covered with sketches of Soviet-run airfields, armories, and military barracks. The maps came with CIA assessments of how best to approach a given target, possible routes of withdrawal, and analysis of how Soviet troops might respond to an attack. Yousaf and his colleagues were dazzled by the details. "They would say there are the vehicles, and there is the [riverbank] and there is the tank," Yousaf recalled. The new efforts focused on strategic targets such as the Termez Bridge between Afghanistan and the Soviet Union. "We got the information like current speed of the water, current depth of the water, the width of the pillars, which would be the best way to demolish," Yousaf said. Pakistani majors and colonels assigned to ISI, which was determined to handle direct training of the Afghans itself, flew off to the United States to learn how to train rebels on new weapons systems such as the Stinger. In the summer of 1986, the CIA set up at ISI headquarters a secret Stinger training facility, complete with an electronic simulator made in the United

States. The simulator allowed mujaheddin trainees to aim and fire at imaginary helicopters and jets tracking across a large screen—without actually firing any expensive missiles. The screen marked the missile's track and calculated whether the trainee would have hit his target. This video missile arcade was enormously popular among the mujaheddin; commanders squabbled among themselves to gain entry.

The rush of technology encouraged farcical speculations about what might actually be accomplished on the Afghan battlefield. Yousaf and his CIA counterparts, for example, spent months trying to figure out how they might blow up the Salang Tunnel, a strategic link in the mountains north of Kabul through which many of the Soviet military and civilian supplies passed. They concocted elaborate plans for mujaheddin to pack an empty fuel tanker with plastic explosives, send it into the tunnel, fake a mechanical breakdown, escape on waiting motorcycles, and then detonate the truck with a remote-control device. Among other difficulties, Yousaf discovered that this was "not the sort of operation popular with the mujaheddin, who preferred the glamour and glory of the battlefield to clandestine sabotage activities. . . . Several times commanders agreed they would do it, but always after a few months I would get word that it was impossible to find the men." Aside from their preferences for noise and loot in war, the mujaheddin often frustrated Pakistani and CIA strategists with their reluctance to destroy what little infrastructure Afghanistan possessed, in part because the rebels did not want civilian clansmen in the government-controlled cities to suffer. Although there were plenty of mujaheddin who thought nothing of lobbing long-range rockets into heavily populated civilian areas of Kabul, there were others who were highly discriminating. Their idea of sabotage—an idea Yousaf said was once implemented in Jalalabad—was to load a camel with plastic explosives, let it wander into a military compound, and then detonate the animal, killing a few enemy soldiers and also spraying fresh camel steaks around for the survivors.

During the mid-1980s, CIA and Pentagon specialists helped ISI establish and supply two secret guerrilla-warfare training schools, including one that concentrated on urban-sabotage techniques. Pakistani instructors trained by the CIA taught Afghans how to build and conceal bombs with C-4 plastic explosives and what Yousaf estimated were more than one thousand chemical and electronic-delay bomb timers supplied by the CIA. The schools were erected in remote desert areas of western Pakistan and

were protected by gauze roofings meant to deceive Soviet spy satellites. Mujaheddin students were bused in and out in darkness so they would not know where the schools were. If a camp was compromised by a local villager's wandering through, the ISI officers would break it down the same afternoon and move it elsewhere. Thousands of mujaheddin were trained at these schools; some used the materials and training supplied by the CIA and ISI to carry out car bombings and other assassination attacks in Kabul under ISI direction. By Yousaf's account, a graduate of the urban-sabotage school nearly blew up future Afghan president Najibullah in downtown Kabul in late 1985. Another time, rebels placed a briefcase bomb loaded with plastic explosives beneath the dinner table of a group of Soviet professors at Kabul University; when it went off, at least several of the teachers were killed. Peter Juvenal, a British television cameraman who traveled extensively in Afghanistan during the mid-1980s, said he once watched guerrillas working for a graduate of the CIA training school prepare bicycle bombs with plastic explosives for use in Kabul. Soviet and Western news reports from the Afghan capital during this period report dozens of unexplained sabotage attacks, car and briefcase bombings around the capital.

"One looks at the war from two different angles," Yousaf explained one afternoon in a small hotel in Düsseldorf, Germany, where I tracked him down in the early summer of 1992 and spent two days talking with him about the secret war. "An act of terrorism may be a question of survival. To my mind, any attempt deliberately made against any civilian—this . . . must be condemned all over the world. Any attempt which is made against a military target is not to be condemned. Neither we nor the mujaheddin ever tried to flaunt anything or any operation in which there was deliberate planning where civilians could have been killed. Never. . . . If you get your own innocent people killed, it would have recoiled back against the mujaheddin."

What, then, explained the seemingly random barrages of mujaheddin rockets that fell on civilians in Kabul throughout the late 1980s, killing hundreds, if not thousands, of Afghan noncombatants?

"If some rocket had gone astray, or they miscalculated, misjudged the distance, the elevation, the angle, and all civilians had been killed, probably it is the war," he answered. "You have to accept. You have to accept."

For Washington's cold warriors, such questions of wartime morality often were viewed as subservient to the greater good of defeating the Evil

Empire. At one point late in 1984, CIA director William Casey flew secretly into Rawalpindi in his specially equipped C-141 Starlifter transport for a tour of the guerrilla training schools. After a dinner with General Zia, Casey rode out to the ISI compound on the Grand Trunk Road and sat in a conference room with the Pakistani spy service's senior generals. Casey shocked the Pakistanis with a proposal that they carry the Afghan war directly into Soviet territory by staging guerrilla attacks north of the Amu River, which divided the Soviet Union from Afghanistan. Yousaf recalled: "He said, 'There's a lot of Muslim population living across the Amu in Turkmenistan and Tajikistan and I personally feel that if we exploit the emotion and sentiment—and they being Muslim and all—we can do a lot of damage to the Soviet Union' . . . roughly words to that effect." Zia feared that a large-scale arms-smuggling program would bring violent reprisals from Moscow, but ISI agreed that it would be a good idea to ship propaganda across the border. Yousaf was already sending trained teams of mujaheddin into Soviet territory to stage small-scale attacks. After Casey's visit, he ordered thousands of Holy Korans in the Turkic language from the CIA. When a sample copy arrived in Rawalpindi, Yousaf shipped it over to an Uzbek acquaintance at one of the mujaheddin radio stations in Peshawar. The Uzbek reported that the CIA translator had made a host of mistakes and had, as it were, put words into the mouth of the Holy Prophet Mohammed. ISI ordered the mistakes corrected and soon the books—along with CIA propaganda tracts about heros of Uzbek nationalism and past Soviet atrocities against religious minorities—were being shipped by mule and camel into the Soviet Union. Casey, Yousaf recalled, "was ruthless in his approach and he had a built-in hatred for the Soviets."

If the CIA specialists were certain about the righteousness of their cause, they did worry about American law, since if this was violated they might well end up in jail, a possibility that hardly seemed remote at Langley headquarters in the late 1980s, as the Iran-contra scandal unfolded. At one stage the CIA's station chief at the U.S. embassy in Islamabad, a young Ivy League graduate who later left the clandestine service for the equally murky world of Wall Street, transmitted a cable to headquarters requesting on behalf of ISI "packages" of long-range sniper rifles, sophisticated sighting scopes, and—by some accounts—high-technology night-vision goggles. The Pakistanis intended to supply the sniper packages to mujaheddin so they could infiltrate Kabul and kill

senior Soviet generals stationed there. As part of the great wave of proposed technological solutions in Afghanistan after 1985, U.S. intelligence pinpointed the residences of leading Soviet generals in Kabul and regularly tracked their movements, as well as those of visiting commanders from Moscow and Tashkent. One of the American specialists involved told me that he once traveled to Kabul and drove over to the Soviet military headquarters with a pair of binoculars. He said you could see the generals just standing in their apartments: how easy it would be to knock them dead with a sophisticated rifle! The trouble was, though, that under a 1970s U.S. law the CIA was prohibited from aiding or carrying out "assassinations" abroad. Particularly in the atmosphere generated by the Iran-contra scandal, there was no shortage of lawyers looking over the shoulders of CIA operations specialists. The debate that ensued about the sniper packages seemed a little half-baked. One official involved told me that Reagan administration lawyers argued that if the CIA station chief in Islamabad provided the rifles to ISI "with the intent to kill specific Soviet generals," then "he will go to jail." The question then arose, "How about if he does it without knowing what they're going to be used for?" But CIA lawyers responded that it was "too late" because the plan to kill specific Soviet generals had been consigned to writing in CIA cables between Washington and Pakistan.

To some involved, such as Cannistraro, the CIA operations officer then posted as director of intelligence at the National Security Council, shooting Soviet generals dead in their Kabul apartments did not seem much different from encouraging mujaheddin to kill Soviet officers in helicopters with antiaircraft missiles. Assassination is "really not a relevant question in a wartime scenario," he said. An additional problem was that President Carter's original "finding," or classified legal authorization for the CIA's covert war, described the purpose of U.S. aid as "harassment" of Soviet forces. Although the Carter finding had been augmented by Reagan's National Security Decision Directive 166, the language in the original finding remained a key legal basis of the covert program. "We came down to, is 'harassment' assassination of Soviet generals?" said an official. "The phrase 'shooting ducks in a barrel' was used," another American recalled of the discussions. Those who favored providing the sniper packages "thought there was no better way to carry out harassment than to 'off' Russian generals in series." Ultimately, a decision was made to provide the sniper rifles requested by the Pakistanis—but with-

out night-vision goggles or intelligence information that would permit effective assassination of Soviet generals. Yousaf remembered receiving more than thirty but fewer than one hundred rifles. He set up a CIA-assisted two-day training course at one of his mobile, camouflaged mujaheddin camps to teach selected rebels how to use the sniper rifles against "military targets."

Not only the weaponry but the doctrinal theories of the CIA-supplied secret Afghan war spilled steadily into the rest of South Asia during the late 1980s. India today accuses Pakistan of plotting covert "proxy wars" in Kashmir, Punjab, and India's northeast. Pakistan accuses India of conducting a secret war with secret commando squads in Sind. Some of these charges are certainly true, but it is difficult to know exactly which ones. In Islamabad during the 1980s, the ISI's involvement in a sprawling $2 billion, CIA-backed conspiracy against the Afghan government seemed to promote the capital's general susceptibility to conspiracy thinking, whether the topic was Zia's death or Benazir Bhutto's political comeback. It became obvious that anybody with money could have a go at secret war. Pakistani markets brimmed with cheap AK-47s, land mines, pistols, and plastic explosives. Sikh and Kashmiri guerrillas crossed the border to scoop up what they could afford, or what the Afghans and ISI were willing to give away.

The U.S. intelligence community believes, despite Indian claims to the contrary, that ISI has not systematically aided Kashmir's anti-Indian Islamic rebels, but that the Kashmir guerrillas have instead hooked up on their own with Afghan mujaheddin and through them obtained training and weapons. As a sweeping assertion, this seemed to me implausible, but ISI has not yet been caught red-handed in Kashmir, and in any event, the distinction U.S. analysts draw may be more semantic than substantive. One time in Srinagar, Kashmir's summer capital, I saw a "sterile" CIA-supplied sniper rifle of the kind ISI and some in the CIA once hoped would be used to kill Soviet generals cradled instead in the proud hands of a Kashmiri guerrilla with the anti-Indian Hizbul Mujaheddin. The guerrilla said vaguely that he acquired it in Afghanistan. Similar sightings of sniper rifles on the Indian side of the Kashmir line recently put the U.S. embassy in New Delhi in the embarrassing position of having to brief the Indian government privately about just how far and how accurately these rifles can be fired by a guerrilla who knows what he is doing. Expertise

useful in the covert promotion of insurgency can be useful as well in the covert promotion of counterinsurgency.

This, unfortunately, was a lesson the Afghan mujaheddin learned anew for themselves in April and May of 1992, when after fourteen years and a million dead—with the cold war officially buried and eulogized in Washington, Moscow, and a dozen European capitals in between—their forgotten mud-rock capital of Kabul at last teetered and fell.

STATES

OF

PROGRESS

14

A Shadow Lifts,
a Shadow Falls

You said that the Cold War was a kind of shadow. I think of it that way. I think that I was in a nightmare. It was a bad dream that has passed.

—*M. Akbar Popal*

"*They're heee-eeere.*"

That was how the cold war ended in Kabul initially, with six or seven dozen foreign journalists and cameramen darting manically around a confused if largely peaceful capital in Soviet-made taxis, flagging each other down, and passing along the day's signature joke, a quote from a Hollywood ad campaign for a film depicting the arrival of aliens on Earth. Reports of recent mujaheddin sightings were freely exchanged. You might think the mujaheddin deserved better after all their struggle against the Soviets and the Kabul Communists, but the members of the first rebel vanguard to enter the city on that Saturday in late April 1992 did look a bit as if they were trying to sort out which planet they were on. They wandered into the city singly or in small groups with rocket-propelled grenade launchers and Kalishnakovs slung over their shoulders. Many had specific instructions from their loosely linked commanders as to which downtown government facility they were to enter and secure, but after fourteen years of living and fighting in remote rock gorges and tiny villages, it was not so easy to find your way around a large and semimodern capital, especially one lacking proper street signs. So the mujaheddin just stood around on corners at first, spinning this way and that, wondering if it was safe to ask directions and assessing whether the

war would be starting again right away, or maybe a little later. With their flowing dark beards and draping robes, stumbling through Kabul's Stalinist architecture and Milan-by-way-of-Prague street fashions, they looked like Hasidic diamond traders just arrived for a convention, uncertain where the hotel might be. Their weapons, however, were a useful defense against anxiety. I spotted one mujaheddin straggler over by the zoo, turning in circles and insisting that anyone who wished to talk with him do so from a distance of ten feet. His name was Syed Munir. "Everyone is friendly," he announced in a tone of pleasant surprise. "But maybe some people want to take my gun."

One of the first things that happened after the mujaheddin's long-awaited triumph in Kabul was that ten of thousands of people went home and changed their clothes. By afternoon it was difficult to find women on the street in the dark skirts and spiked heels that were previously de rigueur in the capital. Instead they wore headscarves, salwars, or the mustard-colored full-length Islamic burkas worn by the purdah-confined refugees in Peshawar. Men tossed their sport jackets with the narrow East European lapels into the closet and pulled out their salwars, stored against the day when tradition might become an urgent necessity. The more prescient among them, evaluating the steady collapse of Kabul's leftist government and the rush of the mujaheddin to the capital's outskirts, had stopped shaving some days before, hoping that the growth on their cheeks would subsume the imitation-Najibullah brute mustaches many of them wore when secular machismo was in fashion. At the hilltop Hotel Continental, where the equally stubbled international press was stationed, government generals arrived in casual attire for evening press conferences to explain how they had really believed in Islam and the mujaheddin all along. The teeming, smoky lobby looked like the union hall of a particularly disreputable Teamsters local. Everybody seemed to be wearing unusual, ill-fitting hats. It was difficult, as my colleague Bill Branigin remarked, to tell the generals from the doormen.

Kabulians had been warned against this day for years by their reigning Bolsheviks. The urgency of the warning was perhaps muted by the absurd language of scientific socialist propaganda through which it frequently was imparted, but the point had settled in nonetheless. If you lived in Kabul, you did not need to accept the stilted formulations about "feudal-reactionary counterrevolutionaries" to be worried about what a mujaheddin victory might mean. Prerevolutionary Afghan codes provided more

than enough cause for concern. Sufficient blood had been spilled in Afghanistan during the previous decade to fertilize centuries of clan- and family-inspired acts of revenge. This was certainly on the mind of former president Najibullah, who had tried as his government collapsed to flee the country with the help of the United Nations, only to be turned back at the airport by unruly Uzbeks armed with grenade launchers and prepared to use them. Najibullah now awaited his fate in hiding at a U.N. safe house in the capital, where we chose to imagine him passing the time with a deck of cards. Around him the ethnic, tribal arrangements that had supported his country's tenuous nationalism for so many years—before Najibullah's Bolshevik book club declared ethnicity and tribalism to be instruments of the oppressive feudal class—looked to be badly, dangerously out of whack.

The northern Afghan minorities—Tajiks, Uzbeks, Shiites—had endured for long years the dominance of the southern and eastern ethnic Pashtuns. Under the leadership of the Tajik mujaheddin commander Ahmed Shah Massoud and the formerly Communist Uzbek general Abdul Rashid Dostam, they were prepared to bid for an enlarged share of power in post-Communist Afghanistan. On the Pashtun side loomed the fearsome reputation of Gulbuddin Hekmatyar, the manipulative, opportunistic Islamic radical whose disciplined performance during the Soviet years of the war had won the respect of the CIA and the affection of the ISI. As a consequence, Hekmatyar received much of the most sophisticated kit from the high-technology covert pipeline in the late 1980s. He was now prepared to use it in service of his ambitions. (A wide range of Pakistanis, Americans, and Europeans involved in managing the secret war told me that Hekmatyar never received much more than a quarter of the weaponry allocated to the mujaheddin, but that what he got was of higher quality than what reached his rivals, in part because Hekmatyar and his men were more willing to accept ISI and CIA training and supervision.) Among the Pashtuns, there were splits within splits, with the long-dominant Durrani tribe now shattered and under challenge from historically less important but now ambitious tribes. Traditional tribal elders and Islamic spiritual leaders found themselves in competition for power with usurping mujaheddin commanders of low birth but high reputation earned on the battlefield. In short, fourteen years of war and destruction had utterly scrambled Afghanistan's political structures, and there were plenty of reasons to be worried about what would happen

when the mujaheddin attempted to unscramble them in the capital city they had long coveted.

Months afterward, as the Yugoslav civil war deepened, racist-nationalist gangs rioted in Germany, the speed train to European political union seemed derailed, clan warlords in post–cold war Somalia enforced a brutal famine, and ex-Soviet subenclaves declared independence from enclaves, which declared independence from republics, which declared independence from each other, I wondered if, in time, I might think back on what occurred during the first twenty-four hours after the fall of Kabul as a kind of fast-forward metaphor for what the end of the worldwide ideological, military, and economic confrontation between the Soviet Union and the United States would mean for my currently indifferent generation. In Afghanistan's capital, the local celebration of this momentous event lasted exactly one day.

By nightfall thousands of mujaheddin had poured into the city from the surrounding mountains. When they found their bearings they entered as subdivided units into military barracks, police stations, and strategic civilian buildings, embraced the neo-Bolshevik government soldiers on duty with brotherly Afghan hugs, stripped them of their weapons and rank patches, and sent them home. Triumphant truckloads of mujaheddin rolled through Kabul chanting "God is great!" Guerrillas tossed flower petals from their trucks. Militiamen inserted tulips in their tank barrels. In this way the streets of Kabul were transformed within hours into a polyglot patchwork of rival mujaheddin parties and ethnic militias in anxious competition to grab the best locales for prospective postideological conflict. Hekmatyar's guerrillas had the interior ministry and parts of the presidential palace. Massoud's guerrillas had patches of the palace, the historic Bala Hissar fort, and many of the key army garrisons. Dostam's fierce Uzbek militiamen controlled the airport north of the city center. Shiites took the formerly Soviet, now Russian, embassy and assured its understandably nervous occupants that, as the commander in charge put it, "we want to respect them and for them to be comfortable." Radical Sunni mujaheddin from a relatively minor party took control of the neighborhood across the way. About them, the Shiite commander was less tolerant. It was one thing to demonstrate to the world that the cold war was history by protecting the Russians, but it was quite another to make peace with Sunni Afghan bastards bent on denying the Shiites their

rightful place at the postwar negotiating table. From our hilltop vantage in the curfew-bound darkness that night, we saw the dazzling visual expression of this paradox. At first the sky above the wide Kabul Valley erupted with a celebratory display of white military flares and streaming, arcing red tracer bullets shot joyfully into the sky. Victory! By the early morning hours, as the noise continued unabated, we wondered if the tracer lines weren't beginning to tilt downward, streaming now in horizontal crossfire instead of vertical celebration. In the disorienting blackness after midnight, it was difficult to tell.

What became an extended, unpleasant stint of ducking and running began the next morning at the downtown palace, where we found the flowers had been taken out of the gun barrels and the new war was well under way. Massoud's mainly Tajik guerrillas had moved on Hekmatyar's mainly Pashtun guerrillas just after breakfast, attempting to drive them off the perimeter of the palace and eventually out of town. Shells crashed and bullets pinged. Buildings burned. A Massoud commander led us quickly into an ornate palace residence near the center of the grounds. We scurried beneath crystal chandeliers, up mahogany staircases covered with intricately woven carpets, past nineteenth-century sculpture, vases, polished green marble tables. Makeshift bunkers had been established on the upper floors. Uzbek militia reinforcements, nominal allies of Massoud's mujaheddin guerrillas, were pouring in from the airport, nabbing loot as they marched in and out—silverware here, a teapot there. Our commander-escort, Ghulam Jam, could not conceal his contempt. "They are uneducated men," he said. "Put them in the zoo."

Jam had been fighting in the northeastern Afghan valleys for more than a decade, first against Communists, more recently against rival mujaheddin. As he led us politely on a tour through his latest battlefield, we asked why the fighting had erupted so quickly and so violently after such a universally celebrated collective victory. "They fired first," he replied. "We didn't let them inside the palace. We want this place to belong to us. They think all this country belongs to them. This group [of Hekmatyar] wants to get the power for themselves."

We asked if he wasn't tired of the war. "For one hundred years we have been fighting," he said. "I will never get tired." We walked on past the sculpture and vases, then paused on a verdant lawn in spring bloom to watch bright orange flames consume a small outbuilding across the palace

grounds. It was strangely peaceful, even with the occasional thudding shells and crackling rifles. "It's a very beautiful place, yes?" Jam asked. In Afghanistan, you grab your aesthetics where you can find them.

For all the potent cold war symbols that Kabul offered, probably the more useful way to think about what has happened in the capital since the mujaheddin's victory is to accept that for Afghans, the imposed ideological aspects of the war faded far more rapidly than occurred in Washington and Moscow, even after Gorbachev's accession. In this sense, the fighting that erupted immediately after Kabul's fall to the mujaheddin, and which has continued since then at the cost of thousands of civilian lives, marked a reckoning of ethnic, tribal, and social conflicts that were well advanced before the rebels entered the capital. That some of these conflicts were created, mutated, and in a few cases explicitly sponsored by the conduct of the superpowers' proxy war is indisputable. That they festered in the last phase of the Afghan war because the outside sponsors could not or would not help to resolve them peacefully is especially tragic, if not an outright case of criminal neglect. Of course, it is hard to know who should be held responsible for what sorts of crimes when you hear reports such as the ones that emanated from Kabul in the summer of 1992, describing rival ethnic mujaheddin commanders who suffocated prisoners of war in railroad boxcars or executed them by driving nails into their skulls. But in any event, to expect that the exhausted, half-bankrupted superpower antagonists of the cold war would rush to the world's far corners and unscramble all the messes they made since World War II was, to say the least, unrealistic. And so today Afghanistan smolders, occupied with its inevitable reckonings, but at the same time justifiably angry, and frustrated by its impotence against the retreating superpowers.

In this environment it is sometimes difficult to recall that the recent conflict in Afghanistan began as a war over foreign ideas. It was my conviction, not always shared by colleagues I respected, that this fact should continue to be a framework for inquiry, even when the ethos of the news shifted in new directions. Ideas and the consequences of ideas did not seem to me a kind of neutral, balanced superstructure, beneath which the "truth" of immutable social history grinds on. Partly for that reason, six weeks before Kabul fell, I traveled to the city to sort out for myself one last time what the end of the cold war meant to those who had constructed one side of the barricade in Afghanistan.

My traveling companion, Mark Fineman, set up a meeting for us with Babrak Karmal, the Afghan leftist who rode the Red Army tanks into Kabul in 1979. Karmal was being held at the time under house arrest, and we found, in the parking lot of his Stalinist apartment block out toward the airport, a large olive army truck with radar wings and eavesdropping gear poking out of the top, pointed at Karmal's window. "I am very happy to see you in our motherland, our fatherland, our heroic Afghanistan," Karmal said at the door in a deep, serious voice as he greeted us with traditional hugs and kisses. For a man widely held responsible for the deaths of more than a million of his own people, he looked serene and fashionable. He wore a white pullover and a gray cardigan against the cold, and his silver hair was combed straight back. He ushered us into his library, which overflowed with books in Russian, Pushtu, Persian, and English. There were tomes on Marxism and the theory and practice of revolution, and a neatly bound set of Shakespeare's *Julius Caesar, Romeo and Juliet*, and *Hamlet*.

Karmal sat in a cushioned armchair, smoked Kent cigarettes, and lectured for two hours about the meaning of the cold war's final act in Afghanistan. Sometimes he banged the table with his hand and made the teacups rattle. (A revolution may not be a tea party, but apparently its deconstruction can be.) This banging Karmal usually performed while arguing that none of the wreckage of war, revolution, and counterrevolution surrounding him in Kabul was his fault. He had simply been overwhelmed, he said, by what he called the "force majeure" of the East-West conflict.

"The tragedy of Afghanistan—it was difficult to forecast," he explained. "These tragedies that happened in Afghanistan do not belong to any party, any person in Afghanistan—it was a rivalry, an antagonism."

But didn't he think that he, personally, made a very serious mistake?

"Do you know anybody in the world, in the history of the world, who has not made a mistake?" Karmal asked whether his enemies in Washington wished to suggest that, at the time he rolled into power in Afghanistan with the backing of the Red Army, "the Soviet Union was not a fact? Communism was not a fact? Socialism was not a fact? To think like this, in German there is a very good word—*Dummkopf*, stupid." The ideological struggle between communism and capitalism, he said, "is a heritage of the history of human beings. Who believed, who did not believe, it is another thing. But it is history."

The afternoon leaked on. Karmal kept banging the table, rattling the teacups.

"This was not Afghanistan's war. We have sacrificed Afghan people because of the cold war between the Soviet Union and the United States. If you kill me, I say this to you. . . . I don't want power. I think sometimes a man becomes evil when he gets power. An angel becomes Satan."

Did that happen to you, Mr. Karmal, during the cold war?

"Actually, I was very sick and weak at that time," he replied. "Now I feel strong and powerful, and to go to the jail or the gallows is all the same to me."

————

You don't hear a lot of anguished reflection in Washington these days about the costs of the cold war. Righteous certitude belongs to the victors. But in Kabul, as the mujaheddin massed in the surrounding mountains in preparation for their victories and their reckonings, you could find the Eastern bloc losers—zealots, professionals, cynics, time-servers—who gave the best years of their lives to a cause now discredited. They sat in the sprawling Soviet compound and the overlarge East European embassies that once provided the external resources for the Afghan war's prosecution. At night, they listened to the British Broadcasting Corporation and the Voice of America on shortwave radio for word of the capitalist revolutions back home. In the old days, most of them were members of the Communist party, privileged apparatchiks. Now they were redefining themselves for what remained of their careers and lives. And a few of them, at least, reflected soberly on the ideological enterprise they witnessed and in some cases directed in Kabul.

There was a distancing that occurred in these reflections, a spinning of abstractions, a need to balance the blame. One afternoon I sat for a couple of hours with Valentin Gratsinsky, Bulgaria's ambassador to Afghanistan. Gratsinsky spent most of the late 1970s and the 1980s in and out of Afghanistan as the director of his foreign ministry's Asia desk and as a diplomat in Kabul. He traveled with the Soviet troops during the war and helped produce documentaries for East European television about the great socialist transformation under way in Afghanistan.

"First, professionally speaking, it was, it has always been, exciting," he said. "But still, you have these psychological scars. I have seen the beginning actually myself. It was by chance. A TV team of Bulgarians

came here and I traveled with them. There were these illusions of a vague, bright future, whatever that means. I never thought what a mess Afghanistan would be, within months only. It was my friend, the TV commentator at that time, who looked around and told me as he was flying out of Kabul, 'No chance without Soviet troops.' I still respect him for that."

I asked him whether he felt guilty.

"As bystanders, sidewalkers, you cannot see very much difference in terms of the guilt or guiltiness [of] either side involved. What depressed us most was the human suffering. I traveled a lot in the countryside and saw what war is like, saw the false events, the illusions, and the claims in newspapers on both sides. Even at that time, people were telling me they were fed up and they just wanted to take care of their crops and families, not more." And yet, Gratsinsky said, he felt "great respect for both fanatics and cynics among the Soviets. Great respect. Because their fanaticism springs from those [Bolshevik] generations and decades of this system. Not a single person individually can be blamed."

He went on to tell a story about traveling at the height of the war with Soviet advisers to a distant outpost manned by Russian troops. "While talking, I asked about their mixed feelings and backgrounds and how they feel about this war and all that stuff. And one of them produced the following sentence: 'We are Soviets, and every generation must have its own Spain,' which was the great Communist struggle against fascism. . . . Ideologically, it was explained to them that they will defend the great idea. I was astonished. 'Every generation must have its own Spain.' "

I asked what he thought the cold war added up to in Afghanistan. There was a very long pause.

"I find myself wrestling with the proportions of international interest here. You see how unfair and unjust the consequences and the heritage of the war here is. Afghanistan was the baby of the cold war, and I [sometimes] think the superpowers have washed their hands, they don't care. 'We're out.' I hope this is not the case. . . . My feelings now are a mixture of human feelings linked to the destiny of this poor, ruined people and the direct connection between the situation here and the changes in the rest of the world, the effort to extinguish the fire, to find a new code of conduct. It's very difficult. I still cannot formulate it for myself. It's not because I do not have the feelings—just the opposite. I do too much thinking."

After the mujaheddin takeover of the capital, when the heavy shelling

began, Gratsinsky retreated to the basement bunker of the Bulgarian embassy. There he hosted a generous, flowing pub-salon for what remained of the city's dwindling tribe of foreigners. Later in the summer, he was wounded by shrapnel. A convoy of vehicles escorted by Dostam's Uzbek militia carried Gratsinsky and dozens of other diplomats, including the by now desperate Russians, north through the treeless mountains, out of Kabul.

———

The cold war decimated Afghanistan, but its effects across the rest of South Asia were more insidious, and so to the east of the Hindu Kush it was possible at the turn of the 1990s to watch the shadow lift and not feel immediately the chill of a new shadow's descent.

South Asian historical writing about the cold war is complex and to me it seemed in many ways untrustworthy. So often factions of the Pakistani and Indian political classes invoked attributed predilections and manipulations of the superpowers to justify and explain arrangements that reflected in large part domestic political, social, and economic competition, or else the reckonings of pre–cold war history. In this way the cold war was described as an enormous, active, shifting series of specific conspiracies directed against South Asia's political centers. Zulfikar Ali Bhutto convinced himself and many of his followers that Jimmy Carter's CIA conspired to overthrow him in 1977 because he was determined to construct nuclear weapons. A decade later his daughter saw the CIA in league with Pakistan's generals to deprive the country of democracy, while some of the generals saw the CIA in league with Benazir to thwart the spread of politicized Islam. Indira Gandhi saw all sorts of "foreign hands" groping beneath Mother India's political clothing. A few such conspiracies did in fact exist. The archives of the dismantled KGB show steady payments to one of India's Communist parties and to some members of the Congress Party. It would be reasonable to assume that the CIA made similar payments on the margins and even occasionally at the center of Indian politics. In this, both sides would have been competing with all of the domestic industrialists, landlords, mafia leaders, and foreign manufacturers who have since independence made the attainment of political office in South Asia so lucrative. No evidence has so far come to light, despite the contrary convictions of many Pakistanis, that the CIA participated in any of Pakistan's recent coups d'état. Without unfettered

access to the facts, it is impossible to be entirely dismissive about such cold war conspiracies, but it is useful to remember that, the Afghan war excepted, the primary purpose of intelligence agencies was and is to gather information, not to shape events. And it is difficult to imagine that the attempted purchase of ideological adherence in South Asia by either Washington or Moscow was anywhere near as large an enterprise as the ordinary domestic purchases of political favors in the state-dominated economies. Both the CIA and the KGB certainly wasted a lot of money on propaganda pamphlets and ideological front organizations to which few Indians or Pakistanis paid any attention. In New Delhi and Islamabad, the rivals also invested enormous sums of money in the narrowest, most incestuous sorts of spy-versus-spy games, pointing elaborate electronic interception equipment across the street at each other's embassy and following each other's deep-cover diplomats around town.

Describing the cold war's importance on the subcontinent in terms of conspiracies, as Indians and Pakistanis frequently do, seems to me a case of missing the forest for the trees. Its greater importance, I think, was that it created an ideologically competitive but structurally uniform system of large-scale financial subsidies that enriched specific South Asian factions and supported corrupt, obstructive political economies on both sides of the Indo-Pakistani border. This, with the East-West conflict's passing, has now changed. In the early 1990s, the overall amount of the subsidies from Washington and Moscow to South Asia fell drastically. At the same time, the green-eyeshade men who controlled the remaining subsidies—primarily at the International Monetary Fund, the World Bank, and in the government of Japan—demanded, as a condition for continuing grants and loans, not geopolitical fealty but the further integration of India and Pakistan into the international market economy. If you believe that the national interest and integrity of India and Pakistan depend on their prosperity—and on their ability to distribute rising income through an egalitarian, expanding middle class—then you have to see this change as of potential benefit, and in the case of India at least, of possibly epochal importance.

The United States government reinforced Pakistan's worst political tendencies during the 1980s by pumping several billion dollars into Zia's martial law regime while in pursuit of cold war objectives along the Afghan Hindu Kush. These direct and large subsidies, in the form of outright military grants and favorable credits, not only enriched and

empowered the Pakistan Army relative to its domestic political competitors, but they reinforced a form of polarized, unforgiving politics that has retarded Pakistan's development since the 1950s. When the United States precipitously cut its cold war subsidy flow in September 1990, nominally because of Washington's concerns about nuclear proliferation but in the broader context of declining concern about preserving Pakistan as a strategically important ally, the immediate short-term effect was to disrupt Pakistan's volatile politics by providing rhetorical grist for the Islamic-nationalist mill. Nawaz Sharif, heading a rightist Islamic coalition, marched from election rally to election rally in the fall of 1990 denouncing the United States as evil and fickle and Benazir Bhutto as Washington's decadent lackey. This tactic, along with Bhutto's myriad failings while in office, helped to carry Sharif to victory.

But what happened once Sharif reached office seemed more instructive about the importance of the cold war's passing than did the opportunistic tones of his campaign rhetoric. Backed by a remarkably broad domestic consensus, he began to preach about the virtues of international, middle-class capitalism. He moved away from the Islamic radicals in his coalition. He challenged in a tentative way some of the army's traditional prerogatives. Of course, between Sharif's grand dreams of a prosperous, self-reliant, capitalist Pakistan—another Asian Tiger—and the realization of such dreams stand his own limits as a visionary, his lack of credibility as a national politician, corruption in his government, disintegration of the state apparatus, endemic poverty, illiteracy, and the polarizing legacies of recent history. These amount to enough obstacles, in short, to make any pessimist credible. But at the very least, the removal of Pakistan's cold war subsidies has altered the range of plausible approaches to these problems. The army is now much less able to afford, in basic financial terms, the costs of undemocratic governance. So too, for that matter, is Benazir Bhutto. The Islamic radicals cannot come up with external subsidies to replace the ones lost by the cold war's demise because the wealthy Islamic states such as Saudi Arabia and Iran will not or cannot afford to provide them. So the loss of the subsidies means Pakistan's domestic political competitors are fenced in by new, pressing economic imperatives. I would not want to predict that what is occurring now within this fence is going to turn out well. But I do believe that it is a framework far more likely to promote the

realization of Pakistani prosperity, nationalism, and independence than was the smothering embrace of cold war alliance.

In India the parallel case is more subtle but more promising. The final disintegration of the Soviet Union in the fall of 1991 made clear how the inequitable, inefficient structures of the Nehruvian state had grown since 1970 to depend in part on direct and indirect subsidies from the former Soviet empire. Measuring these subsidies is more difficult than in the case of Pakistan because they were contained largely in government-to-government trade deals between India, the Soviet Union, and Soviet allies in East Europe, the Middle East, and Asia. These deals included barter, guarantees, and currency conversions that amounted in many cases to effective subsidies from Moscow. How large these subsidies really were is a subject of dispute and it may be difficult for economists ever to assess them accurately and completely. But it is indisputable that because of them, India acquired much of its massive military arsenal on favorable terms, exported shoddy, inefficiently produced goods to markets that basically didn't know any better, and was able for longer than it otherwise might have been to subsidize its sprawling state bureaucracy with hard currency borrowings from the West. In 1991, when the Soviet Union itself disappeared, the rapid deterioration of these Soviet-sponsored trading arrangements, coupled with the accumulation of international debt, provided India with a crucial shock of recognition—just when its middle class was becoming fed up with the recent incompetence and hypocrisy of its traditional, Nehruvian political class. Why did Indian prime minister P. V. Narasimha Rao, having squeaked into office in the chaotic atmosphere that followed Rajiv Gandhi's assassination and the rise of Hindu revivalism, move so suddenly in the summer of 1991 toward free market reform and integration with the international economy? It was not, as Rao made clear to anyone who talked with him, because he was enamored of Western-dominated capitalism; on the contrary, he had spent his entire political life as the author of tracts justifying India's self-styled socialist nonalignment and its "balanced" view of bolshevism, which included among other things virtually unqualified support—in public, at least—for the Soviet invasion of Afghanistan. Rather, it was because Rao recognized that with the end of the cold war, India had little choice but to change. In this recognition he was hardly alone. Fortunately for Rao, the legacy of the Nehruvian experiment includes an energetic class of technocrats,

industrialists who have competed successfully outside of the Soviet bloc, and a populace that has grown used to rising prosperity but is impatient for more. It also includes, not incidentally, a system of governance that makes it possible for those who preach about prospective prosperity to succeed.

15

DEM-o-crah-see

People are not used to the new order.

—*Raj Baral*

O ne of the strengths of democracy in South Asia is its relationship to festival. An election in India or Pakistan transforms the country-side with splashes of color—banners strung across roads, party symbols such as hands or wheels painted onto tractors and buses, graffiti dabbed on walls and houses, patchwork canopies erected for rallies on baking dirt lots. Voters move in clan-sized groups through these fairgrounds, in search of diversion as much as political decision. The election carnivals associate democracy with the most celebratory and hopeful sorts of traditional community events, and in India, with repetition, voting seems in many ways to have become an end in itself, irrespective of the periodic frustrations associated with its outcomes. This is by far the most useful legacy of the besieged Nehruvian political class in India. It managed to nurture the public's sense of entitlement to elections even while it abused the public's trust. By clinging to this principle, independent India created and then stabilized a means of public arbitration that none of its neighbors have enjoyed with the same consistency. The myriad benefits of this path are even more obvious to India's envious neighbors than to many Indians.

Today, for the first time since the British withdrew from South Asia, India, Pakistan, Bangladesh, Sri Lanka, and Nepal all are constitutional, parliamentary democracies, albeit in varying states of repair. Bangladeshis

were the last to achieve this. Late in 1990, they threw out their philandering, golf-loving president-for-life, General Mohammed Ershad. Dhaka's streets erupted with democratic furor, although the agitation was tempered by awareness of Bangladesh's short but brutal history of calamity-in-the-name-of-democracy. Even the ascendant mujaheddin in Kabul talk quixotically about an attempted leap forward from Afghanistan's traditional methods of tribal consensus-building to a new system of one man, one vote. (One woman, one vote appears altogether out of the question.) There are many ways to think about this sudden spasm of democracy in South Asia, depending on your susceptibility to despair. How many steps backward must be taken before the next steps forward is a question beyond the control of democratic revolutionaries dancing in the streets. But if you accept that democracy is a worthy end in itself, then it is hard to see these recent changes as anything other than an exhilarating burst of progress.

South Asians do not require Westerners to explain to them why democracy is useful; since the beginning of the subcontinental independence movements in the nineteenth century, democratic principles have provided the basis for diverse forms of politics of hope. Democracy has become the dominant language of political progress and popular will, and not even the most powerful appeals to predemocratic public ideas such as Islam and politicized Hinduism, or postdemocratic ideas such as Marxist revolution, has yet toppled this ideological enthronement.

The difficulty is that over time, the meaning of ideology depends on its expression through institutions, and here South Asia's experience is more precariously mixed. The Nehruvian state in India has succeeded, for example, in institutionalizing democracy's narrowest mechanisms. Despite occasional, relatively isolated episodes of vote-rigging, India's elections have been free and fair, and the constitutional arrangements around them have proven admirably flexible. But obviously, to measure a democracy's strength by the conduct of its voting is to miss the point of democracy's original appeal. Voters understand that the promise of a democratic system is not merely that the public may hold tyrants and crooks accountable, but that the public will be rewarded in this process with some form of egalitarian opportunity. As long as a democratic nation fails to create such opportunity through its institutions, it remains vulnerable. Prosperity—not raw wealth in itself, but national growth, national momentum—is the tide on which social mobility depends. In

South Asia today, it seems to me, rapidly rising, capitalist-style prosperity is more essential than ever for the consolidation of democracy because the public, state-owned institutions are moribund and broke. They cannot afford to offer new jobs, so they cannot offer social mobility, so they cannot offer hope. And hope is the foundation of democracy, the source of political creation. After four decades of nursing colonial wounds, settling scores, and reckoning with the successes and failures of grand public experiments and international alliances, South Asians of all kinds today are deciding once again where they should go looking for hope. By the time I left in 1992, my own feeling was that a sufficient number already knew where they should begin, if not exactly where they would end. That, at least, was the indelible impression left by the strangely wonderful, unexpected democratic revolution that spilled into the Himalayan mountains as the subcontinent made its epochal turn from the cold war to what lies beyond.

———

Of all the ways in which the cold war's end rippled and washed through South Asia, one of the most charming was what occurred during the fall of 1989 in the dilapidated offices of Kathmandu's major newspapers, and particularly at the *Rising Nepal,* the English-language broadsheet referred to by local libidinous expatriate ex-hippies as the *Rising Nipple,* as in, "Did you see the *Rising Nipple* this morning?" That autumn it was a sight to see. Its beleaguered Nepalese editors were playing a rebellious joke on their king, a sort of game based on the themes of "The Emperor's New Clothes."

Since the eighteenth century, Nepal had been ruled with varying degrees of enlightenment and ruthlessness by a line of kings, the Shah dynasty, and by the Shahs' usurping rivals, the Ranas. The country's history was an epic of court intrigues, alleged poisonings, manipulations, royal coups d'état, and minor-league geopolitics arising from Nepal's position as a Himalayan buffer state sandwiched between India and China. In 1950, the heir to the royal Shah dynasty, King Tribhuvan, conspired with Indian prime minister Nehru to retake power. (Nehru was worried about China's military occupation of Tibet and was looking for a friend on his northern border.) Fitful experiments with Nehruvian democracy and socialism ensued briefly, but Tribhuvan's son, King Mahendra, put an end to them during the 1960s by dismissing parliament, banning all

organized political activity, suppressing non-Hindu religious groups, sending the police to put down demonstrations, and jailing uncooperative newspaper editors. In the decades since then, Nepal had remained a quaint, anachronistic, physically majestic, deeply impoverished Himalayan kingdom under the absolute rule of Mahendra's heir, King Birendra. Tens of thousands of American and European tourists poured through King Tribhuvan airport in Kathmandu each year to trek in the glades and foothills or scale the forbidding peaks, including Mount Everest, the highest mountain in the world. Some urban Nepalese made out well under this regime, particularly the clans of traders and royal relatives who clustered around the monarchy and divvied up franchises in hotels, transport, catering, and other tourist services. But most Nepalese lived in isolated, medieval rural poverty in the hills, dependent on subsistence farming and nominally supported by a dysfunctional welfare state, which was controlled by the king's ministers and funded for philanthropic reasons by Western governments. Any Nepali who objected publicly or persistently to these arrangements was likely to find himself or herself in prison, although by South Asian and broader Third World standards the repression was relatively gentle and easy to ignore. To the degree they thought at all about the place, Western governments tended to like Nepal, not because it was just or dynamic, but because it was stable and neutral, and thus it was easy for the diplomats and the philanthropic contractors to go about their business without much disruption from the locals.

The kingdom's principal iconoclasts were the leaders of its banned political parties—the centrist Nepali Congress and various Communist factions—plus a loose network of urban intellectuals, including unruly university students at Kathmandu's Tribhuvan University and dissident newspaper editors holed up in ramshackle quarters around the capital. These last had been treading a fine line with the king for years, but as their international news wires and shortwave radios crackled in the fall of 1989 with astounding news of the collapse of Eastern Europe's Communist regimes, the impish newspaper editors grasped an opportunity. It was impossible to report on or to advocate popular, democratic dissidence in Nepal itself, but since communism was a royally decreed evil, it seemed more than acceptable to trumpet news of its demise in Europe. Day after day the *Rising Nepal* carried headlines about the democratic people's movements in Poland, Hungary, Czechoslovakia, and East Germany—

mass demonstrations, peaceful calls for democratic rights, student movements inspired by the Chinese students at Tiananmen Square—and the
editors gave the stories front-page prominence that seemed considerably
out of proportion with their interest to isolated Nepalese. (Indian newspaper editors, in comparison, tended to bury the East Europe story, reflecting a general unease in New Delhi about the worldwide tide of popular
disenchantment with leftist state structures.) The circulation of the *Rising
Nepal* and other Kathmandu newspapers was not large enough to have
obvious national significance, but the papers did reach many in the urban
classes living in the Kathmandu valley and the towns in the southern
plains, or Terai. Dissidents in the banned political parties and at the
university later told me that as the news from East Europe went on, the
increasingly bold headlines in the Kathmandu newspapers became a kind
of private code, a signal to the democratic faithful that they could act and
win, as well as an inspiration to the relatively small urban and trading
classes previously reluctant to rock the royal boat.

The king, a baby-faced, generally well-liked man popularly depicted as
the bungling victim of his scheming queen, his ne'er-do-well son at Eton,
and his manipulative ministers, apparently did not understand the implications of this news from afar. Politics did not much interest his royal
highness. Officially decreed to be the living reincarnation of a Hindu god,
Birendra did his bit in public, wandering among the masses to dole out
welfare schemes or cut ribbons at Western-funded infrastructure projects.
But his principal passion appeared to be volleyball, which he played every
day at the Kathmandu palace or at his far-flung hunting lodges. He also
enjoyed swimming and had been trained as a helicopter pilot, potentially
useful skills for a despot uncertain when or how he might need to make
a quick getaway.

By February 1990, the remnants of the Berlin Wall were being scavenged by souvenir hunters and hundreds of students at Tribhuvan
University had banded together to launch a movement for democracy
modeled on the efforts of their Chinese and East European brethren. Their
democracy movement was a direct violation of Nepal's laws against
organized politics, but the students said they intended to go ahead
anyway with street demonstrations, and they set a date to begin. I flew
up from Delhi to see how it would go.

After the sometimes brutal nihilism of Indian religious riots and Sri
Lankan ideological insurgency, the Nepalese democracy movement had

a refreshing air about it. Spared direct rule by British troops during the days of the empire (after a patch of rebelliousness, the reigning Ranas had put their formidable Gurkha soldiers into imperial service during the nineteenth century), the Nepalese managed generally to avoid the institutionalization of brutality in their state apparatus, so while there was repression and even torture of political dissidents in prison, there were relatively few of the routine firings on crowds or extrajudicial killings that had helped to inure democratic India and Sri Lanka to the uses of state violence. In Nepal's embryonic political culture, shooting unarmed civilians in the streets was not yet unremarkable. Added to this was a comparatively pure opposition of eighteenth-century political ideas— constitutional democracy on the one side, absolute monarchy on the other. Of course, many urban Nepalese were aware of the muddling of these opposing ideas in the late twentieth century. The muddle included the king's attempt to establish a "partyless democracy" of district councils, called *panchayats*, through which royal decrees and socialist welfare schemes were implemented. The muddle also included bizarre factionalism and antidemocratic tendencies among the self-proclaimed Nepalese democratic parties, particularly the Nepalese Communists, some of whom were regarded by Beijing as potential levers against the Indian-installed monarchy. But when the students from Tribhuvan University hit the streets that February and King Birendra tried to sort out how he should respond to them, these questions and problems were subsumed temporarily by a greater spirit, a mobilization of sometimes anachronistic political ideas. As an American, to watch this unfold was to be transported into a theatrical Mongolian enactment of dimly recalled elementary school textbooks.

On February 18, the day announced by the students for the start of their demonstrations for democracy, the king and his ministers decided to show their own popular power by mobilizing on the streets of Kathmandu a "spontaneous" demonstration of royalist sentiment. Thirty or forty thousand people streamed onto the cracked concrete bleachers at the National Stadium to prepare for a march. They were mainly government employees or members of civic organizations funded by the king and queen, such as the Boy Scouts and Girl Scouts. Emissaries of the royals handed leaflets and souvenir postcards of their beloved highnesses to all those entering the stadium. There were pictures of the king wrapped

up in orange ribbons, pictures of the king advertising the virtues of democracy, pictures of the king waving to the masses. The king himself felt it imprudent to make a personal appearance, so the next best thing was paraded around the stadium—a larger-than-life-size color photographic cutout of His Majesty in familiar waving pose. Honor guards in red uniforms and large white fur hats toted the royal image in a horse carriage bedecked in flowers and gold braid. The overall impression was of a marginal Peter Sellers movie.

Wandering around the stadium, waiting for the march and the action to begin, I approached a group of primary school teachers in the midst of the crowd. One held a sign that read on one side, "Long Live the Panchayat System of Democracy—Down with the Foreign Alliance," a reference to the Nepali Congress's historic links to its Indian counterpart. The reverse of the sign read, "The Panchayat System Must Be the Best for Nepal." This seemed an odd sentence, potentially ambiguous, but more likely the consequence of South Asian grammar.

I asked the man holding the sign why he had made it. He looked at the sentence stimulating my curiosity, then at me. "Because the panchayat system must be the best for Nepal," he answered.

"Do you think that most people agree with that?"

"No, no, not at all," he said, as if this were obvious.

After an uncomfortable pause, I asked, "Will there be trouble later?"

"Maybe there will."

There was, but it was a modest, relatively playful riot. After a few loops around the stadium track, the carriage carrying the royal cutout departed and ran smack into bands of democracy-movement organizers and squads of truncheon-wielding riot police in the streets of downtown Kathmandu—narrow warrens where swirling Hindu temple architecture blends appealingly with Tibetan influences. The royalists decided quickly to get out of the way; many went home, while others joined the crowds of shopkeepers, office workers, and tourists that formed just west and north of the palace to watch the students break the law. This they did by standing in clusters of two or three dozen at the opposite ends of streets and alleys from the riot police. Wearing blue jeans, bandanas, and track shoes, the students chanted over and over, louder and louder, "We want DEM-o-crah-see! We want DEM-o-crah-see!" At first, I wasn't certain what they were talking about—I thought they might be calling for the

release of some jailed student leader whose name I had somehow missed. For months afterward, the pronunciation echoed in my mind, a sign of my sentimental weakness for hopeful politics.

The students picked up bricks and hurled them at the police. The police picked up bricks and hurled them back. After a while, both sides would stop for another round of chanting. During these breaks I wandered among the students to ask about their plans. As I had no translator and they had little English, our exchanges were limited to blunt declarations, which seemed about right for the mood of the riot. The students said things like, "We are going to break the law! We are going to make it free!" or "We have got the cooperation of the people—this is autocracy, complete autocracy!" or "We will fight so long as our blood is red!" I asked about the king, and a few offered that he was not such a bad man, but he was surrounded by an evil queen and a corrupt court. There was room for forgiveness, if only the king would see the light of DEM-o-crah-see spreading around the world. This day, however, the king seemed determined to snuff the light out, albeit carefully. The police refrained from using guns, at least in the politically sensitive environs of central Kathmandu, but by midafternoon they had had enough of the slogans and the bricks, and they began to charge the students vigorously, emitting guttural screams and wielding their sticks freely on heads and backs. Now adrenaline began to pump and all of us were running and shouting with heightened ability. We white people were supposed to be exempt from police beatings under the general principles of South Asian hospitality to foreigners, but it was necessary sometimes to remind individual policemen loudly of the rules.

By evening the students had pretty much dispersed to tea stalls and campus hostels, vowing to carry on another day. I found myself over by the national museum erected for the preservation of the memory of King Tribhuvan, King Birendra's grandfather, who took back the palace from the Ranas. I went inside for a look. Mainly there were sepia photos of the king on auspicious days of his reign and samples of auspicious clothing he wore on auspicious occasions. There were a few exceptional examples of imperial pomp, such as a snap of His Majesty dressed in a military cap and a Scottish kilt, holding a growling Pekingese while astride a horse. There were photographs of the royal wedding, which took place when the king was only thirteen years old. The ceremony took two days, as Tribhuvan married two women simultaneously, the senior Queen Kanthi

Raja Lakshmi Devi and the junior Queen Ishavari Raja Lakshmi Devi. From later photographs one does not gain the impression of an energetic ménage à trois. But the king does seem enlivened in pictures of his revolt against the evil Ranas, aided by India's Nehru. He stands proudly beside Nehru in one of these photos, decked out in cool jazz shades. They look like a couple of conked swing-era trombonists on leave from a Manhattan hotel.

In the weeks ahead, Tribhuvan's grandson, the Volleyball King, made it plain that he was not anywhere near so hip to the democracy thing. His security forces shot a few students dead and the king's ministers sent the riot police out in greater force. I made an appointment at the palace to ask what the king had in mind. One of his senior aides met me in an office just inside the tall, spiked palace gates.

"The king's idea for twenty-five years is that every institution must keep in tune with the changing times," my informant began. "The king is looked on as the reincarnation of god, but in the Hindu model, where the god is much more of a human figure. To be a reincarnation of god is not really divinity. He has said that he is not divine. He feels the monarchy must keep in step with changing times. He wants to find out what useful role it can play. He sees the role as expediting development and preserving peace."

I asked about the popular impression that the king's court, if not the king himself, was deeply corrupt.

"A great deal of the resentment is exaggerated," my courtier friend answered. "Obviously the contractors do make money and there is corruption in the country and in the palace, but not any more than in other countries. That autocracy thing has been heavily criticized. It's just a rationale for electioneering. The overwhelming impression one has is that the king is a good listener. There's a very strong democratic streak in his temperament. Sometimes he's criticized for not acting quickly enough, but in addition to being democratic and a man who listens, he is a very fair person. . . . He is interested in problems that other people can't solve."

He found one on April 6, the day an estimated two hundred thousand Nepalese in Kathmandu Valley thronged through the streets of their capital to demand multiparty democracy, abandoning their caution about the chanting, brick-throwing university students and joining them at the barricades. It was the largest popular demonstration in recorded Nepalese history. Waving the flags of banned opposition parties, the demonstrators

massed before the downtown palace, pelted stones at a statue of the monarch's father, King Mahendra, and chanted slogans. These included not only the familiar "DEM-o-crah-see!" but now also more focused ones, such as "Birendra the Thief, leave the country!"

Soldiers manning machine guns in pillboxes before the palace gates opened fire. In Kathmandu and at similar demonstrations in other cities, dozens were killed and scores wounded. Anarchy now reigned in the capital's streets.

A clan of us Delhi-based foreign reporters, busy with the usual scattered obligations, had been trying to keep track of the democracy movement's gradual fermentation since its February launching. The sudden swelling of popular demonstration that Friday meant we had to scramble. Seven of us had the last plane into Kathmandu that evening pretty much to ourselves, since the tourists were being told that it was not possible to get from the airport to the downtown hotels because of a nationwide transport strike and an army-enforced night curfew.

King Tribhuvan Airport sits on a plateau above the Kathmandu Valley and the capital city. As we dragged our luggage out of the terminal in the darkness, we could see fires burning for miles and hear shouts of protesters echoing all about. It was eerie and exhilarating. Just below the terminal, teenagers hurled rocks at billboards of the king's visage, painted over "Welcome to Nepal" signs, and burned tires in the road. There were no cars, no buses, no taxis. We decided to walk the two miles to the nearest hotel to see what was happening in the streets and then file our dispatches by telex. So we grabbed a couple of baggage trolleys, loaded all our luggage onto them, and headed briskly down the hill into the revolution—the ultimate in pack journalism.

The revolutionaries were friendly, the police seemed too frightened and preoccupied to bother with us, and for about a mile we rolled along, marveling at the sights. Suddenly a black van came racing up from behind and stopped just in front of us on the main road to Kathmandu. Out jumped a dozen or so riot police with truncheons and a few soldiers holding automatic weapons. They surrounded us. A mustachioed lieutenant with a walkie-talkie pushed through the gun barrels to the front and announced that we were in big trouble.

He was from airport security and he was upset—very, very upset— that we had stolen two baggage trolleys from King Tribhuvan Airport.

We proceeded to have what must be one of the most absurd conversa-

tions in the history of world revolution. He wanted us to give the trolleys back. We said we needed them to get to our hotel. Is it our fault, we asked, that you are having a revolution and so there aren't any porters or taxis to carry our bags? We pointed to broken bricks, glass, and a burning tire nearby and suggested that perhaps he and his men had better things to worry about than our trolleys. Mark Tully, who has not spent two decades in South Asia for the BBC for nothing, reached into his linguistic bag of Hindi curse words, which evidently translated reasonably well into Nepali. But the lieutenant insisted even more adamantly than before that we yield our carts.

Emboldened by what we considered to be the utter implausibility of an army lieutenant's shooting seven foreigners over two baggage carts, our side, led by the large and belligerent Tully-sahib, declared, in effect, No, do what you must, arrest us, shoot us, but we are not giving up our trolleys. Several of us leaned on them meaningfully.

The lieutenant then retreated with his walkie-talkie and yammered in Nepali for what seemed an excessive time. He returned to say, Okay, you can keep the trolleys, but give us your passports. When you return the carts, you can get your passports back.

We responded, Forget it, we need the passports for identification, to check into hotels and change money. There's no way we're giving them up. We offered to make a "deposit" on the trolleys, but he refused—obviously a man of integrity.

In the middle of this, a small band of protestors, in defiance of curfew, king, God, and country, marched by chanting "DEM-o-crah-see!" and something along the lines of "Death to King Birendra!" But the lieutenant paid them no mind. He got back on his walkie-talkie and at our urging, negotiated a compromise. We agreed to give him our visiting cards with our passport numbers written on the back as a guarantee that we would return the trolleys in a few days, when order was restored, if order was restored. The soldiers kept their guns at the ready while they checked our passports to make sure that we wrote down the correct numbers. Before climbing back into his van, the lieutenant turned and announced in his sternest tone, "Be sure of one thing—if these trolleys are not returned, we will lodge a formal protest with your respective embassies."

We pushed off into the night, laughing so hard that it hurt. The Nepalese teenagers wandering around in the night, chanting and setting their symbolic fires, seemed to be having a pretty good time as well.

There was still the problem of the shootings before the palace gates. Kathmandu residents were enraged by the killings. Word spread that renewed and even larger popular demonstrations for democracy would be attempted at the palace on Sunday. Meantime, the king ordered the army into the capital, and by Saturday morning his soldiers had erected bunkers on many street corners to enforce a twenty-four-hour curfew. The silence and emptiness across Kathmandu that day did not portend well for the king. It seemed to me that either His Majesty had to relinquish power quickly and decisively, or else he had better be dusting off his helicopter manuals over at the palace. On Saturday afternoon, I called over to the palace official I had met in February and he agreed to see me. At dusk, I shouted my way past half a dozen bunkers, explaining and gesturing with some exaggeration that I had been summoned by the king. I reached the palace gates and was ushered inside by unhappy-looking Gurkha soldiers in full battle dress.

"The king is consulting a large number of people," my informant explained. "He has seen all the ex–prime ministers, most of the speakers of the old parliaments. He's been just busy meeting important people. What happened Friday was a surprise to everyone. We feel now the process has gone quite far in meeting the widespread desire for change. I think the dialogue is quite serious."

I asked what the king was prepared to accept.

"We're really assessing what they want," he answered, referring to the democratic opposition. "We don't want to force anything down their throat. They haven't raised the question of the king's role yet. Their demand has been multiparty democracy. The king has no personal objection to being a European-style constitutional monarch. He's guided by what the Nepali people want. . . . We'll show a lot of flexibility there." This sounded, in the circumstances, like a very useful capitulation. My informant ended our long discussion with this sentence: "We basically have to keep our people happy."

Four hours later, this enlightened insight of noblesse oblige resulted in the announcement, broadcast over state-owned television, that "on the basis of the international environment and the will of the people," the king had decided to amend the constitution immediately to provide for multiparty democracy, had lifted the ban on political parties, had ordered the release of political prisoners, and had decided to appoint a committee to advise him further on how to change the constitution "as per the will

of the people." The business about the "international environment" seemed a particularly nice touch—here was a monarch who read the newspapers. The king is dead! Long live the king!

The celebration began in the darkness that night and carried on through the next day. By midmorning several hundred thousand people had poured into the streets of Kathmandu. Businessmen, beggars, rickshaw drivers, students, children, and tourists dabbed their faces and clothes with red paint, a Hindu rite of celebration, and then they marched through the city center in great sweeping circles, banging drums and demanding that lackeys of the old regime be hanged. Students rode about in trucks brimming with previously illegal party flags. They stuck flags on rooftops and in the stone hands of the statue of King Mahendra near the palace. That many of these flags depicted Communist hammers and sickles on crimson fields did not, in the emerging international scheme of things, seem a pressing anomaly. Overnight, the anthem of the student movement had been transformed. Now it went, "We GOT DEM-o-crah-see!"

I wandered for hours through the streets in an emotional stupor, drunk on the political joy spilling over everywhere, very much uninterested in the requisite interviews. Anyway, for Western newspapers, the democratic transformation of Nepal was a story with very short legs. And as always, there were reasons for skepticism. There had been a period of political liberalization earlier in Nepalese history and it had failed. It was ridiculous to believe that the new, elected political bosses would perform in office much better than the old bosses, or that the advent of democracy would lead directly to the alleviation of Nepal's crushing rural poverty. But that Sunday afternoon in the streets of Kathmandu, in the sunshine, amid the dancing and singing, none of this seemed terribly important.

16

Bombay and Beyond

Liberalization is not a one-shot deal—that you switch on the lights
and the darkness goes away.

—Aditya Birla

Marketing the bright future of India is today a booming trade, and in India itself there is no shortage of persuasive salesmen. Certainly the best known and arguably the most interesting of these are the Ambanis, a Bombay-based family of self-made industrial tycoons who loom over the political economy the way the Rockefellers did in America a century ago. As was true with the Rockefellers, the principal debate about the Ambanis is to what degree they should be seen as progressive and to what degree as robber barons. In the contemporary ferment of capitalist reform in South Asia, many are inclined to give them the benefit of the doubt, not least because the family's power is difficult to challenge. The Ambanis themselves have proven nothing if not their energetic ability to adapt, so as free market ideology swept India after the cold war's demise, the family tried publicly to disengage a little from the political king-making and socialist wheel-greasing that made them most vulnerable to charges of corruption. Anil Ambani, the young, articulate scion with a master's degree in business administration from the University of Pennsylvania, spent less time dining with politicians in New Delhi and more time wooing investment bankers in New York and Tokyo, carrying with him impressive charts about the financial strengths of the family's $1 billion-plus industrial empire, Reliance

Industries, and about the promise of the emerging Indian economy. But even Anil, who seems to be the family's most outward-looking member, did not neglect his domestic constituency. When he married late in the fall of 1990, he staged his nuptials in a Bombay cricket stadium and invited more than one hundred thousand of his dearest friends. Reliance operatives in New Delhi scoured the capital in advance of the event, carrying gold-embossed invitations by hand and inquiring discreetly of important guests whether they would like to be met at the airport by a chauffeur-driven Mercedes-Benz.

The wedding was a sort of coronation of the emerging order. Much of it represented continuity, particularly the use of a traditional public festival to honor and sanctify the authority of a Big Man. But the throng in the streets of Bombay that day was drawn also by a less traditional worship of Big Money. The Ambanis claimed their financial and political power during the 1980s with astonishing and symbolically important speed. The family patriarch, Dhirubhai, is the son of a schoolteacher who toiled in a remote Gujarat village. Dhirubhai abandoned formal education and built his business by trading commodities and industrial materials between India and the Persian Gulf. By the time he achieved his dynamic fortune in the 1980s, schooled his sons to inherit it, and began to cozy up to India's politicians—particularly those in the dominant Congress Party—the Ambanis had created around themselves an American-style mythology of upward mobility through perspicacity. That the family emerged from a Gujarat trading community with a long, enviable tradition of entrepreneurial success in international business diminished for some Indians the potential universalism of their saga. But nonetheless the tale contained elements of new social imperatives. The most important of these were Dhirubhai's continual assertions that his rapid rise to wealth represented an achievement of Indian nationalism, and that this emerging nationalism was based on hard work, equal opportunity, and a pluralism that could rapidly overtake the old limits of clan and birth status. This self-image was doubtless calibrated for political effect, since the Ambanis were under constant attack from political and business enemies and they needed to come up with some larger justification for themselves. But self-interest did not diminish the power of their words and their example at a time when India was groping for new definitions of its national strength and identity.

"It is much more a nationalistic feeling than anything else that drives

me," Dhirubhai said. "If I slog to build up industry, I will slog in India. I refuse to go abroad, even though there may be a lot of profit in it, because I am not interested in building up other countries. . . . At Reliance we work like anything, leave no stone unturned, work round the clock, to achieve something which is the best. Our people get a kick out of Reliance's achievements because it is their own individual achievement. We have got all communities; it is not only our kith and kin or anything like that. I have a rapport with all my people; they can reach me anytime they want."

This was one self-conscious message of Anil's cricket-stadium wedding—the synthesis of the old patriarchal coronation with the egalitarian imperatives of a competitive economy. India's elegant Old Money—the Tatas, the Birlas, the Wadiyas, who trace their fortunes to collaboration with the British Empire and then the independence movement—would not countenance such a crass public display. But to Anil the crowning moment of the reception was precisely when he spotted two dozen speckled, toothless tobacco sellers approaching him through the great swarm of politicians, businessmen, relatives, and other onlookers. The *paan wallahs* bore gifts—a large silver bowl and some crystal glasses worth five hundred dollars or more. They had purchased these with profits from Reliance Industries debentures, or convertible stock securities, which they had badgered the Ambanis to allocate to them from a special lot.

"They said, 'All of us, you know, you made us such rich people, we are now rich,' " Anil recalled. " 'Each one of us must have made at least eight, ten thousand bucks apiece. And now because you gave your own quota, sir, and so on, so on, so on, so we have all come to greet you and wish you a happy married life, and we come with this gift.' "

A patriarch glowing in the warmth of his adherents' gratitude is perhaps the subcontinent's oldest political image. But when that gratitude depends of the convertible price of a debenture trading in an international capital market, surely an interesting change has occurred. To Anil, the change was contained in his knowledge of what would happen if the capital markets he attempts to influence turned against him and the price of his Reliance debenture fell. At that point, the tobacco sellers "would have given me a kick. They would say 'Let him come out—we'll bash him up' or something." When patriarchal performance has a price and the price is published daily in the financial sections of the Bombay newspapers,

then the pillars of the old obeisance are beginning to crumble. And the tobacco sellers at Anil's wedding are not an isolated example—there are now more than five million individual shareholders of Reliance Industries in India.

One problem is that few potential institutions of capitalism in India—the stock and bond markets, the banks, the export authorities—have yet broken free from the embrace of the Nehruvian state, which means they remain crippled by the hierarchies and corruption of the old order. A version of this problem has certainly impeded Pakistan's reforms. In India, the difficulty became obvious in the spring of 1992 when an ambitious Bombay insurance clerk named Harshad Mehta, attempting to forge a rise modeled on the Ambanis', brought the entire stock market crashing down through a series of speculative manipulations involving state-owned and foreign banks. As Mehta inflated a speculative market bubble and drove prices up, up, up with his manipulations, India's new shareholding class cheered, astonished at the promised magic of capitalism. Nobody, it seemed, was prepared to question Mehta's highly dubious genius because to do so would be to undermine the fragile consensus around the new order. Even *Newstrack,* the independent video news magazine that serves as the middle class's trumpet of accountability, produced an adulatory profile of Mehta that consisted mainly of reporters badgering him for particularly profitable stock tips. When the bubble burst and Mehta went to jail, India was "shocked" at the illusions in which it had invested. Politicians and the media fell back on their traditions of hysterical scape-goating, in which selected examples of official malfeasance are skewered and roasted as if they were somehow exceptions to the rule. (This, of course, is a cycle familiar to anyone who has lived in Washington.) Yet the spirit of reform remained unbroken because there were enough politi-cians in New Delhi, led by finance minister Manmohan Singh, who understood that even this crisis, if properly managed, could advance the reformers' cause.

The inevitable nexus between the new capitalism and the old state lends credibility to those in India who argue that the Ambanis and their Bombay brethren are merely old wolves in new clothes. This argument comes from both left and right. On the left, aside from the tattered remnants of the Communist ideologists, there are scores and scores of caste- or clan-based politicians and mafia leaders who fear they may be unable to compete effectively in the new game if the state drastically

shifts its allegiances to the private sector. Many of these minor thug-politicians have already made their deals with the existing domestic monopolists and oligopolists in the old-line business community and they are deeply uncomfortable about the prospect of a political economy in which they may not be so well positioned to exact their bureaucratic rents. I felt this most acutely one evening with Ram Paswan, deputy leader of the Janata Dal, the left-center opposition party whose main platform these days consists of support for government affirmative action for "other backward classes" and opposition to most forms of capitalism.

We sat in Paswan's New Delhi bungalow, where two dozen suppli-cants had gathered around him to seek favors and discuss political busi-ness. Paswan dismissed the group in order to lecture about international capitalism's many dangers. "This government is the government of the upper castes and big businessmen," he began. "All people and all parties except some big business houses are opposing this reform. The people just realize that acceptance of this new economic policy will jeopardize political and economic sovereignty."

But whose sovereignty? As he spoke, Paswan sat in a thronelike armchair surrounded by a color television, sprawling couches, and spin-ning fans. He wore a well-tailored Nehru coat, a pressed shirt, a gold ring, and a fancy watch. I waved to all this and said, "But you live here in a very big house, with many amenities. Don't you think people all over India want such amenities?"

"This house is very big," he conceded. "Every facility is there. But I never consider that this is my one house. My house is in my village in Bihar. One's hut is more respectable than others' buildings. It's psycholog-ical. . . . The World Bank dictates what will be our village. But what of those who are living in the villages, in bonded labor?"

"But so many other Third World governments are moving in a differ-ent direction these days," I said. "Chile, Argentina, Brazil, Malaysia, Indonesia—and these are proud, independent governments. Don't you worry that they may know something you don't?"

"After ten years, what will happen? They will be shamefaced," he answered. "All of these countries—maybe they have no other alternative. India has got resources. You can develop your industries. You can utilize your manpower. One computer—I agree with you, it is more efficient. But do you realize, one computer makes one hundred persons unem-ployed? In Western countries, European countries, in other parts of the

world, there is a lack of manpower. We have more manpower than we require. The main thing is that you want a market."

He mentioned Pepsi, whose attempt to penetrate the Indian soft drink market had been skillfully impeded by a domestic monopolist who, I was told by Indian politicians, had spread his money around the parliament, purchasing with it such public outbursts of socialist xenophobia as Paswan now offered. I told Paswan that he knew better than I did that the business about Pepsi was all a farce, that the politics around it was bought and paid for by an Indian soft drink manufacturer.

"I don't want to get into that," he said. "But Coke—what about Coke?"

Before we could tackle this philosophical question, the telephone rang. Somebody from Bombay. Paswan had to run.

The sometime masters of politicians like Paswan include old-line manufacturers whose markets have been protected for centuries, first by the imperialists and then by the socialists, and who tend to see nothing terribly wrong with the way things were. At the same time, they worry considerably about industrialists like the Ambanis who seem to be rewarded for their professed contempt for the old arrangements.

In Bombay I once drove out to see Nusli Wadia, heir to his family's three-hundred-year-old shipping and textile fortune. Wadia is a discreet, sophisticated Anglophile who lives in a glorious mansion on the Arabian Sea filled with family heirlooms. Wadia's Bombay Dyeing firm has been in feverish and losing competition with the Ambanis in the textile business—Wadia even accused his rivals of hiring a hit man to assassinate him on his way to work, a charge that the Ambanis denied and that was never proven. But the main point Wadia wanted to make was that the rapid rise of India's New Money did not in any way represent systemic progress, but was rather the last gasp of the old, corrupt system. When true capitalism came to South Asia, he said, the Ambanis would be seen as its victims, not its architects.

"They survived through managing and manipulating the system," he said. "You can make or break any industry by deciding the duty structure. Also, you have to import raw materials. It's not like a free economy. Here what decides your fate is how well you can manipulate the system. The Ambanis have brought about this kind of culture. They were able to sell at enormously high profits. We don't have an SEC [Securities and Exchange Commission] like you do, so you can fool the investor through market manipulation. So long as the manipulation makes money, you do

well. . . . No industrial house in India has got the licenses the Ambanis have. They can get one billion dollars' worth of licenses in a single day. People in this country wait years. It's a question of what sort of business environment you want. You remove these controls and he won't be able to function. His manufacturing is not that efficient. But his manipulation of the political system is more efficient than anyone in the country."

The Ambanis, of course, do not see themselves that way at all. The rapidity with which they have closed $30 million and $50 million deals with Western and Japanese corporations in the aftermath of the announced capitalist reforms suggests at least that they are persuasive about their credentials as pure businessmen. Of course, they do not shrink either from the idea that they possess unusual political influence. I used to talk to the Ambani crowd regularly because they did seem to know, rather well in advance, where the twists and turns of New Delhi's internecine politics would next lead, and for someone who was supposed to keep track of such matters, their prognostications were useful. But by the time I left South Asia in mid-1992, a year after the unveiling of free market reforms, it did seem that the family's attention to New Delhi was wavering. The people I used to call in Bombay now seemed to be traveling abroad a great deal.

After the cricket-stadium wedding, I made an appointment to visit with Anil in his plush, hushed, blue-gray offices in a downtown Bombay tower, to ask what was going on. The Ambanis' headquarters is near to the Gateway to India, the fading arch on the Arabian Sea that once was a symbol of imperial arrival but today seems a passage through which the new Indian industrialists look outward to the future.

"This is just the beginning of the change," Anil Ambani said, speaking with a salesman's manic zeal. "Somebody said it's a watershed. Somebody said it's spectacular. Somebody said it is unheard-of, and so on. I think no amount of adjectives is sufficient to describe this change. I've been in corporate life, after my graduation with my master's from the U.S., now for roughly like ten or eleven years. In those ten years, I have not seen anything like what I've seen in the last six months. The change we are making today is the result of an understanding that India needs to be part of the global economy, and if we get left out now, we'll have only one option—and that is to integrate with Burma.

"The collapse of the Soviet Union has tremendous implications for our politicians, at least in their thought processes. Another very compelling

reason is change in Pakistan. It excites the Indian mind. You know, it lights a fire where it hurts. If Pakistan can change and if they can attract foreign investment and they can privatize banks and they can bring in foreign investment in the secondary market, the stock markets—well, we, India, are a great nation. We have the Taj Mahal. We have people who can do rope tricks. We have good curry. So you know, why are we getting left out? And so I think change in Bangladesh, change in Pakistan, change in Sri Lanka—whether you call it privatization or just the shedding of assets by the government—it has major implications."

I asked him what it was like to take this spiel on the road to New York or Tokyo. How did it play? He answered with his best pitch.

"When the prime minister was recently in the United States for the UN meeting and he met with Mr. Bush in New York, next day on the front page of *The New York Times* was a huge photograph, and guess what it was about? It's not about Mr. Bush meeting Mr. Narasimha Rao. It was sixteen people killed in Punjab. That is the normal association of India— Punjab, Kashmir, terrorism, poor people, rope tricks, flying carpets, these sorts of things. It's nothing state-of-the-art. Nobody talks about eight hundred fifty million people, two hundred million people in the middle class. . . . There are sixty-two hundred listed companies in the capital markets, the second highest in the world after the United States. The language of business is English. We are net exporters of food, one of the largest seafood exporters in the world. We are the largest exporters of pepper in the world, second largest of sugar in the world. Nobody talks about these aspects. The industrial India is not what is exposed to the world, so you get very, very basic questions when you meet lots of people: Do you have roads? Do your phones work? Oh, you have a car. And I have experienced this myself. And senior people abroad have very little or no knowledge, and the only knowledge that they have is about strikes, riots, poverty.

"I think there is a great selling job that has to be done for India as a country."

"How quickly can this India that you want, that you describe, that you think is happening now—how quickly can it deliver meaningful opportunity and growth to the great majority of people who live in the countryside, or the significant majority of people who live in poverty?" I asked.

"Five years," he said emphatically. He was, he admitted, "an optimist."

Toward the end of my tour, I would meet the pessimists back in New

Delhi. They were usually politicians. The most interesting of them were Congress Party careerists who wanted to believe in the Ambanis and in the brash optimism coursing through Bombay, but who worried that the politics of transition might fail. Suspecting that their fears masked the self-interested nostalgia of a political class confronting its own twilight, I usually played the provocateur, arguing that they did not have enough faith that their own people would succeed at capitalism if given the chance. But the most thoughtful responded with a dispiriting, detailed description of just how problematic reform of the Nehruvian state may turn out to be. Licenses and the bureaucracy's control of the economy's commanding heights are the least of it, they said. These are problems that in many cases can be legislated out of existence, and while there may be a bit of scuffling and shouting in the aftermath, the competition to control the new, liberalized economic order will sort itself out and will inject the country with fresh vigor. But what worried them seriously were the sizable sections of the old order that must inevitably be left to crumble.

Nehru's planners deliberately constructed factories, plants, and industrial infrastructure in places where it did not make economic sense to build such things. The purpose of these programs was to provide employment and growth in areas neglected by the British, such as the interior tribal belts, or to dole out patronage rewards in the complex balancing act of socialist democracy. If these factories and other state enterprises are now to be shut down, essentially on the grounds that they shouldn't have been built in the first place, then the government had better be prepared to retrain and relocate the victims. Otherwise, the social and political rebound may be nasty indeed. Just ask the Germans what it has been like since the fall of the Berlin Wall, my informants would typically conclude. And the Germans have the money, the developed economy, to give it a try. India does not. For us, the numbers of people who may languish on the wrong side of transition are just too great. And what will happen if we fail, if we divide our society between those who can make it with the Ambanis and those who cannot? For one answer to that, revisit the Sri Lankans.

Whether Sri Lanka's attempt to shift suddenly toward capitalist liberalization during the late 1970s contributed to its ethnic disintegration beginning in 1983 may be an instructive question in South Asia today, although it cannot be answered with certainty. Direct comparisons between Sri Lanka's small, island economy, which is heavily dependent on

cash crops, and the much larger, more diverse industrialized economies of Pakistan and India would be fallacious. Yet there are obvious similarities. Sri Lanka's postindependence socialist state, its colonial inheritance, and its ethnic and cultural heritage are comparable to India's and Pakistan's. The potential instruction to economic reformers on the subcontinent lies in Sri Lanka's recent history. In 1977, following a long period of socialist stagnation, Sri Lanka attempted a form of shock therapy capitalism that, in its basic policies very much resembled what India and Pakistan are attempting today. The government abolished many currency-exchange controls, import controls, price controls, and its system of licenses, permits, and quotas. It decreed free trading zones and invited foreign corporations and foreign banks to help open the economy. The policies were backed up by the International Monetary Fund and the World Bank. And initially, they worked remarkably well. Between 1978 and 1983, the growth rate of the Sri Lankan economy nearly tripled, to an average of above 6 percent. In some years the growth rate exceeded 8 percent. Unemployment came down from 26 percent to 12 percent by 1983. Inflation dropped into the low single digits. The island was booming.

But in 1983, with the same degree of energy, the island began to implode. Communal riots between Sinhalese and Tamils turned into full-scale ethnic war dominated by radical youth-based guerrilla groups such as the Liberation Tigers of Tamil Eelam. In the Sinhalese south, the Maoist, genocidal People's Liberation Front was suddenly transformed from a marginal leftist political party into a violent and plausible revolutionary force. Obviously these developments were complex. But did the way the government pursued its sudden shift to capitalism contribute significantly to the later violence and revolutionary movements? If so, how?

Sri Lankans themselves have spent no small amount of time and effort trying to sort out the answers to these questions, and at one point I traveled to the island to read their papers and analyses and talk to economists, social scientists, writers, and politicians about what lesson the rest of South Asia could learn from their grisly experience. Nearly everybody I talked to, with the exception of the finance minister who actually devised Sri Lanka's capitalist liberalization, believed that the economic and social changes between 1978 and 1983 had directly shaped the violence that followed. They cited six areas in which Sri Lanka's liberalization had failed: education, language, technology, caste or class, regional disparity, and the broad political management of popular expectations.

In each case they talked about a loss of balance. The Sri Lankan education system, geared for decades toward the service of an overweening socialist state, produced millions of young men and women with impressive degrees, high expectations, but relatively few capitalist skills or attitudes. This produced an "unemployment at the entry level" that remained throughout the initial economic boom, explained the economist Nilam Goonateleke. "It is not classic unemployment with people laid off and families destitute. It is people coming out of universities saying, 'I'm ready' and the country says, 'For what?' . . . It is a political problem. These are not destitute people. You have groups of people with expectations and an ability to articulate frustration. What you have is an extended adolescence in all its virulent forms. . . . The People's Liberation Front didn't even have to articulate the frustration. With the imbalanced economy, everyone felt it."

In attempting to create multicultural pluralism and honor Sri Lanka's ethnic diversity, the state insisted for decades that students be educated in their own languages—not in the English of the British colonialist. In the Sri Lankan south, for example, "the problem with the opening of the economy was that on the one hand, you had a lot of educated people who spoke Sinhala. On the other hand, the international economy demanded English," Goonateleke said. "The young man with ideas and money, he would be looking for trading opportunities. You need English to succeed in the private sector. The problem is that access to English is limited. As you develop a liberalized, outward-looking strategy that emphasizes exports and internationalization and foreign capital, English becomes more and more essential. Yet the Sinhalese see that as an impediment. They see people with English getting ahead of them, and they are angry."

"We have in Sri Lanka an entire generation that is monolingual and monocultural," said Neelan Tiruchelvam, the director of Colombo's Law and Society Trust. "You can imagine what it's like in engineering and technical areas. You have thousands of university students who can't read anything but lecture notes. You gave these rural Sinhala and Tamil students the impression that they not only could gain an educational experience, but could achieve upward social mobility. This, in fact, was not true. Plus, the children of the elite continued to learn English while the other Sinhalas and Tamils didn't. So the children of the elite faced huge opportunities after 1978. You had a middle class grasping the opportunities in the liberalized economy and the other part of that

generation left behind. The liberalization distorted and accentuated these problems.

"The intelligentsia failed to acknowledge the demands of ethnic groups or to understand how the benefits of development had to be distributed," he continued. "You have to enthrone the people."

A monolingual education was often sufficient in the long period of state domination after independence because government business in the bowels of the bureaucracy—and thus access to government jobs—involved only the local language. After 1977, "it wasn't that there was less mobility, it was that the pattern of mobility changed," said Sunil Bastian, of Colombo's Center for Ethnic Studies. "What really happened after 1977 was a changing pattern of opportunity that diminished the power of the state economy. Liberalized economic policies came in conflict with the interests of those who benefited from the old patterns of mobility. In this case, it was the schoolmaster who depended on access to the state against the Tamil businessman or the Sinhalese shopkeeper who did not depend on that access. The battle between the schoolmaster and the shopkeeper was part of the People's Liberation Front conflict." Indeed, when you drove through the southern jungles at the height of the Liberation Front's attempted revolution, it was striking how many of the revolutionary cadres seemed to be schoolteachers.

When it inaugurated capitalist reform, the Sri Lankan state made no attempt to ensure that the shift to free markets was accompanied by a shift in training and educational emphasis. "We misinterpreted the Asian models," said a Tamil economist in Colombo who was writing a doctoral thesis in England about how the mistakes were made. "Taiwan is really the model. But we failed to develop skills behind the [free market] frontiers. You need electronic skills, not just industrial engineering, all this construction and chemical engineering. We needed applied sciences and technological institutes in this country. This technical capacity is the key framework. That's the industrial strategy. At the same time, you need a poverty strategy because even if you do it right, it takes time—twenty-five years at a minimum. In our development, the small entrepreneurs were left out—people with twenty-five employees or less. The banking system in this country is very conservative. All the bank capital goes to the corporations and all the big corporations are controlled by the same families. They're just giving money to the same people—the English speakers. We should be going directly to the Sinhala and Tamil shanty

entrepreneurs, not just with capital but with skills. . . . We were caught up in a euphoria by 1983. We never had it so good. There was no attempt to acquire technological skills to make the growth sustainable. These guys [the new Sri Lankan industrialists] thought they were entrepreneurs, but they were really just traders."

On the grounds of capitalist egalitarianism, Sri Lanka also abandoned efforts to promote caste- or class-based affirmative action programs. Compared with the rest of South Asia, Sri Lanka is unusual in that the historically dominant caste group is in the numerical majority—the reverse of the situation in India. So even the best-intentioned programs of socialist democracy after independence did not promote a rise of lower castes, as in India. Instead, it reinforced the grip of dominant castes. More broadly, the Sri Lankan government rejected affirmative action during the capitalist boom because "we thought we were a much more enlightened society and ought not to acknowledge caste distinctions," as Tiruchelvam put it. "This is essentially an upper-caste illusion. . . . The whole liberalization approach had very little conceptualization about caste or equity. It was growth-oriented, concentrating on sustainable growth. There was no explicit attempt to acknowledge the disparities of caste."

Yet the disparities were obvious to every Sri Lankan. As Ronnie De Mel, the currently exiled finance minister who was the architect of Sri Lankan capitalist reform, acknowledged, "There were aspects of this development strategy that we could have avoided. There was, for example, no reason for the elaborate duty-free complex in downtown Colombo, which led to flooding the country with luxury and consumer goods. That led to a certain frustration among classes that, even if they were employed, could not have afforded these things. We needn't have made certain frustrations so visible. The grandiose schemes, the extravagant and ostentatious and very high levels of consumption in certain sectors of the government also created political and social resentment of a very high order.

"With education and with liberalization, rising expectations come," he continued. "It is very difficult for Third World countries to meet all of those expectations, particularly among the youth. But is that a reason to keep our people backward? I don't think so. You have to take that risk."

But the question that faced Sri Lanka then—and that faces India and Pakistan today—was not whether or not to take the risk at all. In the struggle to create prosperity and national strength, risk is unavoidable.

But there *are* choices to be made about whether and how to manage the risks. This is what dozens and dozens of formerly socialist or Bolshevik states are wrestling with in the 1990s. And this is what Sri Lanka botched in the late 1970s and early 1980s.

One thing the Colombo government failed to do was to persuade the country that some form of capitalism, broadly defined, would provide the basis for unified, equitable Sri Lankan nationalism. Instead, capitalism was decreed, but the nominally socialist political class, hungry for votes, went straight on preaching the old, manipulative sermons. This is exactly what is happening in India, where traditional politicians express even less public enthusiasm about capitalist nationalism than their nominally Communist counterparts in China. Yet at the same time, Indian politicians are vigorously implementing full-blooded free market programs, raising broad expectations in the process.

"The quality of life of the people and their expectations were totally disproportionate to the productive base of the economy," said Tiruchelvam of Sri Lanka's similar experiment. "Looking back, I would place the emphasis on the mismanagement of these expectations. This is a small country. Look, for comparison, at the nature of public discourse in Singapore—a constant obsession with economic indicators, an obsession with their capital reserves. I wouldn't like to live in Singapore, but we belong to the other extreme. Our leaders don't take people into their confidence about the economy, about inflation, budget deficits, and so on. You're not framing meaningful strategies that way."

I spent long hours in New Delhi talking with Indian politicians and planners about the Sri Lankan experience with liberalization and its relevance for the rest of South Asia. We found a few bases for comparison. The problem of entry-level employment—the danger of promoting "extended adolescence in all its virulent forms"—is a palpable part of the continuing rebellions in Punjab and Kashmir. The predicament of those who do not speak English is comparable, although not so stark, since India is not an island nation dependent on international trade, but rather possesses a robust internal economy that revolves around indigenous languages. The imbalances of opportunity that rocked Sri Lanka are already visible in India, particularly in the volatile north, where vast communities of subsidized craftsmen—weavers, locksmiths, cobblers, scissors makers—confront what will be at best a very painful integration into the new, more dynamic market economy.

Yet there seem at least an equal number of reasons to believe that the Sri Lankan lessons will not apply. India's philosophy and practice of nationalism-through-pluralism is far more developed than was Sri Lanka's in 1977. Its education system and its state apparatus have long emphasized the "technical skills behind the frontiers" of a dynamic economy. Its affirmative action programs and its pattern of development have promoted a more diverse middle class. Malaysia, Indonesia, Thailand, even China, have faced similar challenges during the 1980s and have proved, to Sri Lanka's dismay, that with enough capital and dynamism, all sorts of wonderful things can happen very quickly in Asia these days, even with the usual lousy politicians in charge.

In any event, there is no turning back now. South Asia's future belongs to its ascending middle classes. If India's economic and social reformers succeed, their neighbors will have myriad opportunities to rise alongside. If they fail . . .

One of the last architects of the new India whom I met before leaving New Delhi was Amit Judge, a retailing entrepreneur who has accomplished, among other things, the profitable import of Lacoste alligator shirts for the Indian yuppie classes. Judge is the son of a middle-class Nehruvian civil servant. He was educated at "one of those blue-blooded public schools the English left behind," but his mother worked as a hotel clerk to put him through school. As a young man in his family, " 'business' was a very dirty word. I was told not to mix with this guy because he was a businessman's son and made black money. I came from a clean, socialist background and did not mix with businessmen. . . . Business was a big, bad, mafialike thing. My father was one of those idiotic public servants who, if he got a can of Coke from someone, he hurled it back, shouting about bribery, corruption, scandal. I never understood what this can of Coke was all about." A decade later, Judge had built on his own a textile and industrial firm with $40 million in annual revenues and partnerships with several multinational corporations. He still sees his family, including his father-in-law, I. K. Gujral, one of India's best known putatively socialist politicians. But Judge finds himself arguing a lot these days about ideology and progress.

The framework and meaning of these arguments extend far beyond narrow questions about how to implement free market reform in a socialist political economy. The arguments involve fundamental questions about how to distribute power and manage change in a new world. This

is why the debate about capitalist reform in South Asia today is so significant—it is not a debate, as it is in the United States currently, about tinkering with the government's role in the economy, about shifting a marginal amount of resources within a system that is fixed and widely endorsed. South Asia's predicament is much more fundamental because it involves the reconciliation of outdated, narrow, top-heavy political and social arrangements with the swelling, vigorous pluralism of rising middle classes. In this sense, the subcontinent's predicament is comparable to China's, where the paradox of a totalitarian elite and a capitalist middle class is far more extreme than on the subcontinent. The point is that in South Asia, while the public language about reform often focuses on technical questions about business licensing and tax policy, such language disguises a profound, open-ended, even perilous rethinking of the basic rules of the political economy.

Judge summed this up one weekend morning at his office behind a fetid smugglers' market. He wore a knit golf shirt and Western slacks. What he wanted to talk about was India as a kind of blank slate.

"There are eight hundred million people across India," he began. "What you want to do with them is a fantasy. . . . India will go through a phase of 'Look, Mom, what I got!' but we are still a bit scared. We are still spiritually inclined, shy of spending a lot of money on so-called frivolous consumption items. Of course, I don't talk about the Lacoste segment. Those guys, hopefully, will buy things they don't need.

"Before these reforms I was frustrated. I would go to Thailand and see the sea change there. I knew that Indian entrepreneurs are very sharp guys. We move extremely rapidly. This used to frustrate me, these bloody Asian countries. What are they? Nothing. They get four million tourists in Thailand. Why? Because they have planes that go places, that's why.

"But now I'm an optimist that people will be allowed to do business. I had this big argument with I. K. Gujral just last Sunday. I said, 'It's guys like you who ruined this country. For thirty years you went to villages and promised jobs, but you can't create jobs. Only I can. Business can.'

"There's a great, great optimism that business can be done in India now. I for one am extremely surprised by the pace of reform taking place. The headlines in the *Economic Times* today would have had us huddling around at the golf course just a couple of years ago. Now it's mundane news. There is no doubt that this liberalization process is complete in

terms of political will. In India this decade, we can become a major power.

"The only thing which disturbs me is still the politics. Up till now, if you see the statues in this country, they are of some jerk politicians. If J. R. D. Tata [a leading industrialist] dies tomorrow, hardly anyone will notice. But if some jerk politician dies tomorrow, there will be a state funeral and the bloody country will shut down for a day.

"I was arguing with I. K. Gujral the other day about the multinationals. He is against them. But it was our own socialist system that perpetuated this mess. I could very well have been swamped by the system if I had been part of it. When I was younger, I would go to see I.K.'s house when he was a minister, and he had this big bungalow, and all these sycophants. Guys with guns protecting him. It could warp anybody's mind. It gave them a warped sense of power.

"But now at the golf course, these so-called politicians come to play and we don't talk to them anymore. They play by themselves and nobody follows them around. I only hang around you if I need you. I don't need the politician anymore.

"My friends in school who have joined the Indian Administrative Service, they're trying to quit the ministries now. Until now, if you were an IAS officer, you printed it on your card, you tattooed it on your forehead, because this was your passport to power. You had this little flashing red light on your car. What is this? Who is this guy? Why the hell does he need a light on his car? I'm not saying the process is complete, but it is happening rapidly."

We walked into the dirt parking lot. The morning air was humid, sweltering. Shirtless workmen climbed around us on bamboo scaffolding, banging on the concrete frames of new office buildings. Judge climbed into his Indian-made compact car and drove off. He was smiling, pumped up—he was going to play golf. There is nothing quite like golf on a Saturday morning, he said a few times.

I thought about Amit Judge for a long while afterward—about his confidence, his sense of entitlement to India. "Only I can," he declared. I thought about his golf game—Judge and his pals striding around the course, whacking away. If the future belongs to the Lacoste crowd, what besides energetic selfishness can we possibly expect them to deliver? Yet by Judge's own account, for all his brashness, his claim to the future was not arbitrary, but was instead a product of negotiation, of cordial argument with the graying Nehruvian old guard, with people like his father-

in-law, Gujral. In that essentially respectful weekend dialogue, replicated millions of times, lies the potential for a peaceful and democratic transition, and from there—is it too much to wish?—even deliverance from history.

Acknowledgments

This book is in many ways a product of the kindness of strangers. Across my travels, and occasionally in some difficult spots, I was hosted, fed, escorted, aided, advised, protected, harangued, and deservedly admonished by scores of South Asians who had no reason to be helpful other than their own generosity.

Rama Lakshmi, my researcher and translator in New Delhi, contributed immensely to much of the reporting in this book. She found many of the Indian characters who appear in the preceding pages, helped me to interview them, contributed ideas about what they said, and conducted much original research on her own. The reporting on Chopta village, particularly, belongs very much to her, although there and elsewhere she should not be held responsible for my writing, interpretations, and opinions.

Similarly, Kamran Khan, the *Post*'s stringer in Karachi and Pakistan's most accomplished investigative reporter, was an invaluable friend and guide across the border and was the source of a steady stream of tips and ideas that became the basis of reporting and writing in the book.

I also leaned during my travels on the company, ideas, and advice of other talented South Asian journalists and writers, notably Ahmed Ra-

shid, Najam Sethi, Ghulam Nabi Khayal, Surjit Bhalla, Shekhar Gupta, and Dinesh Kumar.

Ned Desmond of *Time* magazine and Mark Fineman of the *Los Angeles Times*, taught me a great deal during the time when this book was reported. Fineman was a frequent and generous traveling companion who contributed in many ways to my work, not least by being a staunch friend. Other colleagues from South Asia's exceptional press corps who went well out of their way to help at one time or another are Michael Battye, Bill Tarrant, Malcolm Davidson, Ruth Pritchard, Anita Pratap, Bob Nickelsberg, Art Max, Bob Drogin, Lyse Doucet, Cathy Gannon, the late Sharon Herbaugh, Peter Heinlein, Tim McGirk, Derek Brown, Ed Gargan, and Chris Thomas. Gary Thomas deserves special thanks for rescuing me several times from the grim fate of boarding at the Islamabad Hotel.

Sumit Ganguly of Hunter College and Philip Oldenburg of Columbia University took time from busy schedules to read the book in manuscript form. They saved me from countless blunders, offered many helpful suggestions, and occasionally managed to straighten out my wrong-headed notions. Both also endured long conversations with me about South Asia, at a point when I was preparing to write. I have pilfered shamelessly some of the ideas generated during those talks. I owe each of them a deep debt, but neither should be held responsible for what I have written.

Others who sat patiently with my tape recorder to talk specifically about some of the material in the book, and whose ideas I have borrowed from, include Neelan Tiruchelvam, Shekhar Gupta, Arun Shourie, Manmohan Singh, and Anil Ambani.

Bob Thompson, editor of *The Washington Post*'s magazine, interrupted what was meant to be a peaceful sabbatical to read the manuscript. As always, his suggestions were graceful and of great value. He also helped to develop some of the material in the book at an earlier stage, as did *Post* editors David Ignatius and Steve Luxenberg. The *Post*'s Glenn Frankel took time from a sabbatical to read the manuscript and offered helpful advice.

Leonard Downie, Bob Kaiser, and Don Graham at the *Post* contributed to my general well-being during the time the book was reported and written. I owe Mike Getler, my boss at the paper, an incalculable debt for his creative management and support.

Ann Godoff at Random House shepherded the manuscript with rare

humor, intelligence, and professionalism. Random House's copy editors were exceptionally thorough and thoughtful. Melanie Jackson performed her usual wizardry as a literary agent and offered advice and support well beyond that role.

To Susan, Ally, Emma, and Max, thanks for all of it.

Index

Abbas, Zafar, 115
Abdullah, Farooq, 179
Abdullah, Tahira, 127–28
Abedi, Agha Hasan, 132–37, 139, 142, 144
adultery, 80–81
Advani, Lal Krishna, 188
affirmative action programs: for lower castes, 37, 211, 214, 215, 278; for Muslims, 205, 214; reactions to, 211–12, 214, 224, 227; results of, 37, 215, 288; Sri Lanka and, 286
Afghanistan, 6, 10; cold war conflict and, 230, 231, 233, 235–36, 243, 247, 252–54, 255, 256; conspiracy theories in, 233, 242, 256–57; democracy in, 262; ethnic conflict in, 75, 79–80, 249; guerrilla warfare in, 176, 232–33, 238–39, 240, 249–50, 251–52; middle class in, 41; mujaheddin rebels, U.S. military support, 88, 100, 113–14, 148, 228, 229, 233–36, 237–42, 249; mujaheddin victory in war, 243, 247–51, 252, 255–56; Najibullah revolution, 230–32; Pakistani involvement in war, 100, 103, 181–82, 233–34, 237, 238–39, 240–42; poverty in, 54; Soviet

invasion of, 8–9, 236, 253, 259; Soviet withdrawal from, 86, 89, 94, 230, 233; warring culture in, 229–30
Africa, 39, 231–32
agriculture, 38–39, 56, 57, 60, 180
Ahiliyabhai (princess), 194–95
Ahmed, Munir, 98–99
Ahmed, Saleem, 205, 207, 209–10
Akbar (Mughal emperor), 193
Ali, Jam Sadiq, 114–15, 116–17, 119
Ambani, Anil, 274–75, 276–77, 280–81
Ambani, Dhirubhai, 275–76
Amin, Hafizullah, 8–9
Andhra Pradesh, India, 144–45
Ansari, Abbas, 182
Anwar, Raja, 8–9
Any Old Iron (Burgess), 171
Arafat, Yasser, 17
Artis, Mark Alphonzo: connection to Iran, 103–4, 106, 110; connection to Zia ul-Haq crash, 100–104, 105, 107–8, 112, 113; detained by Pakistan, 100, 102–3, 107, 108, 109, 111; FBI investigation of, 108, 109–10, 111
Asia Society, 123
Asia Watch, 167
Assam, India, 221

ABOUT THE AUTHOR

Steve Coll was born in Washington, D.C., in 1958. He has been a staff reporter and foreign correspondent for *The Washington Post* since 1985. He is a recipient of the Pulitzer Prize, the Gerald Loeb Award, and, for his dispatches from South Asia, the 1992 Livingston Award for outstanding international reporting. He is currently based in London as an international projects and investigative correspondent for the *Post*. This is his fourth book.